COOPERATIVE EXTENSION

Raspberry & Blackberry Production Guide

For the Northeast, Midwest, and Eastern Canada

Technical Editors

Lori Bushway, Extension Horticulturist
Department of Horticulture, Cornell University

Marvin Pritts, Horticulturist
Department of Horticulture, Cornell University

David Handley, Extension Horticulturist
University of Maine at Highmoor Farm

Natural Resource, Agriculture, and Engineering Service
Cooperative Extension
P.O. Box 4557
Ithaca, New York 14852-4557

NRAES–35
May 2008

ISBN-13: 978-1-933395-18-0

Library of Congress Cataloging-in-Publication Data

Raspberry and blackberry production guide for the Northeast, Midwest, and Eastern Canada / technical
editors, Lori Bushway, Marvin Pritts, David Handley.
     p. cm. — (NRAES ; 35)
  ISBN 978-1-933395-18-0
 1. Raspberries—Northeastern States. 2. Raspberries—Middle West. 3. Raspberries—Canada, Eastern.
4. Blackberries—Northeastern States. 5. Blackberries—Middle West. 6. Blackberries—Canada, Eastern.
I. Bushway, Lori J., date II. Pritts, Marvin Paul. III. Handley, David T. IV. Series: NRAES (Series) ; 35.
  SB386.R3R37 2008
  634'.7110971—dc22

                                                                                    2008005189

To order additional copies, contact:
Natural Resource, Agriculture, and Engineering Service (NRAES)
Cooperative Extension
PO Box 4557, Ithaca, New York 14852-4557
Phone: (607) 255-7654 • Fax: (607) 254-8770
E-mail: NRAES@CORNELL.EDU • Web site: WWW.NRAES.ORG

Contents

Acknowledgments iv

About the Authors v

Introduction 1

1. The History and Biology of
    Cultivated Raspberries and Blackberries 3

2. Site Selection and Site Preparation 10

3. Plant Selection 17

4. Production Methods 28

5. Trellising and Pruning Brambles 39

6. Water Management 51

7. Soil and Nutrient Management 64

8. Insect and Mite Scouting and Management 79

9. Disease Management and Physiological Disorders 92

10. Weed Management 111

11. Spray Application Technology 116

12. Harvesting, Handling, and Transporting Fresh Fruit 132

13. Marketing Bramble Fruits 138

14. Budgeting 148

    Glossary 154

    Table of Conversions 156

    About NRAES . . . . Inside Back Cover

Acknowledgments

The authors would like to thank the following for providing content for earlier editions of this guide:

James Bartsch, Mark Castaldi, Malcolm Dana, Donald Daum, Gene Galletta, Barbara Goulart, William Lord, Ian Merwin, James Mitchell, Steve Spangler, Herbert Stiles, and Catherine Violette.

The authors would like to thank the following for providing helpful reviews:

Adam Dale, Department of Plant Agriculture, University of Guelph, Simcoe, ON, Canada.

Kathleen Demchak, Department of Horticulture, Penn State, University Park, PA.

Gina Fernandez, Department of Horticultural Science, North Carolina State University, Raleigh, NC.

Pam Fisher, Ontario Ministry of Agriculture, Simcoe, ON, Canada.

Sonia Schloemann, Department of Plant, Soil and Insect Sciences, West Experiment Station, University of Massachusetts, Amherst, MA.

Wen-fei Uva, formerly with Department of Applied Economics and Management, Cornell University, Ithaca, NY.

Illustrations by: Marcia Eames-Sheavly and Akemi Ohira except figure 11.8 by Mark L. Kogut.

Editing by Joy Freeman and Marty Sailus; Design by Joy Freeman.

Photo Credits

Photos are referenced by figure number.

T.J. Burr: 9.25

J.F. Dill, Maine Cooperative Extension Service, Orono, ME: 8.7, 8.8, 8.11, 8.23, 8.25, 8.28, 8.29, 8.30, 8.33, 8.35, 8.40

M.A. Ellis: 9.1, 9.2, 9.11, 9.20, 9.24

P. Fisher: 9.4, 9.27 © Queen's Printer for Ontario, 2007. Reproduced with permission.

M.C. Heidenreich: 8.26, 9.3, 9.5, 9.10, 9.12, 9.16, 9.17

S.N. Jeffers: 9.13, 9.14, 9.15

R. Martin: 9.7, 9.8

Entomology Department, New York State Agricultural Experiment Station, Geneva, NY: 8.1, 8.2, 8.3, 8.4, 8.5, 8.6, 8.9, 8.10, 8.12, 8.13, 8.14, 8.15, 8.16, 8.17, 8.18, 8.19, 8.20, 8.21, 8.22, 8.24, 8.27, 8.31, 8.32, 8.34, 8.36, 8.37, 8.38, 8.39, 8.41, 8.42, 8.43, 8.44, 8.45

All other photos provided by the authors.

About the Authors

The chapters each author contributed to are listed in parentheses after his or her affiliation.

Arthur Agnello is an entomologist in the Department of Entomology, Cornell University at the New York State Agricultural Experiment Station, Geneva, NY. (Chapter 8)

Lori Bushway is an extension horticulturist in the Department of Horticulture, Cornell University, Ithaca, NY. (Chapters 1, 2, 4, 5 and 13)

Michael Celetti is a plant pathologist in horticulture crops with Ontario Ministry of Agriculture, Food and Rural Affairs, Bovey Building, University of Guelph, Guelph, ON. (Chapter 9)

Kathleen Demchak is an extension horticulturist in the Department of Horticulture, Penn State, University Park, PA. (Chapter 4)

Larry Geohring is an agriculture engineer in the Department of Biological and Environmental Engineering, Cornell University, Ithaca, NY. (Chapter 6)

David Handley is an extension horticulturist with the University of Maine at the Highmoor Farm, Monmouth, Maine. (Chapter 3,11)

Cathy Heidenreich is a Small Fruit Extension Support Specialist, Department of Horticulture, Cornell University, Ithaca, NY and Research Support Specialist, Department of Plant Pathology, New York State Agricultural Experiment Station, Geneva, NY. (Chapters 8, 9, 11)

Andrew Landers is a pesticide application technology specialist in the Department of Entomology, Cornell University at the New York State Agricultural Experiment Station, Geneva, NY. (Chapter 11)

Greg English-Loeb is an entomologist in the Department of Entomology, Cornell University at the New York State Agricultural Experiment Station, Geneva, NY. (Chapter 8)

Pam Fisher is a berry crop specialist with Ontario Ministry of Agriculture, Food and Rural Affairs, Simcoe, ON. (Chapters 2 and 9)

Bob Martin is a plant pathology research leader with USDA-ARS Horticulture Crops Research Unit, Corvallis, OR. (Chapter 9)

Olga Padilla-Zakour is Director of the New York State Food Venture Center in the Department of Food Science and Technology, Cornell University at the New York State Agricultural Experiment Station, Geneva, NY. (Chapter 13)

Marvin Pritts is a horticulturist in the Department of Horticulture, Cornell University, Ithaca, NY. (introduction and chapters 1, 4, 5, 7, 10, 12, 13 and 14)

William Turechek is a research plant pathologist with the Fruit Laboratory, USDA, ARS, BA, PSI, Beltsville, MD. (Chapter 9)

Chris Watkins is a postharvest physiologist in the Department of Horticulture, Cornell University, Ithaca, NY. (Chapter 12)

Courtney Weber is a plant breeder in the Department of Horticultural Sciences, Cornell University at the New York State Agricultural Experiment Station, Geneva, NY. (Chapter 3)

Anne Verhallen is a soil management specialist in horticulture crops with the Ontario Ministry of Agriculture, Food and Rural Affairs in Ridgetown, Ontario. (Chapter 2)

Wayne Wilcox is a plant pathologist in the Department of Plant Pathology, Cornell University at the New York State Agricultural Experiment Station, Geneva, NY. (Chapter 9)

Introduction

Bramble fruits are the raspberries and blackberries of our farms, gardens, fields, and woodlands. They are fresh fruit favorites and desired ingredients in jams, jellies, sauces, pies, and wines. Raspberry and blackberry fruits are highly nutritious, containing much soluble fiber, vitamins, and minerals. The berries also contain high levels of antioxidants and natural substances that are anti-carcinogenic (cancer preventing).

High demand and market prices for bramble fruit have stimulated much interest among potential and established growers. Demand for bramble fruit is high due to its exotic flavor, its nutritive value, and the growing interest in producing yogurt and juice blends. However, supply of fresh market bramble fruits is frequently low because raspberries and blackberries can be difficult to grow and because the fruit is quite perishable. This presents opportunities for marketing and selling berries through a variety of outlets.

Brambles can be an ideal crop for both large and small farms. Family labor can be employed for many duties on small plantings, but additional hired help may be required on large plantings, particularly in the pruning and harvesting seasons. Because bramble production requires a high initial investment and returns are slow at first, long-term management of capital is required. However, raspberries and blackberries can be sold for a greater price per pound than just about any fruit, and new production techniques allow for year-round berry production.

A bramble grower must consider many factors before investing in a planting. The bramble operation should be compatible with a grower's overall operation in relation to equipment use, time commitment, and seasonality. For instance, brambles which ripen in late summer may fit in well with an operation which also markets early- to mid-summer-ripening vegetables. Other factors include available resources such as land, labor, capital, and management skills of the grower.

The grower's ability to produce high-quality fruit and realize a profit while minimizing negative environmental impacts will largely determine the long-term success of a bramble operation. Establishing an accessible market for the extremely perishable bramble fruits is critical. Without a market for high quality fruit there will be no profit. Maximizing production skills will also help a grower maximize profit.

About This Guide

This guide is intended as a comprehensive resource for both novice and experienced raspberry and blackberry growers as well as crop advisors and educators. It provides information on all aspects of raspberry and blackberry culture for the midwestern and northeastern United States, and eastern Canada. This publication will help raspberry and blackberry growers plan and implement production and marketing decisions. The cultivars mentioned either have performed well in this region or show the most promise. Pest management chapters emphasize cultural controls, since chemical use is regulated at the state or province level. The sample budgets provided in chapter fourteen are based on 2006 costs. A glossary is included to define terms that might be unfamiliar to readers. Throughout this guide the term "bramble" will be used to refer to both raspberries and blackberries when the content applies to both crops. Information on farm food safety practices can be found at www.gaps.cornell.edu. Help on diagnosing common raspberry and blackberry problems can be found at: www.hort.cornell.edu/diagnostic.

Getting Started

Growing raspberries and blackberries is not easy. To succeed, you must be a good horticulturist, labor manager, pest manager, and marketer. Below are some questions to consider before embarking in the bramble business. The information in this guide will help you answer the questions.

1. How do you plan to market the berries? (Perhaps the biggest cause of failure among growers is not planning adequately for marketing the berries.)

2. Are your facilities adequate for the type of marketing you plan to do? For example, do you have cooling facilities for wholesaling or a parking area for pick-your-own customers?

3. Is the soil in your area appropriate for growing berries? Can it be amended to support berry production?

4. Is the soil sufficiently drained?

5. Do you have a large enough water supply for irrigation?

6. Does your land slope enough to allow for air drainage, but not so much that it is difficult to work?

7. Do you have sufficient capital resources to invest in berries—about $5,000 per acre for fall raspberries and $7,000 per acre for summer raspberries? (Keep in mind that a return on investment will be many years away.)

8. Do you have the personal skills necessary to manage laborers and greet customers?

9. Where will you obtain labor during the busy picking season?

10. Do you have land for future expansion and crop rotation?

11. Is your family willing to commit to berry production? (Growing brambles may entail foregoing a summer vacation; working during harvest; and, if retailing, opening the farm to the public.)

12. Have you checked local ordinances regarding zoning, parking, signs, noise, riparian rights, etc., to see if they might conflict with your plans for berry production?

13. Are you set up to keep track of input expenses, payroll, pesticide applications, employee records, yield records, and perhaps customer mailing lists?

14. Have you started a library of resources?

15. Are you certified to apply pesticides?

16. If retailing, have you evaluated your farm's location in relation to population centers, off-road parking, visibility, and competition? Will customers be able to find your farm easily?

17. Have you inquired about membership in state or province and national grower organizations—for example, the North American Bramble Growers Association? See their Web site, WWW.RASPBERRYBLACKBERRY.COM, for membership information.

Further Reading

Grudens-Schuck, Nancy, et al. 1988. *Farming Alternatives: A Guide to Evaluating the Feasibility of New Farm-Based Enterprises*, NRAES–32. Ithaca, NY: Natural Resource, Agricultural, & Engineering Service (NRAES). For more information, visit the NRAES web site WWW.NRAES.ORG, or contact NRAES at 607-255-7654 or NRAES@CORNELL.EDU.

The History and Biology of Cultivated Raspberries and Blackberries

A Brief History

Brambles are a diverse group of flowering plants that belong to the genus *Rubus*, which is a member of the Rose family (Rosaceae). Wild brambles occur on five continents and are common low-growing shrubs in temperate forests and tropic highlands. Some species thrive at cool, high altitudes; others grow well in boggy, tundra areas. They quickly grow and spread in cleared or disturbed land areas. Several hundred species have been identified, but only three to four dozen have edible fruit and only a few of these are important commercially, most notably raspberries and blackberries (figure 1.1).

Raspberries

Raspberries have a long history of cultivation and development. According to legend, the raspberry's scientific name, *Rubus idaeus,* is derived from Mount Ida in Turkey.

It was there that the Greek gods went berrying and returned with raspberries.

Raspberries were possibly cultivated by the Romans of the fourth century. During the sixteenth century, raspberry plants were first collected from the woods for use in gardens in Europe. By the early nineteenth century, more than twenty cultivars of red raspberry were grown in England and the U.S. English cultivars exported to the U.S. were subsequently crossed with North American seedlings leading to improved cultivars. Red raspberries are currently the most widely grown while black raspberries are most popular in certain regions of the eastern U.S. The progeny of black and red raspberries have purple fruits; these types are popular in eastern North America. Yellow-fruited raspberries, caused by a recessive mutation, are also grown on a limited scale for specialty markets.

Patterns of production in North America shifted dramatically in the early 1900s. In 1920, New York State growers harvested more than ten thousand acres of raspberries. Subsequently, the systemic 'mosaic virus disease' infected most of the planting stock, and the raspberry processing industry collapsed in New York. The raspberry processing industry redeveloped on the West Coast with the advancement of virus-indexing nursery stock, breeding resistance to the virus vectors, and the use of mechanical harvesters.

The three major raspberry production regions today are (1) Russia, (2) Europe (mostly in Poland, Hungary, Serbia, Germany, and the UK), and (3) the Pacific Coast of North

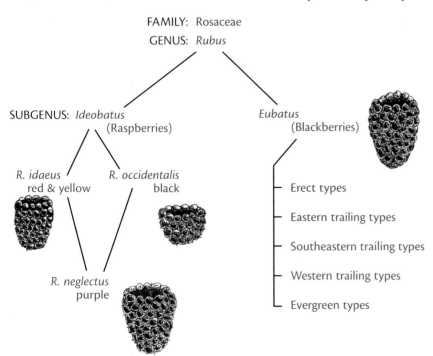

Fig. 1.1 **Relationships between various types of raspberries and blackberries.**

America (British Columbia, Washington, and Oregon). Much of the fruit produced in these regions is harvested mechanically and processed. In eastern North America, nearly all the production is for fresh market. Many other countries, such as Chile, New Zealand, and Australia, also have significant production and supply the fresh market during winter in the northern hemisphere. In both Europe and North America, there is limited greenhouse raspberry production to supply local markets during winter and spring. High tunnel production of raspberries is extensively used in Europe to extend the field season and is becoming common in North America.

Blackberries

Blackberries have been collected from the wild for about two thousand years, ever since the time of the ancient Greeks. They were gathered largely from hedgerows in Europe, where they were used for medicinal and other purposes until the sixteenth century. The cut leaf, or Evergreen, blackberry was domesticated in the seventeenth century. Most of the other cultivars were not commercially produced until the nineteenth and twentieth centuries.

In North America, clearing of forests for agriculture provided the opportunity for native blackberries to spread and hybridize. Cultivation of blackberries in America began sometime between 1850 to 1860. In 1867, eighteen cultivars were listed, most of which were native seedlings and selections. By the late nineteenth century, some notable commercial cultivars had been bred or discovered by private individuals. Production reached forty thousand acres in the U.S. in 1948, mainly in the Southeast.

Today, the Pacific Coast states are all active blackberry and blackberry hybrid producers. The Southeast region is still an important production region. There is active interest in thornless types in the North and much of the East, but fully hardy types have not yet been developed. There are remarkable increases in production, fruit size, and disease resistance among the newer blackberry cultivars. Some also show improved color stability, flesh and skin firmness, better flavor, longer shelf life, and a primocane-fruiting habit.

As with raspberries, tissue culture has greatly improved the blackberry plant supply. The potential for using blackberries in juice has not been fully realized, but the demand for fresh and other processed products is strong, especially in these times of health and nutrition awareness.

Growth and Development of the Bramble Plant

The growth and fruiting habits of different brambles vary. Some brambles are low-growing herbs, and others are woody bushes or climbing vine-like plants. Most cultivated brambles are woody shrubs that have a perennial root system that functions for many years and biennial stems (canes) that emerge every year and live for two growing seasons. Bramble canes may be stiff and upright (erect), free-standing with the top portion arched over (semi-erect), or sprawling over the ground (trailing).

Bramble root systems are perennial, fibrous and relatively shallow. About 70% of the total root weight is in the top ten inches of soil, and an additional 20% in the next ten inches (figure 1.2). Red raspberry roots grow close to the surface far from the parent plant while blackberry roots tend to remain in the location where the parent plant was initially set. Bramble roots are very strong sinks for carbon, meaning that much of the sugar and starch produced through photosynthesis is transported to the roots. Once plants are well established, roots are very tolerant to damage through cultivation.

Bramble canes originate from either crown buds or adventitious root buds in early spring. Bud break on roots is enhanced with chilling. This is why a flush of canes appears in spring, after the root buds have been chilled

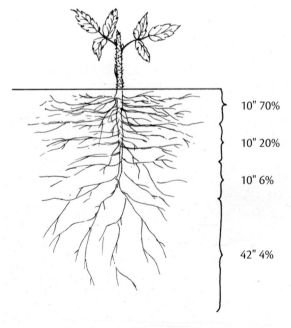

Fig. 1.2 **Typical distribution in the soil of a raspberry root system.**

over winter. Successive root bud break can occur, but often with less vigor after the initial spring flush.

Bramble plants produce new canes (primocanes) every year. Primocanes grow rapidly during spring and early summer. During the summer, axillary buds may break on primocanes and form lateral shoots, especially in primocane-fruiting raspberries and tipped black raspberries and blackberries. Most of these lateral shoots occur on the top one-third of the primocane. In primocane-fruiting types, these lateral shoots will contain flowers that initiate sequentially from the top to the bottom of the cane. If the growing season is sufficiently long, fruit can be harvested from the upper portion of these canes in the late summer and through the fall. During late fall, the buds below the primocane-fruiting zone continue to differentiate into flower buds, but these buds do not normally grow until after winter. In spring, axillary buds on the lower portion of the cane flower and produce a summer crop. Because of this unique growth habit, primocane-fruiting types can be managed to produce two crops per year—one in the summer from the floricanes (second-year canes) and the other in the fall from the primocanes. The term "everbearer" is sometimes used to describe this type, although this name is not an accurate description of the growth habit.

In floricane-fruiting types, as temperatures drop and day lengths shorten in the fall, flower buds begin to form in the axils of leaves, but the buds do not break. With the further onset of cold temperatures, canes stop growing and eventually go into a state of rest called dormancy. At this point plants need an extended period of time exposed to temperatures between 25°F and 40°F (often eight hundred hours or more for raspberries, three hundred hours or more for blackberries). If this period of chilling temperatures has occurred, the buds will break when growing conditions become favorable in the spring. If chilling is insufficient, buds will remain dormant despite the return of warm weather. Chilling requirements vary considerably among cultivars. Long chilling requirements of some cultivars may limit their production in very warm climates. Conversely, cultivars with short chilling requirements may be injured in cold climates if they begin spring growth during a winter warm spell.

After the buds break in the spring, the lateral shoots will grow, producing both leaves and flowers. The most fruitful lateral shoots are those in the middle three-fifths of the cane. After fruiting, the entire cane senesces and dies. While these second-year canes (floricanes) are flowering, first-year canes (primocanes) are growing from the crown or roots.

Flowering and Fruit Development

A typical raspberry flower opens to show five small sepals and five small petals, while blackberry petals can be quite large and showy (figure 1.3). Many stamens are arranged around a center cluster containing many individual pistils inserted on the receptacle (figure 1.4). For pollination to occur, pollen grains must be transferred from the stamen (male part) to the pistil (female part) of the flower. Brambles are self-fruitful so pollen need only be transferred within the same flower to result in fruit set. Honey bee colonies usually are not required for brambles, because the flowers produce huge quantities of nectar that attract both wild and domesticated bees.

Fig. 1.3 **Thorny blackberry in flower.**

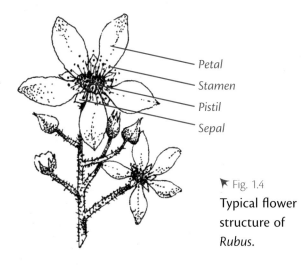

— Petal
— Stamen
— Pistil
— Sepal

▶ Fig. 1.4

Typical flower structure of *Rubus*.

If honey bee colonies are used, two hives per acre are recommended.

Each of the 100 to 125 pistils of a bramble flower contains two ovules. About one month after pollination one of the two ovules will ripen into a mature seed and the other into a fleshy drupelet surrounding the seed. Between 75 and 125 drupelets comprise a mature raspberry (figure 1.5). Raspberries are thus considered aggregate fruits in which each individual drupelet has the same basic structure as a peach, plum, or cherry (botanically these larger fruits are called "drupes"). Considerable variation in fruit size exists, with a range from one to more than ten grams. In the raspberry, the drupelets separate from the receptacle (torus) at harvest, yielding a hollow, thimble-shaped fruit, while in blackberries the torus remains inside the harvested fruit and is eaten along with the true fruit portion. Most raspberry cultivars produce red fruit, but black-, purple- and yellow-fruited cultivars also are grown commercially.

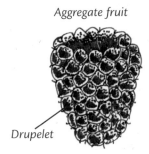

Aggregate fruit

Drupelet

Fig. 1.5 **Typical bramble fruit structure.**

Response to Environment

Cold Temperatures

Although a certain numbers of hours at chilling temperatures (between 40°F and 25°F) are required to break dormancy of floricane axillary buds, temperatures below 10°F can injure the buds of the least hardy cultivars, and temperatures below –15°F can injure the buds of the most hardy cultivars.

Cold-temperature injury occurs when water freezes in the plant's vascular system leading to the buds. When this water freezes, it will expand, which can cause cells to rupture. The buds near the tip of the cane are the least hardy and often rise above the protective snow cover where they are more susceptible to winter injury than buds lower on the cane.

Warmer temperatures later in winter can deacclimate plants and increase their susceptibility to cold temperature. During periods of warm weather, water can begin to move back into the vascular system of a plant as it prepares for spring growth. A significant and sudden drop in temperatures can freeze this water and rupture cells, resulting in plant injury. Consequently,

cold-temperature injury can occur even when plants have been exposed to a mild winter. Fluctuating temperatures in early spring are very detrimental to bramble plants.

Symptoms of cold-temperature injury may not be visible until the weather warms in late spring and the shoot's demand for water increases. The injured vascular system may not be able to provide sufficient water during this period of high demand, and buds or the entire shoot can collapse. However, new primocanes emerge and grow with vigor as underground buds are usually not injured by cold temperatures (figure 1.6).

Warm Temperatures

Warm temperatures can be as detrimental to bramble plants as cold temperatures, although the effects are more subtle. Raspberries, in particular, are susceptible to growth- and yield-suppression caused by very warm

Fig. 1.6 **Winter-damaged floricanes.**

temperatures. Several studies have found that the optimal temperature for raspberry growth is 70°F and that temperatures higher than 80°F suppress growth. In the summer, raspberry photosynthesis may be suppressed in mid-day if temperatures are too hot. The plant then cannot take advantage of the available light, and growth will suffer. The best yields occur under sunny, cool summer conditions. Areas of the world exhibiting the highest raspberry yields (Washington State, British Columbia, parts of Chile, northern Europe) have relatively cool summers and mild winters. Blackberries are more tolerant to warm summer temperatures than raspberries.

Light

The most important environmental factor influencing photosynthesis, growth, and yield is the number of leaves intercepting a high level of light. Yields around the world are highly correlated with ambient light levels when all other conditions are similar. Although the total amount of incident light is beyond a grower's control, the amount of light intercepted in a planting can be manipulated through site selection, planting design, trellising, and pruning.

The slope of the land and the direction that it faces can have a dramatic effect on incident light, particularly in more northern locations. Steep north-facing slopes receive far less light than south-facing slopes, and yields on steep north-facing slopes will be less, all else being equal.

From mid-latitudes to the tropics, a north-south row orientation will intercept more light than east-west rows during summer. Furthermore, a higher number of narrow rows will intercept more light than fewer wider rows. In some situations, growers cannot tighten rows as much as they might like because of equipment such as tractors and mowers that must navigate down the alleyways. In these situations, spreading the canes into a V-shape will improve light interception in the canopy and increase the productivity of lower laterals. Spreading the canes has other advantages, such as improving

spray coverage of floricanes and making hand picking easier, because interference with primocanes is reduced.

When primocanes become too tall or dense they interfere with the light interception of floricanes, reducing the current year's crop. Carbon acquired by primocanes does not move readily into floricanes, so even though total light interception might be greater in a dense planting, the primocanes intercept much of the light and leave too little for floricanes. By regulating cane numbers and height through pruning, a balance between primocane and floricane light interception can be obtained. There is no single rule for pruning raspberries; the optimal system will depend on the length of the growing season, the inherent vigor of the site, the variety, the trellising system, cultural practices, and other factors (see "Trellising and Pruning," chapter five).

Water and Rain

It is rare to see a raspberry planting wilt from drought in the Northeast or Midwest. A well-established bramble root system is relatively large and capable of serving as a significant sink for moisture. Leaf stomata can close during mid-day, allowing the raspberry plant to conserve moisture. These characteristics contribute to the ability

Fig. 1.7 Rain shelter over a raspberry planting.

of bramble plants to survive periods of drought, but insufficient water will significantly reduce fruit production. Insufficient water is first expressed as small berry size, followed by reduced plant growth and primocane production, leaf drop, and then wilting. So for optimal fruit production, the planting site must have access to an ample supply of high-quality water and an efficient irrigation system.

Though adequate water is essential, brambles are particularly sensitive to excessively wet soil conditions. Even temporarily water-saturated soil conditions can cause serious problems, including poor cane growth, increased incidence of soil-borne diseases, and plant death. Choose a site with good soil drainage for bramble production. Installing subsoil drainage can help alleviate problems with excess water as can planting on raised beds.

Raspberry fruit are particularly sensitive to rain. Water on flowers or fruit for an extended period will allow for the development of mold and reduce fruit quality significantly. Rain shelters and high tunnels are increasingly used to prevent moisture damage to fruit.

Wind

The tall, thin canes of a bramble plant are prone to wind damage. Canes that are exposed to persistent wind are significantly shorter and less productive than canes in protected sites. Trellises can relieve some of the stress and cane breakage caused by wind. Winds can be reduced by the planting of windbreaks around a field, usually consisting of fast-growing conifer trees, such as pines or firs or by erecting wind fences. Contact your local Farm Services Agency regarding programs that encourage the planting of windbreaks.

Chemical and Nutritional Composition of Bramble Fruits

The main constituent of raspberry and blackberry fruit is water (85–90%). Of the remaining solids, about 9% are soluble and the rest insoluble. In red raspberries, about 0.1–1.0% of the soluble fraction consists of pectins. Sugars such as glucose and fructose compose the major soluble component of the juice. A typical ripe fruit contains 5–6% sugar. Citric acid is the second largest component of the soluble fraction. Values are similar for blackberries.

The balance between the sugars and acids is important for consumer acceptance. A fruit with a low sugar-to-acid ratio will taste tart; one with a high ratio will taste bland. Fruits with high sugar and high acid generally taste best. Fruits grown in warm, dry summers (daytime temperatures near 77°F, or 25°C) are sweeter, less acid, more aromatic, and more highly colored. Hot weather (temperatures greater than 86°F, or 30°C) will reduce

Fig. 1.8 **Wind fence around a raspberry field.**

the aroma of the fruit, and wet weather will reduce the sugar content.

Bramble fruits are rich in vitamins A, C, and E, as well as folic acid, iron, and potassium (tables 1.1 and 1.2). They are rich in soluble fiber (e.g., pectins), which may help prevent heart disease by lowering abnormally high levels of blood cholesterol. Foods high in soluble fibers also help diabetics by slowing the release of carbohydrates into the blood stream and maintaining a more even blood-glucose level. In addition, berries are high in natural antioxidants, including anthocyanins and phytochemicals such as beta-carotene, and ellagic, coumaric, and ferulic acids. These compounds reduce the effects of damaging free radicals, thereby advancing heart health, reducing the risk of certain types of cancer, and boosting total body wellness.

Table 1.1 **Nutrient content of one cup (123 grams) of fresh red raspberries.**

Nutrition Facts
Serving Size 1 cup 123g (123 g)

Amount Per Serving

Calories 64	Calories from Fat 7

	% Daily Value*
Total Fat 1g	1%
Saturated Fat 0g	0%
Trans Fat	
Cholesterol 0mg	0%
Sodium 1mg	0%
Total Carbohydrate 15g	5%
Dietary Fiber 8g	32%
Sugars 5g	
Protein 1g	

Vitamin A	1%	•	Vitamin C	54%
Calcium	3%	•	Iron	5%

*Percent Daily Values are based on a 2,000 calorie diet. Your daily values may be higher or lower depending on your calorie needs.

© www.NutritionData.com

Table 1.2 **Nutrient content of one cup (123 grams) of fresh blackberries.**

Nutrition Facts
Serving Size 1 cup 144g (144 g)

Amount Per Serving

Calories 62	Calories from Fat 6

	% Daily Value*
Total Fat 1g	1%
Saturated Fat 0g	0%
Trans Fat	
Cholesterol 0mg	0%
Sodium 1mg	0%
Total Carbohydrate 14g	5%
Dietary Fiber 8g	31%
Sugars 7g	
Protein 2g	

Vitamin A	6%	•	Vitamin C	50%
Calcium	4%	•	Iron	5%

*Percent Daily Values are based on a 2,000 calorie diet. Your daily values may be higher or lower depending on your calorie needs.

© www.NutritionData.com

Nutritional data and images courtesy of www.NUTRITIONDATA.COM.

Further Reading

Galletta, G.J., and D.G. Himelrick. 1990. *Small Fruit Crop Management.* Englewood Cliffs, NJ: Prentice-Hall.

Janick, J., and J.N. Moore. 1975. *Advances in Fruit Breeding.* West Lafayette, IN: Purdue University Press.

CHAPTER TWO

Site Selection and Site Preparation

Site Selection

Site selection is an important consideration for berry production. The site will affect not only yield potential but also marketing options. Pick-your-own (PYO) marketing is common in the Northeast and Midwest; but if a potential site is located far from a major highway or population center, then PYO marketing may not be successful. If the site is ideally located for PYO, then perhaps not all of the land can be planted in berries—some must be reserved for customer parking and crop rotation. If the intention is to sell berries through retail outlets, then production fields should be close (preferably less than one mile) to the outlets to minimize the time berries will be in transit.

Choose a site with good internal water drainage. Brambles are particularly sensitive to excessively wet soil conditions. Even temporary water-saturated soil conditions can cause serious problems, including poor cane growth, increased incidence of soil-borne diseases, and plant death. Certain bramble diseases, such as *Phytophthora* root rot, caused by a fungus, are common problems in poorly drained soils. If your site is too wet for berry production, then install subsoil drainage to alleviate problems with excess water. Sometimes brambles can be grown successfully on wet sites if they are planted in raised beds.

Equally important as having good water drainage is the availability of water. Bramble fruit production can be easily affected by insufficient water, so for successful fruit production, the planting site must have access to an ample supply of high-quality water and an efficient irrigation system (see "Water Management," chapter six).

In most locations, the ideal soil for bramble production is a well-drained, sandy loam with a pH of 6.0 to 6.5. Soil pH can be modified and managed on less-than-ideal soils. In some sandy soils, certain micronutrients can

Fig. 2.1 **Raised bed planting with straw mulch.**

become deficient if the soil pH is above 6.0. Heavy clays should be avoided, but sandy soils are acceptable. Stony soils are hard on equipment and difficult to plant in and cultivate.

Brambles should not be grown where tomatoes, potatoes, eggplant, or strawberries have been grown during the previous four to five years. Following corn with raspberries can be a good rotation if certain herbicides with long residual activity, such as atrazine, were not recently used on the corn. Be cautious about following field crops with raspberries unless the full herbicide history is known.

Avoid steep slopes (greater than 5%) as they are vulnerable to erosion, challenging to cultivate, and difficult to irrigate uniformly. Moderate slopes (3 to 5%) allow air to drain, consequently reducing the high humidity around the canes that could promote disease development and reducing the risk of cold temperature injury. South-facing slopes tend to increase the risk of frost injury in spring because plants generally bloom earlier, and west-facing slopes present the greatest risk for winter injury because plants are exposed to persistent, desiccating winds in winter.

Viruses are transmitted among wild and cultivated plants by aphids, thrips, whiteflies, and nematodes. To minimize the chance of viral infections, new brambles should be planted as far as possible from other brambles, wild or cultivated. If feasible, all wild brambles within six hundred feet of a proposed planting should be totally removed. Sites infested with nematodes should also be avoided, or nematode populations eliminated through fumigation or cover-cropping (more details on nematode management follow later in this chapter).

Fig. 2.2 **Sandy loam soil.**

Site Preparation

Weeds

A major step in site preparation is eliminating perennial weeds. This is very important because few herbicides are labeled for use in brambles. The herbicides that are labeled have a limited effect on perennial weeds. Too often growers plant directly into a site where perennial weeds were not eliminated the previous year, and then spend the next several years trying to find the right combination of herbicides to eradicate the weeds. It is much easier to eliminate weeds the year before planting than after planting. A grower that plans ahead and starts site preparation two or three years in advance will be rewarded in future production. Weeds can easily cause more economic loss than diseases and insects combined.

Crop rotation, coupled with a broad-spectrum post-emergent non-residual herbicide the summer before planting, can be an effective approach to eliminating weeds. Cover cropping the site again after applying herbicide will further suppress weed growth while building soil organic matter. Repeated cultivation or covering a site with black plastic for several months also can be effective.

Fumigation can reduce the weed seed bank prior to planting, but this option is expensive. Fumigation as an option is becoming limited due to growing environmental concerns and availability. If fumigation is used, soil should be friable, warm (greater than 50°F), and devoid of decomposing plant material. The best time to fumigate a field is late summer or early fall of the year prior to planting.

See chapter ten for more details on weed management.

Checklist for a Good Site

- ❑ a location close to market
- ❑ good soils
- ❑ good soil drainage
- ❑ a moderate slope (3 to 5%)
- ❑ a source of high-quality water nearby
- ❑ no wild brambles in the immediate area

Nutrient Amendments

Before planting, test the soil for pH, potassium, phosphorus, magnesium, calcium, and boron. Collect 6-inch soil cores from at least ten to twelve locations in a V-shaped pattern within the field (figure 2.3), and mix them together to get a composite sample for sending to the lab. Taking a representative soil sample is crucial to get an accurate soil analysis. After testing, plow the site, add the amount of nutrients recommended by the soil-testing laboratory, and then incorporate the fertilizer. Soil-testing procedures are not standardized between states and provinces. Follow the recommendations from the laboratory where the samples were analyzed. Do not use test results from one laboratory and sufficiency ranges from another unless you know that the laboratory methods and extractants are the same.

If soil test results indicate that the soil pH is below the optimal pH range of 6.0 to 6.5, apply an acid neutralizer such as calcite or dolomite lime to increase soil pH one year before planting. Do not wait until after planting to make a pH adjustment because it will be difficult to incorporate lime at that time. If the soil pH is above 7.0 it will require sulfur to effectively reduce the pH to the ideal range for brambles.

Acid neutralizing agents differ from one another in two important ways, both of which will influence their effectiveness: (1) chemical composition, which affects acid-neutralizing potential and fertilizer value, and (2) particle size, which determines liming efficiency and ease of application. Consider the relative importance of these when selecting a product. For example, even though dolomite has a lower neutralizing value than

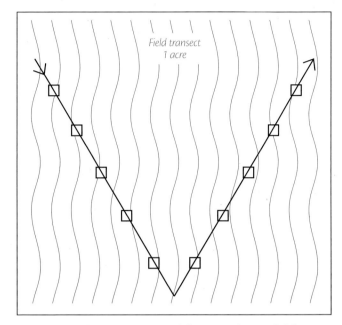

Field transect 1 acre

Fig. 2.3 "V" pattern used for sampling a field.

calcite, it is often used on sites that require supplemental magnesium for adequate fertility. Moreover, finely ground lime is more difficult to apply than coarse particles, but it changes the soil pH more quickly.

Certain nutrients, like phosphorus and potassium, are relatively insoluble in water and move very slowly through the soil. It is important that preplant soil samples be taken and the fertility recommendations followed to ensure adequate levels of phosphorous and potassium in the crop root zone. After the crop is established it is almost impossible to apply these nutrients and get them mixed throughout the soil profile.

Animal manures and legumes offer a good source of slowly released nitrogen. However, animal manures are a potential source of weed seeds. Manure applied to fields should first be well-composted and worked into the soil prior to planting to minimize any risk of fruit contamination from pathogenic bacteria. Chapter seven provides more details on nutrient management.

Irrigation

An irrigation system should be in place and operational before planting brambles for two important reasons: (1) transplants need to be watered

Fig. 2.4 **Lime cannot be thoroughly incorporated when applied after planting.**

immediately, and (2) any pre-emergent herbicide applied after transplanting will need to be watered in by rain or irrigation to be effective. Chapter six, "Water Management," provides details for irrigation design and management.

Preplant Cover and Green Manure Crops

Cover-cropping the site the year before planting is an excellent way to improve soil structure, suppress weeds, and if the proper cover crop is chosen, suppress nematode populations. Cover-cropping benefits are greatest when the soil is sandy and/or the soil's organic matter content is low. Most cover crops will grow well with soil conditions favorable to brambles.

Use minimum seeding rates for cover crops when the objective is to supply a harvestable stand of grain or straw. But when a vigorous, dense stand is desired for weed suppression and organic matter, use a higher seeding rate.

Preplant cover crops are usually either chemically controlled or plowed under in the late fall or early spring prior to planting. Unless the soil and site are prone to erosion, crops with low nitrogen content (grains and grasses) should be plowed under early in the fall to allow enough time for decomposition. Legumes contain more nitrogen and decompose quickly, so they can be turned under within a month of planting. However, legumes harbor several pests and may not be the best cover crop choice immediately before bramble establishment. See the Legumes section later in this chapter.

Some growers are experimenting with planting brambles into a mowed or killed sod of annual rye, rather than planting into bare soil. This method could reduce the need for herbicides.

Many plant species are suitable as preplant cover crops, and each has its own advantages. In some cases, mixtures of crops are used to realize multiple benefits. Listed below and in table 2.1, page 14, are some cover crops that perform well in cooler climates; the list is by no means comprehensive.

Grasses

Grasses have fine, fibrous root systems that are well suited to holding soil in place and improving soil structure. Suitable grass species for cover crops are inexpensive, fast growing, and relatively easy to kill—chemically, mechanically or by winter weather. Grasses do not fix any nitrogen out of the atmosphere, but they can accumulate large quantities from the soil.

Spring cereals

Oats and barley are commonly used as green manure and cover crops. Stands seeded between mid-August to mid-September will have 8–16 inches or 20–40 cm of growth by freeze-up. While seeding can be done outside this time frame, heat and lack of moisture in the summer may interfere with germination. The stand is generally killed by late, hard frosts.

Seeding rate: 90 to 115 lbs/A or 100 to 125 kg per ha

Cautions: Early seeding may result in considerable growth by freeze-up. This can form a mat of dead residue if left untilled. In the spring, this can keep soil cold and wet, interfering with spring tillage.

Annual Ryegrass

Direct seed in spring or late summer. Late summer seedings are more successful when made from early August to early September. Heavy root growth and rapid seeding development make annual ryegrass a very desirable green manure cover crop in areas when good soil-water relations can be maintained.

Seeding rate: 9 to 16 lbs/A or 10 to 18 kg per ha

Cautions: Establishment and growth of ryegrasses can be poor during very hot, dry weather. It can be difficult to kill overwintering ryegrass with only cultivation or discing. The nitrogen tied up in ryegrass releases more slowly than from other cover crops.

Winter wheat

Winter wheat can be seeded in late August through October. It can be seeded outside this time but, similar to spring cereals, weather conditions may reduce top growth. Wheat survives overwinter and begins growing in April. The stand can be killed through tillage or herbicide application. The plant shuts down earlier in fall and begins to grow later in the spring.

Seeding rate: 75 to 120 lbs/A or 80 to 130 kg per ha

Cautions: Generally winter wheat does not return as much green material to the soil as rye, nor does it give the level of weed competition that rye provides.

Winter rye

Winter rye is usually seeded from late August to October, often following field or vegetable crops. It grows until freeze-up, and then begins growth again in February to early April (slightly earlier than winter wheat). Growth rate is very rapid once soil temperatures are above 50° F. The cover crop is generally killed in early spring through tillage or herbicide use. Allow at least two weeks from killing to crop establishment for residue breakdown. Rye can produce significant root and top mass for return to the soil. A rye cover crop suppresses winter annual weeds effectively. Winter rye can be seeded later than any other crop and still survive over winter. For good ground cover and erosion protection, seed at least a month before freeze-up.

Seeding rate: 55 to 115 lbs/A or 60 to 125 kg per ha

Cautions: Kill rye in the fall or early spring to avoid loss of soil moisture and difficulties in incorporation. Rye is an excellent host for root-lesion nematode.

Table 2.1 **Characteristics of green manure crops and cover crops. First frost is assumed to be October 1, so planting dates should be adjusted accordingly.**

Species	Normal seeding time	Seeding rate Lbs/A (kg/ha)	Nitrogen fixed	Nitrogen uptake[1]	Overwintering characteristics	Potential volunteer-seed weed problem	Supports nematodes[2]	
							Lesion	Rootknot
Grasses								
Ryegrass	April to May or August to early September	9-16 (10 -18)	no	medium	Annual & Italian: partial survival; Perennial overwinters	no	—	—
Spring cereals (oats, barley)	mid-August to September	90-115 (100–125)	no	medium	killed by heavy frost	no	+	—
Sorghum sudan	June to August	10-35 (12-40)	no	medium to high	killed by frost	no	—	0
Pearl millet	June to August	8–11 (9-12)	no	medium to high	killed by frost	no	—	0
Winter wheat	September to October	75-120 (80-130)	no	medium to high	overwinters well	no	+	—
Winter rye	September to October	55 – 115 (60–125)	no	high	overwinters very well	no	+[3]	—
Legumes	April to June	species dependent	yes	low	most overwinter	usually not	— to +++	— to +++
Non–legume broadleaves								
Brassicas Mustards	mid-August to early September	5-6 (6-7)	no	high	killed by heavy frost (some species may not)	yes	—	—
Oilseed radish		9-14 (10–14)						
Marigold	May to June	1.3	no	low	killed by heavy frost	usually not	—	—
Buckwheat	June to August	45-55 (50–60)	no	low	killed by first frost	yes	+++	—

1 The potential for nitrogen uptake by individual cover crops is influenced by seeding date, stand and weather.

2 Varietal differences in cover crop species may affect nematode reaction.

3 Rye — whole season rating would be higher (+++).

NEMATODE RATING CODES: (—) poor or non–host; (+) ability to host; (0) some cultivars are non-hosts

Sorghum sudan

Sorghum sudan is an excellent choice for growing as a green manure crop to improve the soil. Root growth is extensive and top growth lush. A preplant herbicide treatment is recommended for crop establishment. Plant in mid-June or after all threat of frost is past. The crop benefits from the warm temperatures of early to mid-summer. Approximately 45 lbs/A or 50 kg/ha of nitrogen helps the crop achieve maximum top growth. Some varieties have nematode-suppressing properties. These varieties do not have to be incorporated green for nematode suppression.

Seeding rate: 10 to 35 lbs/A or 12 to 40 kg per ha

Cautions: Mow sorghum sudan before it reaches 3 ft or 1 m in height. This encourages tillering and ensures stalks are not woody and slow to break down. More than 1 year of a nematode suppressing cover crop may be required to successfully reduce nematode populations.

Forage pearl millet

Forage pearl millet is a warm season grass and is extremely sensitive to frost. It can produce a significant amount of top growth. This makes it a good choice as a mid-summer green manure crop to improve the soil. Root growth is extensive. A preplant herbicide treatment is recommended for crop establishment. Plant in mid-June, after all threat of frost is past. The crop benefits from the warm temperatures of early to mid-summer. Approximately 45 lbs/A or 50 kg/ha of nitrogen helps the crop achieve maximum top growth. Planting certain cultivars of forage pearl millet in rotation with high-valued horticultural crops can reduce nematode populations below economic thresholds. Canadian Forage Pearl Millet 101 reduces nematode populations by inhibiting the ability for nematodes to reproduce in its root system. The pearl millet does not have to be incorporated green for nematode suppression.

Seeding Rate: 8 to 11 lbs/A or 9 to 12 kg per ha

Cautions: Mow pearl millet before it reaches 3 feet or 1 m in height. Do not mow shorter than 6 inches or 15 cm to ensure regrowth. This encourages tillering and ensures stalks are not woody and slow to break down. More than one growing season of this cover crop is necessary for nematode suppression.

Legumes

Legume cover crops can fix nitrogen from the air, supplying nitrogen to the succeeding crop as well as protecting the soil from erosion and adding organic matter. The amount of nitrogen fixed varies between species, although generally, more top growth equals more nitrogen fixed. Nitrogen release from legumes varies from less than 40 lbs/A or 45 kg/ha in poor stands of red clover to more than 90lbs/A or 100 kg/ha with alfalfa plowdown.

Some legume species like alfalfa and sweet clover have aggressive tap roots that can break up subsoil compaction, but this requires more than one year's growth to happen.

Cautions: Legumes are not commonly grown between bramble rows because they provide an inconsistent and season-long release of nitrogen. Too much nitrogen at the wrong time can interfere with fruit quality and winter hardiness of canes. Legumes are also attractive to tarnished plant bugs and most are excellent hosts for nematodes.

Non-legume broadleaves

These broadleaf crops may have a role as green manure crops and in providing different plant species and root systems for soil building. They cannot fix nitrogen out of the air, but they can absorb large quantities from the soil. Most of these crops are not winter-hardy, so additional control measures are not normally required. Do not allow them to go to seed, as the volunteer seed can become a significant weed problem.

Buckwheat

As a cover crop, buckwheat is most commonly seeded in mid-to-late June through to August. It grows very rapidly, reaching flower stage and a height of 18 to 30 inches or 45 to 75 cm in about 6 weeks. It has a relatively small fibrous root system and is completely killed by the first frost. Buckwheat provides rapid soil cover, gives good erosion protection during the growing season, smothers annual weeds, and suppresses perennial ones. It is possible to do repeated plantings of buckwheat during the season. Moderate amounts of fresh organic matter are returned to the soil.

Seeding Rate: 45 to 55 lbs/A or 50 to 60 kg/ha

Cautions: Late summer seedings may be killed by an early frost before providing significant growth. Buckwheat is an excellent host for root-lesion nematode. Buckwheat starts to set seed after 6 weeks, so monitor it closely to ensure the crop is killed before seeds set and germinate; otherwise, a buckwheat weed problem can develop in a subsequent crop of berries.

Brassicas

Brassicas like mustards and oilseed radish are becoming increasingly popular. They are commonly seeded in August or early September. Unaffected by early frosts, they can grow to a height of 20 inches or 50 cm by October. The plant has a thick, short taproot, varying between carrot and turnip shaped, depending on the species. Most brassicas used as cover crops are killed by severe frosts in late fall or during the winter. Brassicas provide rapid soil cover and good erosion protection over winter. It returns moderate amounts of organic matter to the soil. For good growth, this cover crop must have a large amount of available nitrogen. Some brassicas can help to reduce plant parasitic nematode soil populations below economic thresholds. The nematode-suppressing cultivars of oilseed radish and certain mustards must be incorporated into the soil as a "green manure" crop before they will release isothiocyanate into the soil that is toxic to plant parasitic nematodes.

Seeding rate varies with species: mustard 5 to 6 lbs/A or 6 to 7 kg/ha, oilseed radish 9 to 14 lbs/A or 10 to 15 kg/ha

Cautions: Growth will be poor if soil nitrogen levels are low or if soil compaction is severe. Scattered volunteer plants may appear in crops previously planted to brassicas. Some varieties may have a greater tendency to survive winter conditions and germinate the following year. More than one year of a nematode-suppressing cover crop may be required to successfully reduce nematode populations.

Marigolds

Marigolds are used as a preplant cover crop in parts of Northern Europe and to some extent in North America. They can be a useful cover crop for nematode suppression. Certain cultivars of African marigolds produce a root exudate that kills nematodes in the soil directly. Research has suggested nematode suppression from these cultivars can be achieved for up to two years. Shallowly seed marigolds (no more than a ½-inch depth) in the spring once soils have warmed (soil is more than 65°F). Achieving a dense weed-free stand is essential for nematode suppression. Use of the stale seedbed technique for weed control has been successful. Light irrigation may promote more consistent germination. Plants do not have to flower to provide benefits, and they can be plowed under after growing for ninety days or more.

Seeding rate: 1.1 lbs/A or 1.3 kg/ha

Cautions: Seeding of marigold is difficult as the seed tends to bridge in the drill tubes. Seed is expensive. Herbicide options are limited.

Further Reading

Sarrantonio, M. 1994. *Northeast Cover Crop Handbook.* Soil Health Series. Emmaus, PA: Rodale Institute.

United States Department of Agriculture (USDA). 2000. *Managing Cover Crops Profitably.* 2nd ed. Washington, DC: Sustainable Agriculture Publications, USDA. Also available online at WWW.SARE.ORG/PUBLICATIONS/COVERCROPS.HTM.

University of California Sustainable Agriculture Research and Education Program. "UC SAREP Cover Crop Resource Page." Davis, CA: University of California. WWW.SAREP.UCDAVIS.EDU/CCROP. Extensive listings of cover crop species and known scientifically derived characteristics.

Verhallen, A., A. Haynes, and T. Taylor. "Cover Crops: Cover Crop Types." Ontario, Canada: Ontario Ministry of Agriculture, Food and Rural Affairs. WWW.OMAFRA.GOV.ON.CA/ENGLISH/CROPS/FACTS/COVER_CROPS01/COVER_TYPES.HTM. Basic cover crop information and searchable seed source listing.

W.K. Kellogg Biological Station Land and Water program. "Michigan Cover Crops." East Lansing, MI: Michigan State University, Kellogg Biological Station. WWW.KBS.MSU.EDU/EXTENSION/COVERCROPS/HOME.HTM. Extensive information on cover crop establishment and control.

CHAPTER THREE

Plant Selection

The number of bramble cultivars available to berry growers has increased greatly in recent years, thanks to introductions from both new and established breeding programs. Many cultivars have desirable characteristics such as large fruit and high yields (figure 3.1), but many other factors should be considered when selecting cultivars, including hardiness, ripening season, and disease resistance.

Growers in extremely cold, northern climates should plant primarily red raspberries as neither black raspberries nor blackberries have adequate winter hardiness. Alternatively, growers in warm, southern climates, while capable of growing almost all types of brambles, may find consumer demand is highest for a specific berry and should plant accordingly.

Cultivar selection determines the length of the harvest season. A grower can harvest berries continuously from the beginning of the raspberry season in early summer to the first fall frost by selecting early-, mid-, and late-ripening floricane-fruiting cultivars for summer fruit, followed by primocane-fruiting cultivars for fall fruit. A grower more interested in a concentrated harvest season could plant cultivars with similar ripening periods.

Disease resistance is an important factor in cultivar selection. Phytophthora root rot (*Phytophthora* spp.), a root rot fungus, is prevalent in many soils, especially those that hold water because of poor drainage. Plant resistance is the primary method to combat this disease. When choosing bramble cultivars, give priority to cultivars resistant to Phytophthora root rot if you will be planting into a field that has poor drainage or is known to be infested. Planting exclusively nonresistant cultivars could lead to total crop failure, especially during a wet year. Blackberries and black raspberries are less susceptible than many red and purple raspberry cultivars.

The productivity of individual cultivars varies depending on soil type, fertilization, weather, and season. For example, some cultivars are more tolerant of wet soils, while others grow well only in light soils. In all cases, consider where each cultivar has been developed and how extensively it has been tested prior to release. Plant several cultivars to stretch out the marketing season and reduce the risk of loss to one specific disease or pest problem.

Evaluate the performance of new cultivars in small test plantings before placing large orders for plants. Progressive growers provide samples of new cultivars to customers for feedback. While a berry may perform well for the grower, customers may not like the flavor. Ultimately, it is the superior flavor of berries that motivates the consumer to buy.

Order plants from a nursery that offers certified virus-indexed material; this indicates that plants have tested negative for common viruses that may decrease productivity. Certified virus-indexed plants have the best growth and productivity and will generally live longer and be more profitable. Propagation from fruiting fields is not recommended because the disease status of the plants will be unknown.

Fig. 3.1 **Fruit of Titan summer-fruiting red raspberry.**

Three types of bramble plants are generally available from nurseries: bare root (dormant suckers), tip-layered canes, or tissue-cultured plants (figure 3.2). Brambles can be propagated using root cuttings, but this is not a common method of propagation in eastern North America.

Bare root dormant suckers are rooted canes or "handles" with one season of growth that were dug after becoming dormant in the fall (figure 3.3). These conventional transplant types for red raspberries and blackberries are stored until spring shipping. They can tolerate rough handling and can be planted before the danger of frost is over. However, they are large and cannot be put through most transplanters, and their roots cannot be allowed to dry out.

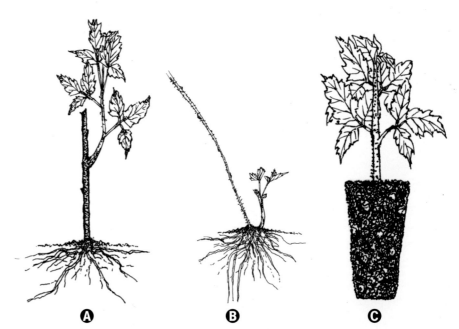

Fig. 3.2 **Types of bramble propagules: Ⓐ** bare root, **Ⓑ** tip-layering, and **Ⓒ** tissue-cultured.

Black raspberry plants are traditionally propagated using a tip-layering method. Tip-layered canes are produced when the growing tips of canes are covered with soil in summer, causing them to root. The new plants are separated from the cane following dormancy, are stored until shipping, and are handled like bare root suckers.

Tissue-cultured plants (figure 3.4) grow more rapidly and uniformly in the field than conventionally propagated transplants and generally produce higher yields early in the life of the planting. However, tissue-cultured transplants are more costly to produce and purchase. Tissue culture is a means of producing whole plants from pieces of plant tissue. Tissue-cultured plants originate in a lab when the growing tips of virus-indexed plants are removed under sterile laboratory conditions and placed in a growth chamber on a specialized medium. The growing tips receive several treatments that cause them to form plantlets. The plantlets are placed in sterile rooting media and grown in the greenhouse. The small tissue-cultured plants are then sold in "speedling"-type transplant trays either as actively growing or dormant plants. This plant type is sensitive to herbicides for several months after planting and non-dormant plants must be set after the danger of frost is over.

Fig. 3.3 **Bare root dormant suckers.**

Fig. 3.4 **Tissue-cultured red raspberry plant.**

Bramble Cultivar Descriptions

Not all available bramble cultivars are included in the following list. Those listed are widely used by growers throughout the northeastern and midwestern United States and eastern Canada, are increasing in acreage, or appear to be the most promising. Cultivars declining in acreage are not listed. The year the cultivar was released is listed after the cultivar.

Red Raspberries, Floricane-fruiting (Summer-fruiting)

Algonquin (Haida × Canby) *1989*
From British Columbia. High yielding with good quality, medium-sized fruit. Fruit may adhere to receptacle and has a dull appearance. Upright canes are numerous, nearly spineless, and moderately hardy. Resistant to the North American aphid, vector to the raspberry mosaic virus complex. Some resistance to Phytophthora root rot and spur blight. Susceptible to cane *Botrytis*.

Boyne (Chief × Indian Summer) *1960*
From Manitoba. Sibling to Killarney. Fruit ripens early, is small to medium in size, somewhat dark, and very soft, but it has good yield, fair flavor, and good freezing quality. Plants are vigorous, spiny and produce many suckers. Plants have excellent winter hardiness but are

susceptible to anthracnose. It is moderately resistant to late leaf yellow rust and tolerant to Phytophthora root rot and crown gall. Susceptible to raspberry fireblight.

Canby (Viking × Lloyd George) *1953*
From Oregon. Fruit ripens mid-season, is medium to large in size, somewhat soft, and bright red with excellent flavor. Plants are tall, nearly spineless, and moderately productive. It has moderate to poor hardiness, and buds may winter kill in cold climates. Susceptible to Phytophthora root rot.

Citadel [Mandarin × (Sunrise × Oregon 420)] *1966*
From Maryland. Fruit ripens late mid-season. Large, medium-long conic fruit are firm and dark red and somewhat difficult to pick. Canes are moderately hardy, vigorous, and resistant to leaf spot diseases.

Claudia [Skeena × (AmosH × NY817)]
(Patent Pending) *2001*
From Maryland. Fruit ripens mid to late season. A late fall crop is common. Large, conical fruit has moderate firmness and good flavor. Produces stout, upright canes but suckers sparingly. It has acceptable cold hardiness for most areas.

Emily [(Southland × Willamette) × Glen Moy]
(Plant Patent #12,350) *1998*
From Maryland. Mid-season fruit with good yield potential. Firm fruit is large with a narrow cavity and mild flavor. Susceptible to Phytophthora root rot. It has a low chilling requirement, is susceptible to fluctuating spring temperatures, and is only moderately cold hardy.

Encore (Canby × Cherokee)
(Plant Patent # 11,746) *1998*
From New York. Latest summer-fruiting raspberry available. Large, firm, conical berries with very good, sweet flavor, medium-red color, and moderate yields. It has vigorous, upright, nearly spineless canes. Good cold hardiness but susceptible to fluctuating spring temperatures. Susceptible to Phytophthora root rot.

Esta (SCRI 8616B6 × Southland) (Patent Pending) *2001*
From Maryland. Fruit ripens in the early season. Large conical fruit has a sweet, intense flavor but can become

soft in hot weather. Needs trellising for ease of picking. Has poor cold hardiness but tolerant to fluctuating spring temperatures. Resistant to leaf hoppers. Susceptible to Phytophthora root rot.

Festival (Muskoka × Trent) 1972
From Ontario. Fruit ripens mid-season and is medium-sized, bright red, and firm, with good flavor. Canes are short with few spines, very productive, and very hardy. Festival is very susceptible to late leaf yellow rust but tolerant to leaf curl virus and spur blight. Resistant to the North American aphid, vector to the raspberry mosaic virus complex.

K81-6 [0.67-245-01 × (Creston × Willamette)]
From Nova Scotia. Fruit ripens very late and is large with average firmness. Canes are medium tall with spines only at the base. Has good cold hardiness. Resistant to late leaf yellow rust. Susceptible to leaf curl virus and raspberry fireblight.

Killarney (Chief × Indian Summer) 1961
From Manitoba. A sibling of Boyne. Fruit ripens early, slightly after Boyne. Fruit is medium-sized, is very bright red, and may crumble. Flavor and freezing quality are good, but berries may soften in warm weather. Good yields. Plants are short to medium, spiny, and produce many suckers. This cultivar is very hardy and is suitable for colder climates. Susceptible to mildew and anthracnose.

Latham (King × Louden) 1920
From Minnesota. Fruit ripens mid-season and over a long period of time. Small fruit has good color, but is crumbly with only fair flavor. Plants are vigorous with few spines and are moderately productive. Very hardy, it is suitable for colder climates. This cultivar is less susceptible to viruses than some cultivars. Considered a standard for Phytophthora root rot resistance. Susceptible to raspberry fireblight and powdery mildew.

Lauren (Titan × Reveille)
(Plant Patent # 10,610) 1997
From Maryland. Productive cultivar ripens in mid season. Large, conic berries with mild sweet flavor may adhere until fully ripe. Canes are nearly spineless and

only moderately hardy with a short chilling requirement. Susceptible to Phytophthora root rot.

Mandarin 1955
From North Carolina. Fruit ripens late mid-season. Red round-shaped fruit with good firmness and flavor and no crumbliness. Plants have shown tolerance to high temperatures and humidity in summer and resistance to injury from fluctuating temperatures in winter, when grown in North Carolina. Very resistant to Japanese beetle.

Newburgh (Newman × Herbert) 1929
From New York. Fruit ripens mid-season and is medium-sized and light red with good flavor. However, berries may be crumbly and fruit tends to ripen unevenly. Plants are moderately productive, tall but not highly vigorous, and have some spines. It is hardy and suitable for colder climates. This cultivar is very susceptible to mosaic virus and is partially resistant to common cane diseases.

Nova (Southland × Boyne) 1981
From Nova Scotia. Fruit ripens in mid-season and is medium-sized, bright red, firm, and somewhat acidic in taste. Considered to have better than average shelf life. Plants are vigorous and upright with long fruiting laterals. Canes have very few thorns. Plants are very hardy and appear to resist some common cane diseases but are susceptible to cane botrytis. May set late fall crop.

Prelude [(Hilton × (Durham × September)) × Hilton)] (Plant Patent # 11,747) 1998
From New York. Earliest summer-fruiting cultivar available. Fruit is medium sized, round, and firm with good flavor. Plants are vigorous with abundant suckers and strong upright canes. Very resistant to Phytophthora root rot. Good cold hardiness. Moderate late fall crop is to be expected.

Qualicum (Glen Moy × Chilliwack) 1994
From British Columbia. Fruit ripens mid season. Large, firm berries have a pleasant flavor and very good quality with extended shelf life. Nearly spineless canes. Not cold hardy for northern areas. Susceptible to Botrytis, anthracnose, Phytophthora root rot, and crown gall. Resistant to mosaic virus complex.

Reveille [(Indian Summer × Sunrise) ×
September] *1966*
From Maryland. Fruits ripen early and are medium to
large with good flavor but very soft. Sunburn can be a
problem on exposed fruit. Fruit has poor shipping and
freezing quality and is recommended for pick-your-own
markets. Plants are vigorous, producing many suckers,
and are high yielding. It is hardy and suitable for colder
climates.

Taylor (Newman × Lloyd George) *1935*
From New York. Fruit ripens late and is medium to
large, with excellent flavor, good color, and good firmness.
Plants are vigorous with some spines. It is moderately
hardy, but very susceptible to mosaic virus, leaf spot,
and fungal diseases.

Titan [Hilton × (Newburgh × St. Walfried)]
(Plant Patent # 5404) *1985*
From New York. Fruits ripen mid-to-late season and are
extremely large and dull red, with mild flavor. Berries
are difficult to pick unless fully ripe. The plants produce
large canes with very few spines,
and suckers emerge mostly from the
crown, so it is slow to spread. With
only fair hardiness, Titan is for moderate climates. Plants are susceptible
to crown gall and Phytophthora root
rot but are extremely productive.
Resistant to raspberry aphid vector
of mosaic virus complex.

Tulameen (Nootka ×
Glen Prosen) *1989*
From British Columbia. A late raspberry producing very large, glossy,
firm fruit. It is very productive with
an extended season. Plants are not
adequately hardy for field production
in northern areas. It is recommended
for winter greenhouse production.
Has resistance to aphid vector of
mosaic virus complex.

Fig. 3.6 **Black raspberry fruit.**

Black Raspberries, Floricane-fruiting (Summer-fruiting)

Black raspberries may winter kill to the snowline if
temperatures drop to −5°F in combination with dry
winds. They are also quite susceptible to viral infections,
Verticillium, and rusts. It is difficult to remove all viruses
from the planting stock. Black rasp-
berries have a shorter harvest season
than red raspberries.

Fig. 3.5 **Titan summer-
fruiting red raspberry.**

Allen (Bristol × Cumberland) *1963*
From New York. Fruit ripens early to
mid-season and very uniformly so the
harvest period is short. Fruit is large
and very attractive with mild flavor.
Plants are vigorous and moderately
high yielding. Moderately hardy.

Blackhawk (Quillen ×
Black Pearl) *1954*
From Iowa. Fruit is medium-large
and glossy with good firmness and
flavor. Plants are vigorous. High
yielding and relatively hardy. Resistant to anthracnose.

Bristol (Watson Prolific ×
Honeysweet) *1934*
From New York. Fruit ripens early
and is medium to large and firm,

with excellent flavor. Plants are vigorous and high yielding. Bristol is hardy but should not be grown north of Pennsylvania without testing on the site. Susceptible to anthracnose. Tolerant to powdery mildew.

Cumberland (Gregg open pollinated) *1896*
From Pennsylvania. Fruit ripen mid-season and are medium sized with fair flavor. Plants are vigorous and moderately productive but not particularly cold hardy.

Haut [Manteo × (Bristol × Bristol)] *1987*
From Maryland. Fruit ripens early but over a long period. Berries are medium-sized and firm with good flavor. Plants are vigorous with good productivity.

Jewel [(Bristol × Dundee) × Dundee] *1973*
From New York. Ripening in mid-season, the fruit is firm, glossy, and flavorful. Plants are vigorous, erect, and productive. This cultivar appears to be more disease resistant than others, including resistance to anthracnose. This is a hardy black raspberry cultivar.

Mac Black (Parentage Unknown) *2000*
From Ontario. Ripens in late season, extending the black raspberry season by 7–10 days. Medium-large fruit is soft and slightly purple with a waxy appearance possibly from

some red raspberry ancestry. Flavor is mild and good. Has good cold hardiness. Canes are vigorous and erect.

Munger (Shaffer open pollinated) *1897*
From Ohio. Standard cultivar in Oregon. Fruit ripens mid-season with most other black raspberries. Shiny black fruit is medium to large with good firmness and flavor. Moderately vigorous with adequate cold hardiness.

Purple Raspberries, Floricane-fruiting (Summer-fruiting)
Purple raspberries are hybrid berries derived from black and red raspberries. Fruit is often intermediate in color, soft fleshed, and retains much black raspberry flavor. In general, purple raspberries are not adequately hardy to be commercially viable in the colder climates of the Northeast (Maine, New Hampshire, and Vermont) or Canada.

Brandywine (NY 631 × Hilton) *1976*
From New York. Fruits ripen later than most red cultivars and are large, reddish-purple, and quite tart. Berries are best used for processing. This is a high-yielding cultivar. Canes are very tall with prominent thorns, and suckers grow only from the crown so the plant will not spread. Hardy to USDA Hardiness zone 4. It is susceptible to crown gall but partially resistant to many other diseases.

Estate (Parentage Unknown) *2000*
From Minnesota. Ripens very late. Fruit is more red than purple, large, and round with good flavor. Plants are tall and thorny. Suckers emerge from the crown, so plants are slow to spread. Has acceptable winter hardiness.

Royalty [(Cumberland × Newburgh) × (Newburgh × Indian Summer)] (Plant Patent # 5,405) *1982*
From New York. This cultivar is considered the best purple raspberry for fresh eating. Fruit ripens late and is large and reddish-purple to dull purple when fully ripe. Berries tend to be soft, but sweet and flavorful when eaten fresh. Excellent for processing. Can be harvested when fruit is red. Canes are tall and vigorous, with thorns, and are extremely productive. Hardiness is acceptable for northern growing areas. Royalty is immune to the large raspberry aphid, which decreases the probability of mosaic virus, but it is susceptible to crown gall.

Fig. 3.7 **Royalty purple raspberry.**

Red Raspberries, Primocane-fruiting (Fall-fruiting)

Cold hardiness is not a consideration for primocane-fruiting (everbearing) raspberries since most growers cut canes to the ground after the leaves drop in late fall or early the following spring. However, since the primocane crop ripens in the late summer or early fall, certain cultivars may fruit too late to bear a crop in cold climates. Primocane-fruiting raspberries can be made to flower and fruit earlier than usual by applying a lightweight row cover over the row in early spring after last year's fruiting canes are mowed to the ground, or by growing them under high tunnels (see chapter four).

Autumn Bliss (Complex *Rubus* Hybrid)
(Plant Patent # 6,597) *1984*

From England. Early ripening, 10 to 14 days before Heritage. Large, highly flavored fruit is somewhat soft and dark. Much of the crop is produced within the first two weeks of harvest, which is an advantage in northern climates. Short canes with few spines. Susceptible to raspberry bushy dwarf virus. Good resistance to Phytophthora root rot.

Autumn Britten (Complex *Rubus* Hybrid)
(Patent Pending) *1995*

From England. Early ripening with large, firm, good flavored fruit. Taller than Autumn Bliss with better fruit quality but slightly lower yields. Somewhat less vigorous than Autumn Bliss with fewer suckers than Heritage.

Caroline [(Autumn Bliss × Glen Moy) × Heritage]
(Plant Patent #10,412) *1999*

From Maryland. Ripens 7 to 10 days before Heritage. Large, good flavored, conical fruit with good firmness and color. Tall upright canes. Short fruiting laterals can be challenging to pick. Good resistance to Phytophthora root rot.

Dinkum (Autumn Bliss × Glen Moy)
(Plant Patent # 9,477) *1992*

From Australia. Early fruit ripens 7 to 10 days before Heritage. Shelf life can be extended by harvesting before fully-ripe. Fruit is good flavored and firm. Canes are spineless, stout, and strongly erect. Moderately resistant to late leaf yellow rust. Susceptible to Phytophthora root rot and raspberry bushy dwarf virus.

Fig. 3.8 **Primocane-fruiting Heritage red raspberry.**

Heritage [(Milton × Cuthbert) × Durham] *1969*
From New York. Considered the standard for fall-bearing cultivars. Ripens relatively late. Fruit is medium in size and has good color, flavor, firmness, and freezing quality. These tall, rugged canes have prominent thorns and are very high yielding. Due to its late ripening, this cultivar is not recommended for regions with cool summers or a short growing season with frost before September 30. Can be double cropped. Resistant to most diseases but susceptible to late leaf rust.

Josephine (Amity × Glen Garry)
(Plant Patent #12,173) *1998*

From Maryland. Late ripening fruit ripens mid-season, after Heritage. Large berries are firm and cohesive with excellent flavor. Plants are upright and vigorous needing little containment trellising. Resistant to leaf hopper.

Polana (Heritage × Zeva Herbsternte)
(Patent Pending) *1991*

From Poland. Very early season, 14 days before Heritage. Medium-sized fruit with good flavor. Short, productive canes with multiple laterals per node. Higher levels of nitrogen are recommended to increase cane height. Susceptible to Verticillium wilt and Phytophthora root rot.

Redwing (Heritage × Fallred) *1987*
From Minnesota. Productive and ripens just after Autumn Bliss, up to two weeks before Heritage in northern climates. Ripens closer to Heritage in more moderate climates. Fruit is medium in size and somewhat soft. Susceptible to the aphid vector of the raspberry mosaic virus complex and susceptible to anthracnose.

Ruby (cv. Watson) (Heritage × Titan) (Plant Patent # 7,067) *1988*
From New York. The primocane crop ripens slightly ahead of Heritage. The fruit is large, but flavor is mild. Plants are moderately vigorous with good productivity. The cultivar is suggested for fresh market or shipping in areas with longer growing seasons. Ruby is moderately susceptible to root rot and susceptible to mosaic virus complex. Resistant to late leaf yellow rust and powdery mildew.

Summit (ORUS 1838 × ORUS 1842) *1989*
From Oregon. Fruit ripens 10 to 14 days before Heritage. Firm, medium-red berries are medium to small sized with good flavor. Vigorous primocanes have few spines. Resistant to Phytophthora root rot and plants do well in heavier soils. Susceptible to raspberry bushy dwarf virus and to the North American aphid vector of the raspberry mosaic virus complex.

Yellow Raspberries, Primocane-fruiting (Fall-fruiting)

Yellow fruit is more susceptible to sun burn since it lacks dark pigments that absorb ultraviolet light.

Anne (Amity × Glen Garry) (Plant Patent # 10,411) *1998*
From Maryland. Ripen mid-to-late season, 7 to 10 days before Heritage. Large, conic, pale yellow fruit have very good flavor and texture. Tall upright canes sucker sparsely requiring higher planting density. Resistant to Phytophthora root rot. Susceptible to leaf hoppers and Botrytis.

Fig. 3.9 **Primocane-fruiting Fallgold yellow raspberry.**

Fallgold [NH 56-1 × (Taylor × *Rubus pungens oldhami*) F2 open pollinated] *1967*
From New Hampshire. The primocane crop ripens relatively early, 10 to 14 days before Heritage. Fruit is medium-sized, yellow with a pink blush, and soft, but has excellent flavor. It is poor for freezing or processing. Canes are very vigorous and produce many suckers. Susceptible to raspberry fireblight.

Golden Harvest (Parentage Unknown) *1992*
From New York. Late fall season similar to Heritage. Firm yellow berry with good flavor. Small fruit size with average yield potential. Good plant vigor.

Goldie (cv. Graton Gold) (Heritage Sport) (Plant Patent #7,625) *1987*
From California. Ripens relatively late. Amber sport of Heritage, similar in all characteristics except fruit color. Fruit blushes pink when overripe. Fruit is medium-sized and has good flavor and firmness. Tall, rugged canes have prominent thorns and are very high yielding. Due to its late ripening, this cultivar is not recommended for regions with cool summers or a short growing season with frost before September 30. Can be double cropped. Resistant to most diseases.

Kiwigold (Heritage Sport) (Plant Patent # 11,313) *1988*
From New Zealand. Ripens relatively late. Amber sport of Heritage, similar in all characteristics except fruit color. Fruit blushes pink when over ripe. Fruit is medium-sized and has good flavor and firmness. Tall, rugged canes have prominent thorns and are very high yielding. Due to its late ripening, this cultivar is not recommended for regions with cool summers or a short growing season with frost before September 30. Can be double cropped. Resistant to most diseases.

Blackberries, Thornless (Summer-fruiting)

Thornless blackberries have vigorous canes which must be trellised. They ripen later than most red raspberries and are not hardy below 0°F, so most cultivars are not commercially viable for much of the Northeast without winter protection.

Apache (Ark. 1007 × Navaho)
(Plant Patent # 11,865) 1999

From Arkansas. Ripens mid-season with high production. Fruit is conical with good quality and flavor and is well presented for picking. Erect, strong canes are self-supporting, vigorous and prolific. Resistant to orange rust.

Arapaho [(A-550 × Cherokee × A-883)]
(Plant Patent # 8,510) 1992

From Arkansas. Earliest ripening thornless cultivar. Fruit is medium-sized and glossy with a short conic shape, good flavor, and noticeably small seeds. Canes are erect and self-supporting. Moderately vigorous and moderately hardy.

Black Satin (Thornfree × Darrow) 1974

From Illinois. Ripening late, the berries are large, firm, dull black when ripe, and slightly tart. Fruit is excellent for jams, jellies, and pies. These plants are very vigorous, semi-erect, productive, and resistant to anthracnose. More hardy than Thornfree.

Chester Thornless (Thornfree × Darrow) 1985

From Illinois. The late-ripening fruit is somewhat difficult to pick but is of high quality with little breakdown. Fruit is large with mild flavor. Vigorous canes are semi-erect and hardier than most other thornless cultivars. It is resistant to cane blight. Flowers are lavender colored. The most successful thornless blackberry in the North.

Doyle Thornless (Pedigree Unknown) 1975

From Indiana. Chance seedling that is known for an extremely high yield potential and good fruit flavor. Berry size can be small, particularly when plants are heavy-cropping. Fairly good adaptation to soil types and climate zones.

Hull (SIUS 47 × Thornfree) 1981

From Illinois. The plants produce fruit in mid- to late season after Black Satin. Berries are very large and firm,

Fig. 3.10 **Thornless blackberry fruit.**

and they hold color under high temperatures. They are sweeter than most other thornless cultivars. Canes are trailing and moderately hardy.

Navaho (Thornfree × Brazos) × (A-550 × Cherokee)
(Plant Patent # 6679) 1988

From Arkansas. Berries are late ripening with good shelf life. Fruit is medium-sized, sweet, and firm, with very good flavor and small seeds. The fruit is presented well for picking. Canes are semi-erect, but the plants have low vigor. Moderately hardy but not recommended for colder climates. Moderately resistant to anthracnose and rosette.

Ouachita (Navaho × Ark.1506) (Patent Pending) 2003

From Arkansas. Berries ripen in mid-season. High yielding with large, firm, sweet fruit. Canes are vigorous and erect, needing support during full harvest. Hardiness is moderate for a blackberry. Resistant to double blossom and orange rust. Tolerant to anthracnose.

Thornfree [(Brainerd × Merton Thornless) × (Merton Thornless × Eldorado)] 1966

From Maryland. Fruits in the mid-to-late season with firm, tart berries with good flavor. Medium-large fruit are blunt conic with glossy black skin and adhere strongly. Semi-upright canes are vigorous. Very susceptible to cold damage.

Triple Crown (SIUS 68-2-5 × Ark. 545) 1996

From Maryland. Large, sweet aromatic berries with excellent flavor. Very productive. Canes are semi-erect, vigorous, and sturdy, but have insufficient cold hardiness for most northern regions. May be useful for protected culture.

Blackberries, Thorny (Summer-fruiting)

Erect blackberries have tall, rugged canes with prominent thorns. The plants give similar yields to thornless types but are somewhat less susceptible to low temperatures in general. Most cultivars are not recommended for commercial production in most of the Northeast without winter protection.

For many years, plants of a sterile type, which bloom but do not set fruit, have been distributed. These plants are triploid (a genetic condition) and should be discarded. Such mixtures are difficult to prevent. Viral infections may also cause sterility in blackberries.

Black Butte (ORUS 830-4 × ORUS 728-3)
From Oregon. Very large, somewhat tart fruit. Fruit is long and cylindrical. Trailing canes are moderately thorny and vigorous. Not considered cold hardy enough for northern regions.

Chesapeake (Shawnee × *Rubus cuneifolius*)
(Plant Patent #13,878) 1974
From Maryland. Very large fruit with sweet flavor. Very vigorous, erect canes. Extremely thorny but presents fruit well for picking. Cold hardiness may not be adequate for northern regions but hardier than most blackberries.

Chickasaw (Ark. 842 × Ark. 1246)
(Plant Patent # 11,861) 1999
From Arkansas. Ripens in the early season with an extended fruiting season. Productive cultivar produces large, long, cylindrical fruit of good flavor and quality. Very vigorous grower that can be managed as a hedge. Resistant to orange rust and moderately resistant to anthracnose.

Choctaw (Ark. 526 × Rosborough)
(Plant Patent # 6,678) 1988
From Arkansas. Very early season. Fruit is medium sized with a mild flavor and excellent quality. Fruit is short conic with small seeds. Canes are erect, vigorous, and prolific. Immune to orange rust. Moderately susceptible to powdery mildew.

Comanche (Darrow × Brazos) 1974
From Arkansas. Early ripening with very large, firm fruit that are excellent for processing or fresh market. Not as productive as Cherokee or Cheyenne. Canes are vigorous and semi-erect.

Darrow [(Eldorado × Brewer) × Hedrick] 1958
From New York. Fruit is large, long conic and often irregular. Black, glossy fruit is mildly subacid with good quality. Secondary fruiting laterals produce fruit into late August and September in New York. Thorny canes are vigorous and hardy for a blackberry.

Illini Hardy (NY95 × Chester Thornless)
(Plant Patent #8,333) 1988
From Illinois. Ripens in the late season. Fruit is medium sized with good flavor and quality but acidic. Canes are erect, very thorny, and vigorous with good hardiness. Suckers mainly from the crown. Resistant to Phytophthora root rot.

Kiowa [(Thornfree × Brazos) × Comanche] ×
[(Ark. 557 × Wells Beauty) × Rosborough]
(Plant Patent # 9,861)) 1996
From Arkansas. Ripens mid-to-late season with an extended harvest season. Moderately firm fruit is very large with excellent flavor. The glossy black, oblong fruit is well presented for picking. Erect, self-supporting canes are moderately vigorous. Immune to orange rust, moderately resistant to anthracnose.

Lawton (Unknown Parentage from the Wild) 1834
From New York. Ripens late season. Berries are medium sized and sweet and become dull after picking. Very soft when ripe. Canes are vigorous and hardy for a blackberry. Susceptible to orange rust.

Shawnee [Cherokee × (Thornfree × Brazos)]
(Plant patent #5,686) 1985
From Arkansas. Fruit ripens in the late season and is very large with long conic shape. Fruit is flavorful and well presented for picking over an extended period. Moderately firm and shiny black. Canes are vigorous, erect, and productive. Immune to orange rust, moderately resistant to anthracnose, and susceptible to rosette. This cultivar is recommended for southern locations.

Blackberries, Primocane-fruiting (Fall-fruiting)

Primocane-fruiting blackberries are now available. Arkansas has released Prime-Jim and Prime-Jan. These blackberries have not been extensively tested in the northeastern United States or Canada. Preliminary trials indicate that they fruit very late, so may have to be grown in protected culture in northern areas.

Raspberry × Blackberry Hybrids (Summer-fruiting)

The genus *Rubus* contains many species that can hybridize to some degree. Chance seedlings and controlled crosses by breeders have been used to develop hybrid berry cultivars that have shown some promise in certain areas. Most are hybrids between red raspberry and various blackberry species. Fruit is generally similar to blackberry with the receptacle remaining with the fruit when harvested. Fruit color varies from a red wine color to a black similar to most blackberries. Most cultivars are not hardy in northern growing regions but may have potential in milder climates or in protected culture systems.

Boysenberry (Western Blackberry/
Raspberry Hybrid) *1935*
From California. Late season fruit is very large and tart but good flavored. Fruit similar to blackberry. Excellent for processing. Thorny canes are vigorous and trailing and require trellising. Similar to Youngberry. Poor cold hardiness.

Loganberry [Raspberry (Possibly Red Antwerp)/
Western Wild Blackberry Hybrid] *1885*
From California. Ripens in the late season. Long, dark red berries, similar in form to blackberry. Excellent for processing. Vigorous trailing canes are thorny and require trellising. Poor cold hardiness.

Fig. 3.11 **Tayberry fruit.**

Tayberry (U.K. Aurora (Blackberry) × SCRI 626/67 (Raspberry)) (Plant Patent #4,424) *1980*
From Scotland. Large fruit is long conical with good flavor. Fruit similar in form to blackberry. Canes are vigorous, hardy, highly productive, and very thorny. Plant is semi-spreading. Susceptible to leaf and bud mite.

Wyeberry (Eastern Blackberry/Raspberry Hybrid) *2000*
From Maryland. Large, fairly firm fruit. Fruit similar to blackberry in form. Vigorous canes are semi-erect and thorny. More cold hardy than other hybrid berry cultivars.

Thornless Boysenberry (Boysenberry Sport) *1938*
Similar to Boysenberry without thorns.

Youngberry (Mayes × Phenomenal) *1925*
From Louisiana. Very large fruit with very sweet flavor with high yield potential. Fruit is reddish colored, similar in form to blackberry. Excellent for frozen pack and jam. Trailing canes are vigorous and thorny. Susceptible to anthracnose and rosette. Poor cold hardiness.

Further Reading

Cornell University Department of Horticulture. "Cornell Nursery Guide for Berry Crops." Cornell Fruit Resources. Ithaca, NY: Cornell University. www.fruit.cornell.edu/Berries/nurseries.

Weber, C. "Strawberry, Raspberry, and Blueberry Cultivar Review." Cornell Fruit Resources. Ithaca, NY: Cornell University. www.fruit.cornell.edu/Berries/genprodhtml/berrycult.html.

CHAPTER FOUR

Production Methods

Throughout the north, brambles are commonly grown in field plantings for fresh market. By selecting an early-ripening, a mid-season and a late-season floricane-fruiting cultivar, and a primocane-fruiting cultivar, a grower can harvest berries continuously from early summer through the first fall frost. Bramble plants are adaptable to a variety of production systems besides field production, including high tunnels and greenhouse production, allowing the harvest season to be extended nearly year-round. These protected systems offer potential increases in yield and fruit quality as compared to field production, but they require significantly more investment in technology and operating capital. High-tunnel and greenhouse systems are of particular value where a premium market exists for high-quality fruit produced with little or no pesticide use.

Which type of bramble and production systems you should choose depends on the time of year you wish to produce berries, the quality of the market in your area (are consumers willing to pay top dollar for high-quality, off-season produce?), and your aversion to risk.

Field Production

Layout

Commercial field plantings of brambles are set out in rows for ease of management and maximum production. Narrow row widths and closely spaced rows produce the highest yield. Before deciding on a row orientation, growers should take into account slope, soil erosion potential, wind movement, soil drainage, and sunlight interception. North-south rows intercept sunlight more evenly than east-west rows; hence sunscald is less problematic, and fruit ripens more evenly. Rows that run with the wind will dry more quickly than those that block the wind. The best orientation for each site will vary. For example, a grower on a breezy site with winds from the west may decide to orient the rows east-west, while a grower on a site that is mostly calm is likely to find north-south rows preferable. In heavy soils or wet sites, use raised beds that are 10 to 12 inches high at the peak and 4 to 6 feet wide at the base (figure 4.1). Raised beds are more prone to drying out, so it is critical that plants in raised beds receive adequate moisture as fruit size and vegetative growth are negatively affected by shortages of moisture in the soil (see "Water Management." chapter six).

It is usually better in the long run to purchase equipment to match the optimal row spacing than to establish row spacing around equipment. The optimal row spacing to achieve the greatest yield per acre is about 9 to 10 feet between rows. Some growers base their spacing on the size of equipment; for example, if a grower's mower is 8 feet wide, then the rows are at least 11 feet apart to

Fig. 4.1 **Raised bed planting with straw mulch.**

Fig. 4.2 **New raspberry planting with trickle irrigation.**

dividing this number by the distance in feet between plants within the row. For example, in a field with a ten-foot between-row spacing and a three-foot within-row spacing 1,452 plants per acre would be required (i.e. 43,560 square feet per acre ÷ 10 feet = 4,356 feet of row per acre; 4,356 feet of row per acre ÷ 3 foot within-row spacing = 1,452 plants per acre).

For successful establishment of a new bramble planting, the moisture in the root zone needs to be greater than 50% of the field's water-holding capacity throughout the early growing season. It is critical that a trickle irrigation system be in place before planting to ensure water delivery to the young plants (see "Water Management," chapter six).

accommodate the mower and a 3 to 4 foot weed-free strip. When a V-trellis or T-trellis is used, the distance between rows may have to be even greater than if an I-trellis is used (see "Trellising and Pruning," chapter five). In greenhouses and high tunnels where equipment (e.g. a mower) does not have to move down the row, rows can be as close as 6 feet. This is not a recommended spacing for field plantings.

Red raspberries are typically planted 2 to 3 feet apart within the row. Red raspberry cultivars tend to produce many suckers (new shoots originating from root buds) and will form a fairly uniform hedgerow of canes within two years of planting. Cultivars that do not produce many suckers, such as Titan and most yellow raspberries, should be planted 2 feet apart, while vigorous cultivars, such as Boyne, can be set up to 4 feet apart.

Black raspberry plants do not spread far from the original plant, and hence do not fill in the row in the same manner as red raspberries. However, considerable space is needed for each plant because they produce new canes from the crown area, as well as strong lateral branches when pruned properly. Plant black raspberries about 3 to 4 feet apart within the row, and plant the more vigorous purple raspberries 3 to 5 feet apart in the row.

Most thorny blackberries produce suckers profusely and should be planted 3 to 4 feet apart to form a uniform hedgerow of canes. Thornless blackberries do not produce many suckers, but their growth is vigorous and new canes develop from the original crown. Plant thornless blackberries in a hill system with each plant set 4 to 6 feet apart within the row.

Determine the number of plants required per acre by calculating the number of feet of row per acre, then

Planting Details

Order plants from the nursery well ahead of time to insure adequate quantities of desired cultivars. As the time for planting nears, notify the nursery of the preferred time for delivery. Bramble transplants are most commonly obtained in a dormant state or as tender tissue-cultured plants. Dormant stock typically originates

Fig. 4.3

Tissue-cultured plant (*at right*) and dormant suckers (*below*).

from either material that was propagated in the field (dormant suckers or tip-layered canes) or material that was propagated by tissue culture then grown briefly in the field and harvested after the plants became dormant in the fall (nursery-matured plants). See "Plant Selection," chapter three, for additional details on bramble transplant types.

Transplanting Dormant Stock

It is ideal if the transplants remain dormant until planted, but do not allow the roots to dry out before planting. If the plants arrive too early, those packed in polyethylene-lined boxes can be held in cold storage at about 35°F (1°C) for several weeks. Other plants may be heeled in for temporary storage. Dormant plants may be transplanted by hand into trenches or individual holes. Transplanting machines also may be adapted to perform this task. Be sure that plants are set vertically as plants set at an angle do not grow well. Apply water immediately after planting.

Plant red raspberry and thorny blackberry dormant suckers in early spring with their stems at the depth they were in the nursery. Spread roots laterally from the sucker stem and place the roots slightly deeper than they were in the nursery soil. Prune the dormant transplant to a height of 5 inches, and then remove this woody portion once new shoots emerge from the soil.

Plant tip-layered canes, i.e., black or purple raspberry and thornless blackberry dormant transplants, in early spring with the tips of their crown buds pointing upwards. Place the center of the crown about 3 inches below the soil surface, so that bud tips are approximately 2½ inches deep. If buds have begun to grow before planting, their tips should be closer to the surface. Spread roots laterally and slightly downward and pack soil firmly around roots to minimize air spaces. However, avoid damaging buds when tamping the soil. Cut off the handle (the piece of the stem extending above the soil) close to the ground once new shoots emerge from the soil.

Transplanting Tissue-cultured Plants

Planting greenhouse-grown, tissue-cultured plants can be easy and quick since some kinds of semi-mechanized vegetable and tobacco transplanting equipment can be adapted for use with these types of transplants. Growth of tissue-cultured bramble plants is also more uniform

Fig. 4.4 **Plastic mulch in a new bed.**

and vigorous than dormant transplant material. However, not all cultivars are available as tissue-cultured plants. Further, tissue-cultured plants have shallow root systems, which are sensitive to dry soil and herbicides, and the transplants are susceptible to frost damage.

Delay transplanting of tissue-cultured plants until damage by late-spring frosts is no longer a hazard. Cover the top of the root ball with field soil to a depth of ¾ inch. Pack soil to ensure good contact with the root ball. Apply water in the transplant hole, and irrigate the entire planting immediately after transplanting. Avoid herbicide applications and disturbances of the root system in new plantings.

Nurseries sometimes produce purple and black raspberry stock by rooting semi-hardened, leafy cuttings. This stock is often sent while actively growing if the time and method of sale is appropriate. Handle these transplants in the same manner as greenhouse-grown, tissue-cultured plants. If cuttings are dormant, however, they may be handled by the same methods as tip-layered plants.

Root Cuttings

Alternatively brambles can be grown from root cuttings. Root cuttings are generally planted in spring after they have been dug in fall and stored in a refrigerator during winter. For raspberries, place roots of variable lengths and ¹⁄₁₀ inch or larger in diameter about 3 inches deep in soil, with approximately 2 ounces of root per hill or per 3 feet of hedgerow. For blackberries, plant pencil size (6 inches long and ⅜- to ⅝-inch diameter) root pieces.

Early Care

Help maintain soil moisture around the delicate roots of bramble plants by amending the soil with compost or another source of organic matter prior to planting. After planting, a light layer of straw mulch will help retain soil moisture during plant establishment. Alternatively moisture may be retained and weeds managed by planting brambles in plastic mulch, although this mulch will have to be removed at the beginning of the second year to allow new primocanes to emerge (figure 4.4).

Minimize weed competition in a bramble planting but avoid cultivation or herbicides until the plants are well established. Fertilizer should not be applied to brambles immediately after they are planted; root systems are very delicate at this time and fertilizers will likely burn them. The use of dilute liquid fertilizer is generally fine for a new planting.

Most first-year growth occurs in the root system. First-year primocanes rarely reach an adequate height to produce a significant harvest. For convenience, many growers mow first-year canes to the ground in the fall or early spring. Eliminating the first-year short canes reduces the time and expense of managing and harvesting their nominal crop and allows the second-year primocanes to grow unimpeded.

To manage between-row weeds, most growers either use clean cultivation between rows (figure 4.5) or plant grass and mow the alleyways. Some growers plant flowering species between rows to attract beneficial insects (figure 4.6). A good time to seed grass is the fall of the planting year when soil temperatures are still warm, yet rainfall and soil moisture are generally higher. Leave a 3- to 4-foot unseeded strip around the bramble plants to minimize competition between the bramble plants and grass. Perennial ryegrass, dwarf fescues, bluegrass mixes, or a combination of these, make an attractive and durable ground cover. Avoid faster-growing and more aggressive mixes such as conservation or contractor's mixes.

Once plants are well established in fall of the planting year, herbicides may be applied, if necessary. Do not leave any straw or plastic mulch on raspberries after the first year as the excessive moisture may increase the incidence

Fig. 4.5 **Using clean cultivation between rows to control weeds.**

Fig. 4.6 **Planting Alyssum between rows to attract beneficial insects.**

of *Phytophthora* root rot. On drier soils, other mulching materials, such as wood chips or shavings, applied in a layer 4 to 6 inches thick may be used to retain moisture and prevent weed seed germination. The use of mulch on wet, heavy soils is generally not recommended.

Using Rowcovers

Rowcovers can be used to accelerate the flowering and ripening of primocane-fruiting raspberries (figure 4.7, page 32). The harvest of primocane-fruiting types such as Heritage frequently is truncated by fall frost. By applying rowcover in early spring, growth is accelerated and flowering and fruiting can occur 10–14 days earlier than normal, resulting in a much larger harvest in fall. Apply rowcover after the snow melts but before the new canes emerge from the ground. Be sure to anchor it well as high and persistent winds often occur this time of year. Keep the rowcover in place until mid-May or until the

Fig. 4.7 **Rowcover in primocane-fruiting raspberries.**

canes are about 18 inches tall, whichever comes first. Keeping the rowcover on longer than this can actually delay harvest as raspberries are sensitive to heat. Be sure to allow slack in the rowcover to accommodate the growth of canes underneath.

High Tunnel Production

A high tunnel is a large plastic hoop house covering plants that are usually set directly into soil. The plastic covering is a type that allows light to penetrate, traps some heat, and is durable in sunlight. Rapid advances are being made in plastic coverings, so consult a specialist for the latest recommendation before purchasing a cover. Tunnels are less expensive than greenhouses for extending the season and protecting plants from adverse weather. Temperature inside the tunnel is regulated by rolling the sides up or down and opening or closing the end walls. For the most part, tunnels do not contain heaters, lights, or any source of power. High tunnels offer the opportunity for bramble growers in northern climates to harvest early in the season (May for some floricane-fruiting cultivars) and to stay in production later in the season (November for some primocane-fruiting cultivars). High tunnels also provide protection from rain and hail and can reduce disease and pest pressure. With good

planning, cultivar selection, and detailed management, this system can greatly extend the harvest season.

Layout

High tunnels need to be large enough for the grower to plant, monitor, and harvest the crop from inside the structure. Standard tunnel dimensions vary with the manufacturer. One common tunnel size is 14 feet wide, 96 feet long, and 7½ feet tall at the center, while others are 30 feet wide, 15 feet tall and 96 feet long. A minimum peak height of 9 feet is recommended, and installing post extensions as high as 4 to 5 feet may be necessary to improve air circulation and reduce heat accumulation in the tunnel. Wider tunnels also can make management easier, but tunnels should be no wider than 30 feet. Long tunnels have limited cross ventilation, and the potential stresses caused by the weight of snow can become an issue. Tunnels longer than 96 feet also may pose a psychological barrier to pickers.

The frame consists of metal bows made by bending steel pipe or tubing (figure 4.8). Frames with a peak will shed snow better during the winter and are recommended over a more gradual bend (Quonset-style frames). Metal pipes are driven into the ground approximately 2 feet deep and set every 4 feet of the high tunnel length, providing support for the frame. The bows fit into the ground pipes and are attached by bolts. The ends of the structure

Fig. 4.8 **High tunnel structure.**

can be plastic or wood on a wood stud frame, but should be removable or be able to open to allow access for tillage equipment and to increase ventilation in the summer. The structure is typically covered with a single layer of 6-mil polyethylene with IR trapping and UV protection, with provisions for rolling up the sidewalls. (Some growers have reported better production with special light-diffusing plastic that increases light interception on lower laterals.) The plastic is secured onto a batten board on each side of the high tunnel about 5 feet above the soil line. A vertical sidewall helps to keep rain out of the tunnel and when rolled up, provides ventilation. A pipe is then attached to the loose bottom end of the plastic along the length of the structure. A T-handle on the end of the pipe is used to roll the plastic onto the pipe to open the sides (figure 4.9).

Fig. 4.9 **Side ventilation in a high tunnel structure.**

The key to successful use of the high tunnel is to spend the time laying out and preparing the site for construction. The better the tunnel is constructed, the easier the sides will roll up, and the easier it will be to ventilate. During periods of cold weather the sides are lowered in the afternoon to hold heat and then raised in the morning to vent before temperatures inside get too high. The floor of the structure may be covered with a layer of black weed barrier. This helps to raise the temperature inside the house, controls weeds, prevents evaporation of soil moisture, and allows excess water to drain. Excess moisture will raise humidity in the tunnel and may lead to disease problems. Humidity of the air will increase at night as the air cools down. Venting in the morning will allow drying of any condensed water and reduce humidity.

Planting Details

In a high-tunnel system, bramble plants may be grown either in the ground or in containers using media as for greenhouse production. If plants are grown in the ground, the high tunnel needs to be dedicated to bramble production unless the tunnel is moveable. Containers offer the advantage that a different crop can be grown within the high tunnel early in the year, after which the bramble plants can be moved into the tunnel. Place bramble plants in the high tunnels from bloom through harvest. Protecting plants from rain during this time period helps to control gray mold without fungicides.

If plants are grown in the ground, set plants in rows at least 6 feet apart. Vigorous growth produced by the bramble in tunnels makes management at closer spacing a challenge and increases considerably the amount of time required to manage the planting. Within the row, however, space primocane-fruiting raspberries more closely than the 3-foot recommendation for field production, as vigorous growth in the first year makes it possible to harvest a significant crop the year of planting. To maximize first-year harvest, plant transplants as early in the spring as possible, at least four weeks earlier than field production if the tunnel is covered.

While extensive evaluation of cultivar suitability has not been done, characteristics desired may be somewhat different than for field production. For example, if a market that commands a choice price is to be targeted, size and flavor may be more important than resistance to foliar diseases since plant foliage is kept dry. For primocane-fruiting raspberry cultivars, Autumn Britten, Heritage, Caroline and Josephine have performed well, with Autumn Britten fruiting about two weeks earlier than Heritage and Josephine fruiting later. A high-tunnel system may also be used to produce primocane-fruiting raspberries later in the season than would be possible in an open field if the plastic is not applied until early September. Cultivars that produce a bit too late for field production in some regions (e.g., Josephine) can produce a significant crop in high tunnels.

Culture

The use of high tunnels does require an increase in both the level and the amount of management required to grow the crop. In particular, the sides must be raised and lowered to regulate temperature and humidity in spring and fall. Temperatures under high tunnels are managed differently depending on the targeted window for harvest. For example, if floricane-fruiting raspberries are to be fruited in May or June, then shade cloth may be required beginning in May to reduce temperatures and reduce solar injury on fruit. If primocane-fruiting raspberries are to be fruited in November, then plastic may be removed entirely for the summer to reduce heat stress, and replaced once flowering begins. Unless supplemental heat is provided, the tunnel may not be able to provide adequate protection to the plants after mid-November, although rowcovers can be used within tunnels to protect plants on cold nights.

Pruning, trellising, and tipping canes is different under tunnels than for open-field production. For example, tipping primocanes to delay harvest may be desirable in a high tunnel, but is probably undesirable in the field. Chapter five provides details on cane management under tunnels.

High tunnels can reduce the incidence of some diseases and insects, particularly if trickle-irrigation tubing is used, as no water (rain or irrigation) gets onto the foliage to transport spores or otherwise encourage disease development. Keeping air flowing through the tunnel when possible will also minimize

Fig. 4.10 **The fruits of winter green house raspberry production.**

the likelihood of disease development. Season extenders such as floating row covers or screens can be used as physical barriers to keep insects off the crop. Fruit harvested from tunnels without any fungicide applications is usually of higher quality than field-grown fruit that has received regular fungicide treatments.

Some disease and insect damage can occur in high tunnels. Scouting must begin when the plants are set out. Powdery mildew and two-spotted spider mites are a common pest under protected culture. Scout for two-spotted mites at least weekly, and more often if the weather is hot. The use of beneficial insects may be the most practical way to deal with mite problems. Mite populations can explode, so if two-spotted mites are observed, order and release predatory mites immediately (see "Insect and Mite Scouting and Management," chapter eight).

The potential for nutritional deficiencies to occur in high tunnels is greater than in field production as plant growth is significantly increased. A yearly complete-tissue-nutrient analysis is needed to best guide a fertilization program. Preplant compost incorporation will also help ameliorate potential deficiencies. If the tunnel is covered year-round, irrigation will be required very early in spring since rain and snow are excluded.

Bumblebees may be required to maximize production in the early and late part of the season when the sides are rolled up infrequently. The bees flying in and out of their boxes will visit the various flowers on their way in and out each day, which should provide adequate pollination. However, in the fall, bumblebees are attracted to the warm, dry environment of a high tunnel, so purchasing bees may not be necessary at that time of year.

Greenhouse Raspberry Production

Greenhouses offer raspberry growers in northern climates the opportunity to provide the consumer with high-quality fruit in the middle of the winter (figure 4.10). Compared to field production, greenhouse-produced berries are larger, firmer, and much less prone to fruit rot.

Growers can use greenhouses to

extend the season of primocane-fruiting raspberries in fall, produce floricane-fruiting raspberries in early spring, and by staggering the date when dormant raspberries are moved into the greenhouse, produce raspberries year-round.

Staggering the production of raspberries requires a cooler since plants must be held at a temperature near 30°F (–1°C) prior to their use in the greenhouse. The following describes how a greenhouse is used to produce early spring raspberries without the use of a cooler. Variations on this scheme are provided in the Greenhouse Raspberry Production Guide available on the web at WWW.FRUIT.CORNELL.EDU/BERRIES/GHRASP.HTML.

Fig. 4.11 **Tulameen fruiting in the greenhouse.**

Fig. 4.12 **Irrigation system in greenhouse production.**

Layout

A greenhouse with a heat source is required for maintaining warm temperatures of up to 70°F inside while the weather is cold outside. Coolers and venting may be necessary for late spring production. Other materials needed include a clean water source with low salinity, a fertilizer injector, an irrigation system, min/max thermometers, growing media, and containers. Other supplies that are valuable include growing lights, humidity gauges, and a weed barrier for gravel greenhouse floors.

Supplemental lighting is not necessary for successful greenhouse raspberry production, but if lights are already installed in the greenhouse, supplemental light can accelerate harvest by a couple of weeks and may increase yield by 20–30%. The expense of adding supplemental lighting just for raspberries may not be offset by higher yields.

The use of inexpensive box fans on the greenhouse floor will provide air circulation around the plants to help reduce pockets of high humidity that encourage disease. The relative humidity should be maintained between 65–75%. Relative humidity below 65% will encourage mite infestations as well as poor pollination, and relative humidity greater than 90% will encourage fruit mold and poor pollination. Humidity levels will vary depending on whether the greenhouse floor is gravel or concrete. Concrete floors tend to absorb moisture much more and therefore may need to be sprayed with water during the day in order to maintain sufficient humidity.

The greenhouse provides an excellent environment for pests and disease organisms to thrive. The greenhouse must be thoroughly cleaned before any raspberries are moved in. Maintaining an empty greenhouse at temperatures greater than 104°F and relative humidity at less than 50% for three to four days will eradicate many insects.

An irrigation system is necessary for greenhouse raspberry production (figure 4.12). Usually one or two spaghetti tubes in each pot from a plastic irrigation line are adequate. Water pH and EC (electrical conductivity, or soluble salts in the water) will vary from one region to another. A water analysis can be done to determine if your water source falls within the optimal pH and EC ranges for raspberries (6.0 to 6.5 pH, < 30 ppm sodium, < 50 ppm chlorine, with an EC < 3 mS/cm). For more detailed explanations on water and nutrient aspects of greenhouse operations, please consult *Water and Nutrient Management for Greenhouses* (see Further Reading at the end of this chapter).

Measure the available greenhouse space to determine

how many containers can fit about two feet apart within rows, with a minimum of 5½ to 6 feet between rows for floricane-fruiting cultivars and 4 feet for primocane-fruiting cultivars. Closer spacing may result in higher yields per house, but disease pressure will be greater. Leave space for a trellis support system as well as 3 feet to access both sides of the outside rows for harvesting.

Three-gallon containers provide sufficient room for root and primocane growth and are fairly easy to move in and out of the greenhouse, though some growers use five- or seven-gallon containers or bags of peat. Regardless of the container chosen, a well-drained potting medium rich in organic matter with a pH between 5.5 and 6.5 is needed. Cornell Greenhouse Raspberry Soilless Mix (see sidebar) and premixed media such as Metromix or ProMix have been used successfully.

Planting Details

For reasons not yet understood, cultivars that are proven to be reliable producers of high-quality fruit in the field do not necessarily perform similarly under greenhouse production. The floricane-fruiting Tulameen has proven to be an outstanding cultivar that consistently produces

Fig. 4.13 **Titan fruiting in the greenhouse.**

Cornell Greenhouse Raspberry Soilless Mix

Combine:
- 2 bushels peat
- 2 bushels vermiculite
- 1 bushel sand (adds weight to keep the containers from tipping over too easily)

Add nutrients:
- 14.5 ounces lime
- 3 ounces triple super phosphate
- 3 ounces calcium nitrate
- 4.5 ounces Micromax trace elements
- Slow release fertilizer (optional)

---

a high-quality raspberry in the greenhouse with few insect and pathogen pest issues (figure 4.13).

Tissue culture virus-indexed transplants have the best growth and productivity and will generally live longer. When planting, the top of the root ball should be covered with a soil medium to a depth of ¾ inches. Medium should be pressed to ensure good contact with the root ball. Fill containers two-thirds full, applying a few inches of compost to the pot surface to retain moisture and begin irrigating immediately after transplanting.

The containers can be placed outdoors for the first growing season if danger of spring frost is past. Pest management materials are usually easier to apply outdoors in comparison to a greenhouse. Place the plants in full sun, out of the wind, and on a growing bed with a weed barrier and automated drip irrigation. A north-south orientation is preferred for better light interception. Sufficient spacing between the rows of at least 8 to 10 feet should be allowed for maximum sun exposure on the lower portions of the canes. If the plants are too close together, the lower buds will not produce fruiting laterals once they are moved into the greenhouse.

During hot, sunny, and/or windy days, the containers may need to be watered more than once a day. Irrigation is adequate when there are no dry spots in the container root zone and water has moved through the entire container. Fertilize with a complete soluble fertilizer solution containing 100 ppm of nitrogen at least once a week. Once moved inside and flowering begins, reduce the overall rate to 50 ppm to avoid excessively lush canopy growth and soft fruit. Raspberries appear to grow best with a higher proportion of nitrogen relative to the phosphorus and potassium found in commercial formulations. Therefore, it may be necessary to use two stock solutions to obtain the right balance between nitrogen and the other nutrients (see sidebar). Remove any weeds growing in the containers as they are a source of competition for nutrients and moisture.

As the primocanes grow during that first season outdoors, support stakes will be necessary to keep the canes upright in the wind. This upright stability can be achieved through relatively simple measures such as running a series of twine support lines between strategically located bamboo stakes.

Outside insects and diseases should be minimal. Scout weekly especially to monitor for Japanese beetles, oriental beetles, and raspberry sawfly larvae (see "Insect and Mite Scouting and Management," chapter eight). Conventional pest control measures can be used when plants are outdoors.

In early fall cut back on watering and fertilizing, but do not allow the containers to completely dry out. After leaf drop, move the pots closer together and surround them with bales of straw to protect them from cold temperatures. In most regions, the chilling requirement (800 to 1200 hours of temperatures between 28°F and 45°F) is usually met by late December, and containers can be moved into the greenhouse. To ensure that a sufficient number of chilling hours has been achieved, plants can be moved into a cooler (that does not contain other fruit that can produce ethylene gas) for eight weeks prior to moving them into a warm greenhouse. If natural chilling is relied upon and fall temperatures are mild, then chilling may not occur until later than desired. To avoid cold injury, less hardy cultivars such as Tulameen may have to be moved into an unheated greenhouse or building if temperatures are forecast to fall below 20°F for several consecutive hours.

Some nurseries may be able to provide "long canes" or bare-root canes that are dug from the nursery after the chilling requirement is fulfilled. These plants can be directly potted and fruited without waiting one or two years for fruiting canes to develop from young plants. Shipping costs will be high, however.

Nutrient Management of Greenhouse Raspberries

Stock solution #1:
- 1 lb 6.5 oz calcium nitrate
- 4.5 oz ammonium nitrate
- 10 gal water

Stock solution #2:
- 2 lb 11 oz soluble 5-11-26 fertilizer (e.g., Peter's Hydrosol 5-11-26)
- 10 gal water

Add both stock solutions in equal proportions, diluting each to a ratio of 1 part fertilizer to 50 parts water to obtain a 100 ppm nitrogen solution to deliver to the plants. Once flowering begins, reduce overall rate to 50 ppm by reducing solution to water ratio to 1:100. The EC of the fertilizer solution should be a maximum of 1.5 mS/cm and the pH should be 6.5.

Initial temperatures in the greenhouse should be maintained at 50°F at night and about 65°F during the day. Once plants fully leaf out, the temperature can be maintained as low as 55°F during the evening and as high as 70°F during the day. The plants will flower in approximately five to eight weeks. Proper pollination is essential for optimal fruit set. Purchase bumble bee hives as these pollinators function better at cooler temperatures and under cloudier skies than do honey bees. Bumblebees are also relatively docile and will not sting unless provoked.

Pruning and trellising recommendations are different in a greenhouse than in the open field. Details can be found in chapter five.

A two-year-old mature plant will produce between 10 and 15 half-pints or more of fruit over about an eight-week period. Fruit size will be exceptionally large and of high quality. Ninety percent or more of the fruit should be marketable since it should be free of disease and insect infestation. Primocanes can be tipped during the harvest period so they will not interfere with picking. They will regrow after harvest is complete.

Some growers use primocane-fruiting cultivars in the greenhouse to obtain fruit over a longer period of time without moving plants in and out of the greenhouse as frequently. Once a primocane fruits, the fruiting portion of the cane is removed, and lateral buds lower on the cane will break and flower, producing more fruit several weeks later. This process continues until the entire cane is expended. New canes will grow, allowing for an extended period of fruit production.

Scout for insects and disease weekly in the greenhouse. No chemical pesticides should be required with careful monitoring, temperature control, and the use of cultural and biological controls. United States Environmental Protection Agency policy currently states that a pesticide can be used in a greenhouse as long as the target crop and organism are listed on the pesticide label, unless the label specifically restricts use in greenhouses. Pesticides cannot be used in the greenhouse if there is a specific greenhouse prohibition on the label. The predominant pest problem in greenhouse raspberry production is two-spotted spider mites. An application of a fine horticultural oil before bud break can reduce early outbreaks of spider mites, as can the use of certain predatory mites available from various biological pest control suppliers.

After the harvest season has ended, the fruiting canes can be completely cut off at the soil level and discarded. Once the risk of killing frosts has passed, the containers with the newly growing primocanes can be moved outdoors for the summer and the cycle can be repeated for about three fruiting years.

Further Reading

Heidenreich, C., M.P. Pritts, M.J. Kelly, and K. Demchak. 2008. "High Tunnel Raspberries and Blackberries." Cornell Fruit Resources. Ithaca, NY: Cornell University. WWW.FRUIT.CORNELL.EDU/BERRIES/BRAMBLEPDF/ HIGHTUNNELSRASP.PDF.

Koester, K., and M.P. Pritts. 2003. "Greenhouse Raspberry Production Guide: For Winter or Year-Round Production." Cornell Fruit Resources. Ithaca, NY: Cornell University. WWW.FRUIT.CORNELL.EDU/BERRIES/ GHRASP.PDF.

Penn State College of Agricultural Sciences. "Center for Plasticulture." University Park, PA: Pennsylvania State University. HTTP://PLASTICULTURE.CAS.PSU.EDU.

Weiler, T.C., and M. Sailus. 1996. *Water and Nutrient Management for Greenhouses*. NRAES-56. Ithaca, NY: Natural Resource, Agricultural & Engineering Service (NRAES).

CHAPTER FIVE

Trellising and Pruning Brambles

Trellising and pruning brambles are essential for maintaining quality and productivity over the long term. Proper trellising and pruning allow a grower to manipulate cane growth and positively influence plant growth rate, fruit quantity and size, soluble solids (sugars), disease susceptibility, ease of harvest, and spraying efficiency.

Primocane-Fruiting (Fall-Fruiting) Red Raspberries

Primocane-fruiting raspberries produce fruit at the top of first-year canes in late summer. If allowed to overwinter, these same canes will produce fruit again in early summer of the second year on lower portions of the same cane (double-cropping). However, the quality of the early-summer fruit is inferior to both the late-summer primocane crop and the summer crop of floricane-fruiting types. Also, harvesting the early-summer crop from primocane-fruiting types is difficult because new primocanes grow among the fruiting canes, making harvest difficult. Likewise, the late-summer primocane crop is smaller when the second-year canes are allowed to fruit in summer. Consequently, with primocane-fruiting raspberries most growers favor managing canes for a single late-summer primocane crop. Additional advantages of a single-cropping system are that it eliminates cane thinning, detailed pruning, tying, cold injury and winter damage from rabbits or voles; it reduces spur blight, anthracnose, cane blight, and sap beetle damage; and it makes applications of fertilizers and pesticides easier.

Trellising

A temporary trellis for primocane-fruiting raspberries during the harvest season will allow easy movement between plant rows, keep the top-heavy canes from drooping over to the ground, and make harvesting

fruit easier. A simple T-trellis works well. It consists of T-shaped wooden or metal posts (e.g., rebar), approximately 7 feet tall, with a 2-foot cross arm (figure 5.1). The ends of the cross arms have a screw eye or other hardware to hold a length of baling twine. The baling twine is cheap and disposable, yet strong enough to temporarily hold canes upright. Each T-shaped post is set into a hole in the center of each row; holes are placed 25 to 30 feet apart within rows. The holes should be 2 feet deep and slightly wider than the diameter of the base of the posts. A 2-foot section of plastic PVC pipe can be set into the holes immediately after they are dug to prevent them from collapsing.

Just before harvest, T-posts are slid into the plastic-lined holes. The baling twine is strung from pole to pole and pulled tight to lift canes upright. After harvest, the twine can be cut and the posts removed and stored for another year. Since the plastic pipe is buried, it can remain in the ground where it will not interfere with cane-cutting operations.

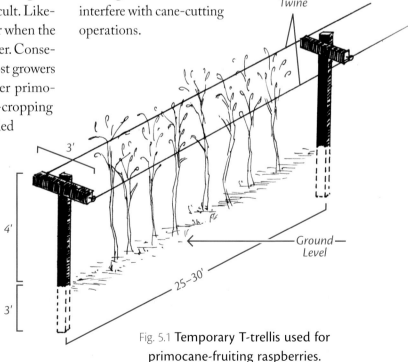

Fig. 5.1 Temporary T-trellis used for primocane-fruiting raspberries.

Pruning

To prune primocane-fruiting raspberries for a single late-season crop, cut them to the ground each year. New canes will grow and fruit in late summer and the cycle will continue. It is important to cut old canes as close to the ground as possible so that new buds will break from below the soil surface. If canes are not cut low enough, fruiting laterals may form on any remaining cane portion. These fruiting laterals are not healthy; they are entry sites for insects and disease pathogens. Also, any fruits that form will most likely rot, attracting pathogens and creating a source of inoculum (disease-conducting material) for the late-summer crop. All canes that are cut from the planting should be removed from the area and destroyed. In warm climates, the primocane crop can be delayed by mowing the young primocanes a second time when they are approximately 6 inches tall. Pinching the primocanes (removing the growing tip) to stimulate growth of laterals will also delay fruiting. This is sometimes done in the South to delay harvest until after the intense heat of July.

The timing of cane cutting is also important. Carbohydrates move from plant leaves into the crown in autumn, and from the crown to the buds in early spring. If canes are cut before all the carbohydrates reach the crown in autumn, the new canes may not be as vigorous the following year. Canes can also be cut too late, after carbohydrates have moved into the buds. From December through February, most carbohydrates are in the crown, so this is the ideal time to cut canes.

Yield of primocane-fruiting types is largely influenced by the number of canes per unit area, up to about 15 per square meter (10 square feet). Since large numbers of canes do not seem to decrease fruit size in the fall crop of primocane-fruiting raspberries, growers generally do not thin canes. Some benefit may be realized by removing weak canes, but the effort may not be economically justified. Row widths of 12 to 18 inches are considered ideal for harvesting. Narrow rows generally result in higher yields per planted area, so small equipment is often more desirable.

Floricane-Fruiting (Summer-Fruiting) Brambles

Floricane-fruiting brambles produce fruit only from buds on second-year canes. Unlike primocane-fruiting raspberries, these canes must remain intact throughout the winter and following growing season, until the completion of harvest. Also, during second-year flowering and fruiting on floricanes, new first-year primocanes are growing. These primocanes can interfere with spraying and harvesting, shade the leaves and laterals of floricanes, and compete for water since they share a single root system. Cane winter damage and primocane interference and competition must be minimized through trellising and pruning to obtain a high yield of fruit each year.

Trellising

Many methods of trellising floricane-fruiting bramble canes exist, including an I-trellis, which ties plants to a single wire 3 to 4 feet above the ground, or a T-trellis, which ties plants to two wires 3 to 4 feet above the ground. Some growers angle posts into the ground, forming a V, but the V-trellis and T-trellis are functionally similar. An I-trellis will help prevent cane breakage, but since it

Fig. 5.2 **I-trellis system used with black raspberries.**

Fig. 5.3 **Four-wire T-trellis with two cross arms.**

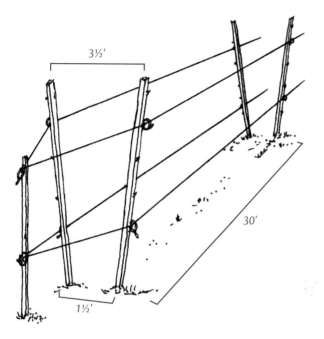

Fig. 5.4 A V-trellis system used on raspberries.

Fig. 5.5 T-trellis system used with purple raspberries.

allows little light to reach the lower portions of canes, primocane growth is forced toward the aisles where it can greatly interfere with spraying and harvesting operations. It also makes adjustments for annual variations in cane height difficult. The disadvantages of the I-trellis can be addressed with a split canopy trellis (T or V). Cane interference and competition can be reduced and yields increased by separating the fruiting canes from vegetative canes.

With the V-trellis system, anchoring posts are placed at thirty-foot intervals at a 20° to 30° angle along the outer margins of each plant row to form a V-shaped structure. Monofilament plastic wires are strung at two heights along the posts through screw eyes or other inexpensive hardware and pulled taut (figures 5.4 and 5.5). Fruiting canes are tied to wires on the outside of the V, and primocanes are permitted to grow in the center of the V. Spraying, harvesting, and pruning operations are made easier since floricanes are outside and accessible, and primocane interference is minimized. Also, the presence of primocanes in the center of the row forces fruiting laterals to grow outward. Yields of several cultivars of raspberries have increased when plants are V-trellised, primarily due to increased light interception by the plant canopy. The V-trellis allows adjustments in wire heights to be easily made at any time.

Several types of V-trellises are used throughout the world. In some places, half of the floricanes are tied to each side of the V. Elsewhere, growers tie floricanes to one side of the V and train primocanes to the other side. Some growers use a V-trellis and mow alternate halves of the row lengthwise every year. In these cases, fruiting canes are tied to only one wall of the V.

Fig. 5.6 V-trellis system used with black raspberries where floricanes are all trained to one side of the V.

Modifications of the Gjerde system developed in Norway can be used to change an I-trellis shape to a V-trellis (figure 5.7) by adding a crossbar as on a T-shaped trellis (figure 5.8). Two wires are strung across the top of the crossbar. From early spring until the beginning of flowering, floricanes are held vertically in an I-trellis configuration with the wires close together. When flowering begins, the wires and the attached floricanes are moved to a wider position, making a V configuration, while primocanes take the center position. Additional wires on a lower crossbar may be needed to support the fruiting canes. Care must be taken not to damage the fruiting laterals when spreading the floricanes. The outward direction of the fruiting laterals, which results from spreading the floricanes during flowering, makes harvest easy and efficient. After harvest, the outer wires are removed and the dying fruiting canes are bent out at right angles to the row and cut, while middle wires hold the primocanes erect.

For thornless blackberries the double curtain V-trellis has been very successful. Fruiting canes are tied to one side of the V and primocanes to the other. Primocanes and floricanes alternate sides of rows across the field, so each alleyway is bordered by canes of the same age. This pattern makes spraying and harvesting easier.

A swinging-arm trellis can facilitate harvest in thornless blackberries and other flexible-caned brambles. This system has a single arm that swivels on a post about 3 feet off the ground. Primocanes are trained up the post, then over on the swinging

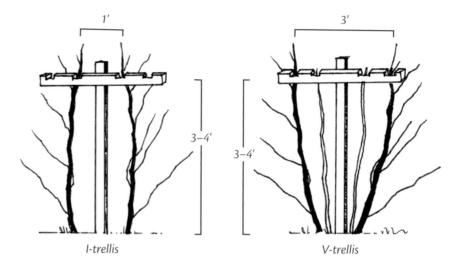

Fig. 5.7 **The Gjerde system used on raspberries in Norway.**

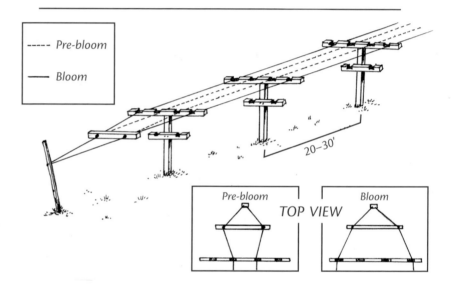

Fig. 5.8 **Converting a trellis from an I to a V configuration.**

Fig. 5.9 **Shift trellis for thornless blackberry production.**

arm that now is in a nearly horizontal position. The swinging arm may support several wires that catch and hold the growing primocanes. Canes overwinter in this position. In the spring, fruiting lateral buds will break and grow upwards towards the light. Once fruit set occurs and flower petals drop, the entire trellis arm is shifted about 135 degrees to the other side of the row. All of the fruit is now leaning out towards the pickers, making harvest easy. Once the fruit is harvested, the floricanes are removed, the arm is shifted to horizontal, and the growing primocanes are brought up onto the swinging arm where they will remain until next year.

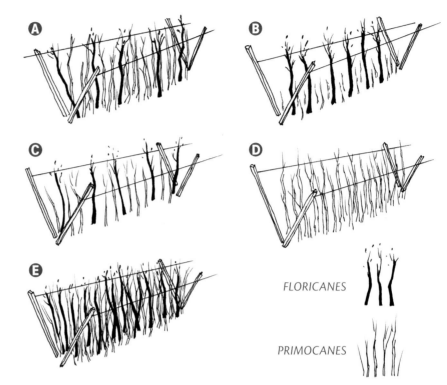

Fig. 5.10 **Raspberry management systems as they would appear in mid-summer.**
Ⓐ Selective pruning with no mowing or suppression of primocanes.
Ⓑ Primocane suppression. Ⓒ Partial primocane suppression.
Ⓓ Alternate-year mowing, 1st year. Ⓔ Alternate-year mowing, 2nd year.

Pruning

Five general methods of pruning floricane-fruiting brambles for field production are described below. Each method will produce different results in the growth of primocanes and floricanes. For all methods, maintain row widths at no greater than 12 inches to concentrate new cane growth under the trellis, and to prevent canes from growing in the alleyways.

In the following descriptions, mowing refers to removal of all canes at ground level. Suppression refers to removing or chemically suppressing the first flush of primocanes when they emerge in spring, forcing the plant to produce new canes later in spring. Selective pruning refers to the removal of floricanes in early spring, generally by removing weak spindly canes and retaining thick fruitful canes.

Selective Pruning with No Mowing or Suppression of Primocanes

This training system is traditionally used by bramble growers in the Northeast. Primocanes emerge and are permitted to grow throughout the season. The following year, they become floricanes, flowering and fruiting as new primocanes emerge (figure 5.10A). Immediately after fruiting, however, the floricanes are cut at ground level and disposed of. Some carbohydrates are lost by cutting canes in summer. However, this loss is offset by the advantages of reduced disease inoculum and a reduction in dormant-season pruning. In early spring of the following year, all remaining canes are topped (headed back) to a convenient height for picking, since little vegetative growth occurs in the second season. Fruiting canes are thinned to a desired number (see details for each crop below). When thinning, the most vigorous canes should be selected to produce the next crop—those with good height, a large diameter, and no visible symptoms of disease, insect damage, or winter injury.

Primocane Suppression

The highest long-term yields and largest berry sizes have resulted from a combination of selective floricane thinning and suppression of primocanes in late spring (figure 5.10B). If primocanes are suppressed when reaching 6–8 inches tall, shading on the lower portions of floricanes is reduced and energy is diverted into fruiting canes. Harvesting is easier because smaller primocanes cause less interference. Primocane suppression has also been reported to increase hardiness.

Fig. 5.11 *Left:* Rampant growth of purple raspberries.
Right: Same field of purple raspberries the following year with primocane suppression.

Since there is less shading and fewer demands for water, fruit size and productivity of lower laterals are increased. Primocanes of vigorous cultivars can still grow to a sufficient height for adequate fruiting the following year.

Primocanes should not be suppressed until the planting is at least three years old. Primocanes contribute large amounts of carbohydrates to the bramble plant, and repeated suppression will reduce carbohydrate levels. Therefore, suppression should be skipped every third or fourth year to allow the planting to recover from the general reduction in vigor. Weak hills or sections of rows should not be suppressed at all.

There are conditions under which suppression of primocanes is not recommended. If a fruit-crop load is particularly heavy, primocane growth may decrease naturally as developing fruit demands all the plant's resources. Also, if primocanes are suppressed in regions with short growing seasons, they may be too short at the end of the growing season. Suppression is not recommended under the above conditions, or whenever the plant is stressed from a lack of moisture or a nutritional imbalance.

Advantages of primocane suppression are: (1) increases in fruit size and quality, (2) increases in production, and (3) reduced cane numbers. Disadvantages are: (1) long-term reductions in stand vigor and (2) expenses involved with primocane suppression or elimination. Furthermore, there are no universally accepted methods of suppressing primocanes chemically.

Partial Primocane Suppression

Yield and quality may be increased without suppressing all the primocanes in a planting. Removing all but 4 or 5 primocanes per linear foot of row will increase yield and fruit quality in some cultivars.

For this method, growers select the primocanes in late spring which will be carried into the following year for fruiting. Rejected primocanes are cut to ground level when 8 inches tall. The raspberry plant uses resources for the current fruiting canes and the remaining primocanes, rather than for many primocanes which would eventually be removed with the conventional system.

Primocane regrowth is ignored until the dormant season when these short canes are removed (figure 5.10C). Advantages of this system are: (1) selected primocanes grow for an entire season instead of the partial season under complete primocane suppression, (2) rejected primocanes are removed when small, succulent, and easy

Fig. 5.12 **Selective thinning of primocanes in early summer.**

to handle, as opposed to large and thorny, and (3) fruit size and quantity in the current season is increased. The major disadvantages are: (1) primocane selection is difficult when leaves are on the plant, and (2) suppression of undesirable canes requires much labor.

Alternate-Year Mowing

One method that growers use to reduce the expense of selective cane removal (by hand) is to mow the planting to the ground (by machine) during the dormant season. This technique does not permit any yield the year canes are mowed, but concentrates the crop in the year after mowing. By mowing half the planting in any one year, growers can still harvest annually.

With alternate-year mowing, primocane interference among floricanes is reduced. In the spring after mowing, primocanes will emerge and grow without interference from fruiting canes (figure 5.10D). The following year, the floricanes will flower and fruit (figure 5.10E). Although primocanes will also grow in the fruiting year, all canes will be cut to the ground during the next dormant season. Advantages of this method are that no detailed cane thinning or pruning are required, and spray material costs are reduced approximately 50%. Disadvantages include a reduction in fruit quality, berry size, and yield of approximately 30% for most cultivars, since only half the planting is fruiting in any one year.

Alternate-Year Mowing with Primocane Suppression

The reduction in yield caused by alternate-year mowing can be partially offset by removing all primocanes from the plant row during the fruiting year. After the first few flushes of growth are removed, primocanes eventually will be allowed to grow, but practically, the system is biennial. Primocanes grow without interference from floricanes, and floricanes grow without interference from primocanes.

The advantages of this method are: (1) the ease of pruning when done in early spring, (2) a reduction in spray materials cost, and

(3) reduced canes diseases. Disadvantages are: (1) a small reduction in yield over the long-term, since only half the planting is fruiting in any one year, and (2) the cost of primocane suppression (labor, materials).

Red (and Yellow) Raspberries

Productivity in summer-fruiting red and yellow raspberries is most closely related to the number of canes. Unlike the situation with primocane-fruiting raspberries, however, fruit size decreases as cane numbers increase. Growers must maintain a high number of canes, but not high enough to greatly reduce fruit quality. In general, three to five large canes per linear foot of row is the optimal range, with a plant row width of 12 inches and a between-row spacing of 9 feet (figure 5.13). A greater density is optimal if between-row spacing is wider.

On summer-fruiting raspberries, buds at the top of a cane often winter kill because they are less mature and less hardy than buds lower on the cane. Spring pruning should be delayed until winter injury on canes can be identified, usually by mid-March. Canes should be topped as high as the trellis and harvest operations will permit, but below the point of winter injury. Severe topping will increase fruit size but will greatly reduce yield. To prevent a loss in yield, no more than the top one-fourth of a cane should be removed.

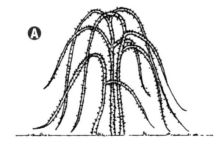
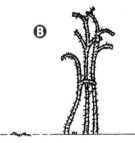
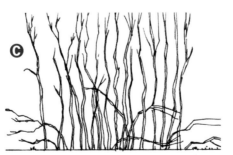
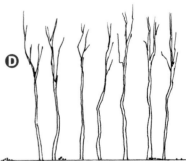

Fig. 5.13 **Before and after winter pruning for red and black raspberries.**
Ⓐ Black raspberry before winter pruning; **Ⓑ** Black raspberry after winter pruning.
Ⓒ Red raspberry before winter pruning; **Ⓓ** Red raspberry after winter pruning.

Growers may choose any of the five general pruning methods presented above for summer-fruiting raspberries (figure 5.10, page 43). Each method will produce different effects on yield and productivity. After pruning, canes are tied loosely to the trellis wire to prevent wind damage of laterals after bud break. Canes should be spaced evenly along the trellis wire and equally divided between sides of a V-trellis.

Tipping (pinching off the tips) of red raspberry primocanes during the growing season to promote lateral growth is not recommended for field production. This procedure slows cane development, does not stimulate much branching, and makes the plant susceptible to winter injury and cane diseases.

Black Raspberries

In contrast to red raspberries, black raspberries respond well to primocane tipping. Many more fruiting buds are produced on black raspberry lateral branches than on the main cane, so when primocanes reach about 28 inches, pinch them back to stimulate lateral branching from the main cane. At least 4 inches of tip should be removed during pinching. Several passes through the field may be required since canes grow at different rates. Ideally, primocanes should be tipped just above a bud. Tipped canes can be a site for cane blight infection, especially if wet weather follows tipping.

Some growers tip black raspberries mechanically by shortening fruiting canes to a height of 22 inches in early spring. Later in the spring, several passes are made with a sickle bar mower at 24 inches. Although this method is less labor intensive than tipping, primocanes will be more susceptible to cane blight infection since there is little control over wound size or the amount of dead wood between the cut and first bud.

At the end of the first year, black raspberry primocanes are branched with long laterals. These lateral branches should be supported by trellis wires before October since wet snow tends to break them off of the main cane. Also, canes are more

flexible in early autumn than in late autumn and are less prone to breaking from the crown during trellising.

A large portion of lateral branches may be killed during the winter since black raspberries generally are not as hardy as red raspberries. Laterals are shortened (headed back) in early spring to remove winter-damaged wood and to maintain berry size. Some growers shorten laterals to less than 10 inches. The choice of lateral length depends on cultivar vigor and the relationship between crop size and fruit size. The relationships among productivity, fruit size, and lateral length are not well known.

Whatever general pruning method is chosen, leaving 4 to 6 canes per crown should give most growers acceptable yields of large fruit (figure 5.13). Black raspberries will respond well to partial primocane suppression. Full suppression is not recommended because black raspberries produce few primocanes.

Purple Raspberries

Purple raspberries perform best if pruned similarly to red raspberries (figure 5.14). Purple raspberry primocanes may be tipped, like black raspberries, but wounds are often an entry site for cane diseases which kill part of the cane.

If a grower chooses not to tip or suppress purple raspberry primocanes, the canes will grow very tall (see figure 5.11). Often these canes are shortened in winter so the trellis can support this vigorous growth. Some natural branching will occur near the base of primocanes

Fig. 5.14 **Brandywine purple raspberry before (*right*) and after (*left*) dormant pruning.**

Table 5.1 Recommended strategies for pruning and trellising specific brambles.

Species	Plant type	Pruning options during the growing season	Trellising method	Pruning during the dormant season
Field Production				
Red/yellow raspberry *Rubus idaeus*	Primocane/ fall fruiting		T-trellis prior to fall harvest	cut canes to ground (December to February)
	Floricane/ summer fruiting	• Selective floricane pruning • Alternate year mowing • Mowing with primocane suppression • No mowing with primocane suppression • Partial primocane suppression	V-trellis floricanes in spring	In mid-March thin to 3–5 large floricanes per linear foot of row; top canes as high as the trellis
Purple raspberry *Rubus neglectus*	Floricane/ summer fruiting	• Selective floricane pruning • Alternate year mowing • Mowing with primocane suppression • No mowing with primocane suppression • Partial primocane suppression	V-trellis primocanes with long laterals before October	In mid-March thin to 3–4 large floricanes per linear foot of row; shorten laterals
Black raspberry *Rubus occidentalis*	Floricane/ summer fruiting	• Pinched back 28" primocanes • Selective floricane pruning • Alternate year mowing • Partial primocane suppression	V-trellis primocanes with long laterals before October	In mid-March thin to 4–6 large floricanes per linear foot of row
Blackberry *Eubatus* spp.	Thornless trailing	• Pinched back 24" primocanes • Partial primocane suppression • Selective floricane pruning	V-trellis floricanes in spring	In mid-March thin to 6–8 large floricanes per hill; top canes as high as the trellis or weave on wire: shorten laterals; remove lower laterals
	Thorny erect	• Tipped when 3–4 feet high • Alternate Year Mowing • Selective floricane pruning	V-trellis primocanes with long laterals before October	In mid-March thin to 2 large floricanes per hill; shorten laterals
Greenhouse/High Tunnel Production				
Red/yellow raspberry *Rubus idaeus*	Floricane/ summer fruiting	• Suppress first flush of primocanes • Pinch primocanes to 36"	I-trellis floricanes	Thin to 4 large floricanes per pot
	Primocane/ fall fruiting	• Greenhouse—continuous removal of expended fruiting portion of the cane • High tunnel—may pinch primocanes to delay fruiting	I-trellis primocanes	

← Fig. 5.15
Shortened Royalty primocanes in winter that were not pinched in summer.

Fig. 5.16 →
Royalty primo-canes in winter with shortened lateral branches.

when growing conditions are favorable. These canes may be removed or allowed to fruit.

If primocanes are tipped to keep the plant short and compact, it should be done when primocanes reach a height of 32 inches. At least 4 inches of tip must be removed. Many lateral buds will break near the top of the cane, and fewer near the base. Lateral branches should be shortened below any winter damage in early spring.

Tipped plantings without cane diseases will generally produce higher yields, but berries on the long laterals are more difficult to harvest. Also, long lateral branch or cane length generally results in smaller fruit size. Larger fruit can be obtained by shortening canes or lateral branches in early spring, but at the expense of yield.

Pruning methods that leave three to four fruiting canes per linear foot of row produce acceptable yield and quality of fruit. Purple raspberries respond favorably to primocane suppression but do not respond well to mowing.

Thornless Blackberries

For two years after planting, thornless blackberry primo-canes tend to grow along the ground, like a vine. Grow-ers may have to move trailing canes in the direction of the row to allow room for cultivation. After two years, however, canes become more erect and are naturally branched. Thornless blackberry canes are thicker and more flexible than raspberry canes.

Because of the poor hardiness of thornless blackber-ries, northern growers must take special precautions to protect canes during winter. Although canes are somewhat flexible, they will not bend to the ground after the third

year to be covered with mulch or straw. Some growers tip thornless blackberry primocanes when they reach a height of 24 inches so that low-growing laterals are more easily protected during winter.

In spring, the canes should be tied at least 3 feet above the ground to trellis wires. Fruiting canes are either shortened to the top trellis wire or woven around the wire. Woven canes should overlap no more than 2 or 3 feet with an adjacent plant. Lateral branches are

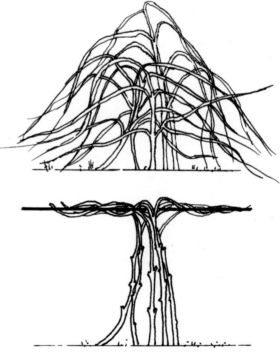

Fig. 5.17 **Before and after pruning for thornless blackberries.**

shortened to approximately 18 inches, and laterals on the lower 2 feet of cane are removed. Thinning canes to six to eight per hill will maintain acceptable production (figure 5.17). Partial primocane suppression is recommended for thornless blackberries.

Thorny Blackberries

Thorny blackberry primocanes are tipped when 3 to 4 feet high to stiffen canes and cause lateral branching. The laterals are shortened to 12 to 16 inches in early spring, and canes are thinned to two per linear foot of row. Longer lateral branches will produce more but smaller fruit than will shortened laterals. Growers may choose alternate-year mowing methods to avoid the difficult task of pruning the thorny canes.

Trellising and Pruning Greenhouse Raspberries and High-Tunnel Brambles

A trellis support system is absolutely required in greenhouse and high-tunnel production, as the fruiting laterals will become heavily weighed down with the production of the fruit and make transit through the closely-spaced rows difficult. Several options are recommended. One is an I-trellis consisting of wooden or metal posts, approximately 7 feet tall, with either no or short cross arms.

Fig. 5.18 **Greenhouse I-trellis system.**

The ends of the cross arms have a screw eye or other hardware to hold a length of monofilament plastic wire or twine for containing the canes. In the greenhouse, where posts cannot be driven in the ground or attached to the house frame, buckets filled with sand can be placed on the trellis frame for stabilization. The wire is strung from pole to pole and pulled tight to help keep

Fig. 5.19 **Short cross-arms for retaining primocane-fruiting raspberries under a high tunnel.**

Fig. 5.20 **Greenhouse trellis system with sand buckets for stability.**

Fig. 5.21 **Greenhouse trellis system with wires to keep canes upright.**

the canes upright. Bamboo posts or a similar product inserted into each pot and secured to the trellis or to the greenhouse ceiling or frame also can help maintain upright stability of raspberry canes. Although a V or T trellis may capture more light, they also require more space. In a greenhouse or high tunnel where space is at a premium, narrow rows should prevail.

Floricane-fruiting cultivars

New emerging primocanes can grow as much as 15 feet in the first season and must be pinched back or the first flush removed so they do not become a major source of competition with the fruiting floricanes or get in the way of harvesting the fruit. Remove the smallest and the largest primocanes at the soil level, leaving only four healthy primocanes (about ½ inch in diameter) for next year's crop. Alternatively, remove the first flush of primocanes and allow the second flush to grow. When the primocanes reach a height of approximately 3 feet, pinch their tips. This will temporarily halt the primocane's growth and limit primocane interference when harvesting fruit from floricanes. The primocanes will break a bud below the pinched area and once again continue to grow later in the season. Under warm, sunny conditions, multiple pinching may be required, perhaps every three weeks.

Primocane-fruiting cultivars

In the greenhouse, primocane-fruiting raspberries will flower and fruit several months after planting. To promote additional flowering, remove the expended portion of the cane. New fruiting laterals will break below the cut, and additional flowering and fruiting will occur. New primocanes also may emerge for additional fruiting in several months.

In a high tunnel, flowering can be delayed until late fall by tipping the primocanes before they flower, usually when canes are between 24 and 36 inches tall. The earlier the canes are tipped, the longer the delay. This is desirable when a late market is available for raspberries.

Further Reading

Crandall, P.C. 1995. *Bramble Production*. Binghamton, NY: Food Products Press, an imprint of The Haworth Press, Inc.

Galletta, G.J., and D.G. Himelrick. 1990. *Small Fruit Crop Management*. Englewood Cliffs, NJ: Prentice-Hall.

Koester, K., and M.P. Pritts. 2003. "Greenhouse Raspberry Production Guide: For Winter or Year-Round Production." Cornell Fruit Resources. Ithaca, NY: Cornell University. WWW.FRUIT.CORNELL.EDU/BERRIES/GHRASP.PDF.

CHAPTER SIX

Water Management

Water is essential to produce bramble fruit. The increase in berry size from fruit set through ripening is due primarily to an increase in cell size, rather than to division of existing cells in the undeveloped fruit. This increase in cell size (called cell expansion) is highly dependent on water availability. A raspberry plant growing vigorously in the summer can evapotranspire up to a quarter of an inch of water each day and can deplete all available moisture within just a few days after a heavy rainfall. Though excessive moisture must be avoided to discourage soil-borne disease, bramble plants require a continuous supply of water throughout the fruiting period.

Do not plant brambles without an irrigation system in place. While total rainfall statistics in many regions might prompt one to believe that irrigation is unnecessary, rainfall distribution is often uneven, with long, dry periods occurring in the summer months in most of the United States and Canada. For example, figure 6.1 shows

average monthly precipitation and potential evaporation for Oregon, Michigan, and New York. In Oregon, the precipitation is low at times of high evaporation demand. In Michigan and New York, monthly precipitation is more uniform and generally adequate, but long periods of water deficits still occur during the summer.

Problems associated with water deficits can occur even during years of normal, abundant rainfall. For high-value crops, irrigation is beneficial even in humid climates and is cheap insurance against catastrophic loss. For example, in the Northeast, there are on average five days between significant rains. For a sandy soil, which cannot store adequate water for more than a few days, drought stress may occur even under these circumstances. In one out of every two years, a ten- to fifteen-day period without rainfall is likely. As a result, just one water application could provide significant yield benefits to brambles in at least half of the years, particularly if water stress occurs during blossom and fruit set or the

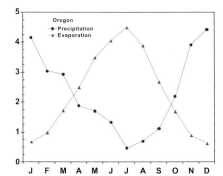
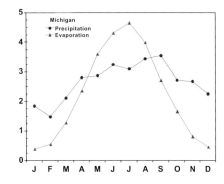
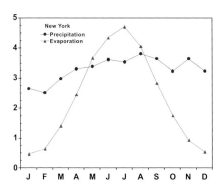

Fig. 6.1 Average monthly precipitation and potential evapotranspiration for Oregon, Michigan, and New York.

berry enlargement period. Periods of twenty to thirty days without significant rainfall may occur two or three times every twenty years somewhere in northeastern North America. A drought lasting this long during the prime growing season would result in catastrophic yield losses. In the upper Midwest, the average number of days between rains is six or seven, and the drought frequency is greater.

In the lower Midwest, the South, and Pacific Northwest, significant periods of drought occur nearly every year.

Along with soil, markets, and terrain, you must consider water management during the initial site selection process to minimize future problems. In many cases, the water available for irrigation determines whether the site is suitable for bramble production.

Table 6.1 Comparison of various chemical injection methods.

Injector	Advantages	Disadvantages
Centrifugal Pumps		
Centrifugal Pump Injector	Low cost. Can be adjusted while running.	Calibration depends on system pressure. Cannot accurately control low injection rates.
Positive Displacement Pumps		
Reciprocating Pumps		
Piston pumps	High precision. Linear calibration. Very high pressure. Calibration independent of pressure.	High cost. May need to stop to adjust calibration. Chemical flow not continuous.
Diaphragm pumps	Adjust calibration while injecting. High chemical resistance.	Nonlinear calibration. Calibration depends on system pressure. Medium to high cost. Chemical flow not continuous.
Piston/ diaphragm	High precision. Linear calibration. High chemical resistance. Very high pressure. Calibration independent of pressure.	High cost. May need to stop to adjust calibration.
Rotary Pumps		
Gear/lobe pumps	Injection rate can be adjusted when running.	Fluid pumped cannot be abrasive. Injection rate is dependent on system pressure. Continuity of chemical flow depends on number of lobes in a lobe pump.
Miscellaneous Pumps		
Peristaltic pumps	Very low cost. Injection rate can be adjusted while running.	Short tubing life expectancy. Injection rate dependent on system pressure. Low to medium injection pressure.
Pressure Differential Methods		
Suction Line Injection	Very low cost. Injection rate can be adjusted while running.	Permitted only for surface water source and injection of fertilizer. Injection rate depends on main pump operation.
Discharge Line Injection		
Pressurized mixing tanks	Low to medium cost. Easy operation. Total chemical volume controlled.	Variable chemical concentration. Cannot be calibrated accurately for constant injection rate.
Proportional mixers	Low to medium cost. Calibrate while operating. Injection rates accurately controlled.	Pressure differential required. Volume to be injected is limited by the size of the injector. Frequent refills required.
Venturi Injectors		
Venturi Injector	Low cost. Water powered. Simple to use. Calibrate while operating. No moving parts.	Significant pump pressure required to operate the system. Does not provide a constant parts per million concentration in the irrigation water.
Combination Methods		
Proportional Mixers/Venturi	Greater precision than proportional mixer or venturi alone.	Higher cost than proportional mixer or venturi alone.

Source: Haman, et al. 1990. Chemical Injection Methods for Irrigation. Florida Cooperative Extension Service

Irrigation Systems for Chemical Injection

Irrigation systems used in bramble production can also be used for chemical injection (chemigation). Any chemical, including fertilizers or pesticides, that is soluble in water can be applied through an irrigation system (see "Soil and Nutrient Management," chapter seven, table 7.8, page 75). However, only certain fungicides are labeled for chemigation in brambles. Other pesticides that are not labeled for this application method in brambles should not be used this way.

Nutrients, particularly nitrogen fertilizer, are frequently injected through irrigation systems. There are several advantages to this method of nutrient application. It is often less expensive, since the cost is limited to placing the nutrient solution in an injector. The soil compaction that results from driving machinery over a field is avoided as well. Fertilizer distribution is highly dependent on the injector and flow rate used. A comparison of injectors is detailed in table 6.1.

Irrigation systems used for chemigation should apply water and chemicals uniformly. Furthermore, backflow prevention devices are required any time chemicals are injected into irrigation water. These devices may be quite expensive if you use municipal water supplies, but they are critical for protecting the water supply.

Fig. 6.2 **New raspberry planting with trickle irrigation.**

Table 6.2 Advantages of trickle irrigation in bramble plantings.

Irrigation Factor	Trickle as Compared to Overhead
Water storage capacity	Trickle irrigation requires about half the water needed by overhead systems. Water is used more efficiently since it is applied to the root zone.
Pump and pipe network	Trickle requires lower flow rates and operating pressures, so less energy is required for pumping. Smaller pumps and pipes are required.
Water use efficiency	Plants are supplied with the water they need, not an excessive amount.
Disease/weed management	Diseases that develop when free water is on leaf and fruit surfaces do not develop with trickle irrigation, since water is applied directly to the root zone. Weeds are less problematic between rows or in non-irrigated areas. However, weeds can occur at the emitters.
Labor/ automation	Trickle irrigation generally requires less labor (particularly when compared to portable overhead pipe, which needs to be moved periodically) and can be extensively automated.
Wind	Water can be applied efficiently under windy conditions.
Fertilizer	Trickle requires less fertilizer, since fertilizer is distributed only near plant roots.
Rodents/insect/ people damage	Though trickle systems may be eaten/damaged by rodents and insects and damaged by routine field operations, they are relatively easy to repair.

Trickle Irrigation Systems for Water Application

Trickle (drip) irrigation is the preferred system for most bramble growers as it offers many advantages (table 6.2). In trickle systems water is most often delivered via a tube that runs along the length of the row (figure 6.2). This delivery system is more efficient than overhead sprinklers because water is delivered directly to the soil surface surrounding the plant. No water is applied between rows, and less water is lost to evaporation. For most on-farm uses, trickle systems are rated at 80 to 90% efficiency and sprinkler systems around 60 to 75%. System efficiency is especially important when the water supply is limited or expensive to access. Trickle systems also keep the plant foliage and fruit drier, which can help discourage the development of fungal and bacterial diseases.

Planning an Irrigation System

Many growers consult professional irrigation designers (either from private companies or state/provincial

Cooperative Extension System specialists) before planting bramble crops rather than plan every aspect of the trickle irrigation system themselves. Be prepared for such a consultation with the following information:

1. An aerial photograph of the entire farm (optional). The Natural Resources Conservation Service can often provide a copy of an aerial photograph, with a normal scale of 1 inch being equal to 660 feet. Photographs showing water features (ponds, streams) and the major soil types are useful for planning. One web source for aerial photos is available at HTTP://TERRASERVER.MICROSOFT.COM/.

2. A topographic map showing changes in elevation. The topographic lines often show either 10- or 20-foot variations, adequate for planning purposes. More detailed surveys may be needed later for installation. Area libraries may have a map that you can copy, or you can obtain a map by writing or visiting your local Natural Resources Conservation Service. If neither of these sources can help you, request ordering information from the Branch of Distribution, U.S. Geographical Survey, Federal Center, Denver, Colorado 80225. The web address is HTTP://TOPOMAPS.USGS.GOV/INDEX.HTML. These maps are also available in computer software (DeLorme Topo USA, National Geographic Topo, Maptech Terrain Navigator).

3. A detailed sketch of the fields and management data, specifically:

   a. Diagram showing fields with their dimensions and location relative to other fields and laneways. Water location and power sources should also be detailed.

   b. Approximate elevation variation in the field(s).

   c. Type of soil and soil texture.

   d. Plant type and details that relate to timing and amount of water required for that type of plant.

   e. Length of rows.

   f. Row direction.

   g. Number of rows per field.

   h. Distance between rows.

   i. Spacing of plants in the row.

4. Water supply information.

   a. If the water supply is a pond, the approximate size and depth of the pond, the source of pond water (springs or streams), and the history of the pond's water-holding ability through the summer. You should also be able to approximate how long it takes for the pond to refill if water is used from it. Finally, a description of the pond's cleanliness (weed growth, algae on the surface, silt buildup) should be provided.

   b. If the water supply is a well, the capacity (gallons per minute at zero pressure), size (diameter) of the well casing and the water pipe inside, depth, standing water level, and well identification number. Well drillers often provide this information, or a pump test may need to be done. Have the water tested for pH, iron, manganese, total dissolved solids, sodium, calcium, magnesium, and bicarbonates; and note whether there is hydrogen sulfide, sand, or silt in the pumped water.

   c. If the water supply is a stream, the availability of water through dry months, the approximate flow rate in gallons per minute, and a description of the water cleanliness during the summer season. To test for cleanliness, take a water sample and allow it to settle.

5. Existing equipment information, including pump specifications.

6. Electrical power availability. If possible, note the voltage and phase available, the distance of the electricity from the pump site, and the power company's address and phone number.

7. Any consideration of your future irrigation needs.

To summarize, the system designer will need to first determine the plant water requirements and how the water can be delivered. Then the designer will compare the water supply capacity to the crop demand and look at other design factors.

Water Supply Considerations

An adequate and dependable supply of good-quality water must be available at a reasonable cost throughout the growing season if irrigation is to be successful and cost-effective. The water source should be as close as possible to the area to be irrigated to minimize the pumping and supply line cost. Large ponds, lakes, streams, springs, groundwater, municipal water, and recycled water are all potential water sources.

The legal right to withdraw large quantities of water for irrigation must be verified. Water rights in the eastern United States are called *riparian* or landowner's rights because anyone is entitled to use any water associated with land ownership. However, a riparian owner's rights are not absolute and are subject to reasonable use interpretations. In many western states, water is available only through appropriative rights. In some areas, permits or water use reporting are required before surface water or groundwater can be withdrawn for irrigation. Contact your state or provincial agriculture department for information on water use regulations.

Water sources must be able to provide water as often as it is needed. Stream flow and shallow groundwater sources are strongly influenced by climate, so they may not provide enough water during the dry part of the year when irrigation is needed most. Sometimes municipal water systems allow connections for irrigation purposes. However, this option may be expensive if water-use prices are high or if large areas need to be irrigated. Furthermore, if the municipality enforces water rationing, it may not permit irrigation during droughts. Although wastewater sources are generally poor quality and may not supply enough water to fulfill crop needs, they are being used more frequently for irrigation.

The irrigation water supply must be large enough to replenish the moisture taken from the rooting volume. Since irrigation is not 100% efficient, the water supply rate must be higher than the crop water use rate. Crop water requirements depend on climate, plant type, and soil moisture availability. Water supply systems are generally evaluated using two criteria, seasonal water demand and daily water demand. The water supply must be sufficient to satisfy the requirements of the irrigation system and must supply enough water to meet crop needs.

Pumping and pressurizing water can be expensive (table 6.3). The energy required is often overlooked by growers. Pumping 1 acre-foot of water from a well 100 feet deep with a pump running at 70% efficiency costs about $100 (at $0.10 per kilowatt hour). The energy cost

to pressurize surface water to 43 pounds per square inch (psi) is the same as lifting the same volume of water 100 feet. There is also a trade-off in the pumping cost versus the initial pipe cost because it takes more energy to pump water through small diameter pipes.

Seasonal Water Demand

Seasonal water demand is the average amount of water a crop will need for the entire growing season. Growers find this amount useful for sizing water supply systems where water is stored for irrigation, such as in ponds. In the northern United States and Canada, typical floricane-fruiting raspberry plants require about 1 to 2 inches of water per week, or about 25 to 30 inches per season. Demand tends to be higher in the warmer coastal areas. For a thirty-day drought period, or a growing season with 15 inches of rainfall, an additional 10 to 15 inches of water would be required to meet the seasonal demand. In the north, growers should store from 3 to 13 acre-inches of water for each acre irrigated during the season. In the Pacific Northwest, growers should store the entire seasonal demand because precipitation is minimal during the summer. An acre-inch is a unit of volume equal to 1 inch of water depth over an entire acre and is equivalent to 27,154 gallons of water.

Because trickle irrigation systems are not 100% efficient (they are usually around 80 to 90% efficient), the rule of thumb is to store 32,000 gallons of water for every 1 acre-inch application. For example, a 5-inch seasonal demand would require 160,000 gallons per acre

Table 6.3 Cost to pump 1 acre-foot (325,850 gallons) of water 1 foot in elevation, assuming $0.10 per kilowatt-hour.

Pump Efficiency	Energy Requirement (kilowatt hours)	Cost
100	1.02	$0.102
75	1.37	$0.137
60	1.71	$0.171
50	2.05	$0.205
40	2.56	$0.256

Pumps generally run at 60 to 80% efficiency, depending on the type, impellor wear, and operating conditions relative to its capacity.

(5 inches × 32,000 gallons per acre-inch) if irrigated with a trickle irrigation system. To irrigate a 10-acre parcel, a total of 1.6 million gallons (160,000 gallons per acre × 10 acres) should be available in storage. To store this water, a grower would have to have a 150-foot-by-150-foot pond that can store water to a depth of 10 feet (1 cubic foot = 7.48 gallons), or have a smaller pond with a rapid recharge rate.

Peak Evapotranspiration Rate (Daily Peak Use Rate)

At some time during the growing season, environmental conditions and crop characteristics will demand peak water-use, or peak evapotranspiration rates. The peak evapotranspiration (ET) rate is another useful value for sizing water supply systems such as continually flowing springs, streams, wells, or municipal systems. Both the water supply and the irrigation system must be capable of supplying water at the peak rate. Irrigation schedules based on the daily peak use ensure that enough water is applied when needed.

Peak ET rates are the highest in July and August (table 6.4). Since these rates represent long-term and monthly averages, demand during any single day could be another 25% higher, especially under hot, windy conditions. To use the information in table 6.4, look up the location closest to the site to be irrigated, select the peak ET rate value, and convert it to the appropriate units of interest. For example, at Harrisburg, Pennsylvania, the potential peak ET rate averages 0.22 inch per day. To irrigate 1 acre to a depth of 0.22 inch during a twenty-four-hour period will require about 5,970 gallons (27,154 gallons per acre-inch × 0.22 acre-inch). This will require an irrigation system that can supply a minimum of about 4 gallons per minute (gpm) to each acre irrigated (5,970 gallons ÷ 1,440 minutes per day), providing the system is operated for the entire 24 hours. With the recommended drip irrigation system, this is an overestimate of irrigation need because only the planted row is watered, not the whole field. If watering is restricted to a 4 foot strip of row and approximately 8 feet between the row is not being watered, the calculated irrigation need above would be reduced by approximately two-thirds.

If these values are increased 25% to account for higher single daily peak uses in the months of July and August,

Table 6.4 Monthly average potential evapotranspiration or peak-use rate of water (inches/day) for July and August at various locations in the United States and Ontario, Canada.

State	Location	Avg Peak Use Rate
Arkansas	Fort Smith	0.24
	Little Rock	0.23
	Texarkana	0.22
California	Bishop	0.45
	Eureka	0.16
	Fresno	0.39
	Mount Shasta	0.39
	Oakland	0.22
	Red Bluff	0.43
	Sacramento	0.36
	San Francisco	0.26
	Stockton	0.38
Connecticut	Bridgeport	0.22
	Hartford	0.21
	New Haven	0.20
Delaware	Wilmington	0.22
Idaho	Boise	0.38
	Lewiston	0.35
	Pocatello	0.36
Illinois	Cairo	0.21
	Chicago	0.24
	Moline	0.22
	Peoria	0.22
	Springfield	0.23
Indiana	Evansville	0.22
	Fort Wayne	0.22
	Indianapolis	0.23
	South Bend	0.23
Iowa	Burlington	0.22
	Des Moines	0.22
	Dubuque	0.21
	Waterloo	0.19
Kentucky	Lexington	0.23
	Louisville	0.23
Maine	Caribou	0.17
	Portland	0.20
Maryland	Baltimore	0.25
Massachusetts	Boston	0.24
	Blue Hill Observ.	0.23

State	City	Value
	Nantucket	0.20
	Pittsfield	0.22
	Worcester	0.22
Michigan	Alpena	0.20
	Detroit	0.25
	Escanaba	0.20
	Flint	0.21
	Grand Rapids	0.24
	Lansing	0.24
	Marquette	0.19
	Muskegon	0.22
Minnesota	Duluth	0.21
	International Falls	0.20
	Minnesota–St. Paul	0.22
	Rochester	0.22
	Saint Cloud	0.21
Missouri	Columbia	0.23
	Kansas City	0.25
	St. Joseph	0.22
	St. Louis	0.23
	Springfield	0.23
New Hampshire	Concord	0.20
	Mt. Wash. Observ.	0.15
New Jersey	Atlantic City	0.22
	Newark	0.23
	Trenton	0.23
New York	Albany	0.20
	Binghamton	0.17
	Buffalo	0.22
	New York	0.23
	Rochester	0.21
	Syracuse	0.21
North Carolina	Asheville	0.18
	Cape Hatteras	0.20
	Charlotte	0.20
	Greensboro	0.20
	Raleigh	0.20
	Wilmington	0.21
Ohio	Akron	0.22
	Cincinnati	0.23
	Cleveland	0.24
	Columbus	0.22
	Dayton	0.24
	Sandusky	0.24
	Toledo	0.25
	Youngstown	0.21
Oklahoma	Oklahoma City	0.28
	Tulsa	0.25
Ontario*	London	0.18
	Ottawa	0.20
	Ridgetown	0.20
	Simcoe	0.22
	Trenton	0.20
	Toronto	0.19
	Vineland	0.20
Oregon	Astoria	0.15
	Eugene	0.24
	Medford	0.33
	Pendleton	0.38
	Portland	0.22
	Salem	0.25
Pennsylvania	Allentown	0.21
	Erie	0.21
	Harrisburg	0.22
	Philadelphia	0.22
	Pittsburgh	0.19
	Williamsport	0.21
Rhode Island	Block Island	0.19
	Providence	0.21
Tennessee	Bristol	0.19
	Chattanooga	0.21
	Knoxville	0.22
	Memphis	0.22
	Nashville	0.23
Vermont	Burlington	0.21
Virginia	Lynchburg	0.21
	Norfolk	0.20
	Richmond	0.21
	Roanoke	0.22
Washington	Olympia	0.20
	Seattle	0.21
	Yakima	0.33
West Virginia	Charleston	0.20
	Elkins	0.15
	Parkersburg	0.20
Wisconsin	Green Bay	0.20
	LaCrosse	0.21
	Madison	0.22
	Milwaukee	0.22

*Source: Best Management Practices: Irrigation Management. 2nd edition. 2004. Agriculture and Agri-Food Canada/ Ontario Ministry of Agriculture and Food.

Table 6.5 Infiltration rates of overhead irrigation for various soil types.

Soil Texture	Infiltration Rate (inches/hour)
Coarse sand	0.75–1.00
Fine sand	0.50–0.75
Fine sandy loam	0.35–0.50
Loam or silt loam	0.25–0.40
Clay loam	0.10–0.30

Note: Do not apply water faster than the soil can absorb it, unless irrigating for frost protection.

Table 6.6 Maximum irrigation period (hours) with trickle irrigation for various soil textures, assuming 50% moisture capacity at the beginning of the cycle.

Flow Rate (gal/hr/ 100 ft)	Soil Texture				
	Loamy sand	Sandy sand	Clay loam	Silt loam	Loam
12	5.0	8.0	11.5	15.5	17.5
18	3.5	5.0	7.5	10.5	11.5
24	2.5	4.0	5.5	8.0	8.5
30	2.0	3.0	4.5	6.5	7.0
36	1.5	2.5	4.0	5.0	6.0
42	1.5	2.0	3.0	4.5	5.0
48	1.5	2.0	3.0	4.0	4.5

Table 6.7 Water-holding capacity of various soil types.

Soil Type	Inches Water/ Inch Soil
Sand	0.02–0.06
Fine sand	0.04–0.09
Loamy sand	0.06–0.12
Sandy loam	0.11–0.15
Loam	0.17–0.23
Silty clay loam	0.14–0.21
Clay	0.13–0.18

then the average peak use rate becomes 0.28 inch per day with a requirement of 5.3 gpm per day per acre [(27,154 gallons per acre-inch × 0.28 acre-inch) ÷ 1,440 minutes per day]. Thus, a spring, stream, well, or municipal water source would have to supply 4 to 5 gpm continuously for each acre irrigated to meet the peak demand in the summer months.

Round-the-clock irrigation is not always possible or desirable, so growers must make the numerical adjustments for the number of hours they plan to irrigate. For example, if a grower wants to irrigate for only ten hours a day with a trickle irrigation system operating at 85% efficiency, then the water supply must be capable of delivering approximately 14 gpm per acre to meet the daily demand discussed in the previous paragraph.

Water Quality

In most bramble production areas, water quality is generally good enough for irrigation. However, quality should always be a concern when a water source is assessed. Water quality includes its physical, chemical, and biological constituents.

Physical constituents refer to sand, silt, or other suspended materials in water. While the physical constituents are usually not damaging to fruit crops, they can damage or clog the irrigation system. For example, a high sand content damages pumps, and suspended materials can clog trickle systems including screens and disc filters.

Carefully evaluate your pond or river water, use filtering, and frequently back flush screens. A media (sand) filter works best for surface water, because it has more capacity for trapping particles and the media is lifted during backwash to flush the debris out.

Chemical constituents of water refer to pH, dissolved material, proportions of dissolved ions, and any organic compounds such as oil. Although generally not a problem, organic solvents or lubricants in the water can damage plants. If water pH is high (7.0 or above), lower it with sulfuric acid to prevent nutritional problems in the field. Certain pesticides can be deactivated by high-pH water, so it is important to be aware of the water pH when using the irrigation system to add chemicals. In arid areas, the total dissolved solids and sodium content of the water can add to the soil salinity and affect soil permeability. Saline and sodic soil conditions will limit production potentials. Trickle irrigation systems are susceptible to clogging when large amounts of calcium, bicarbonates, iron, manganese, and/or hydrogen sulfide are present.

Biological constituents such as bacteria and algae are often present in surface water. They are usually not harmful to fruit crops and can be controlled under most circumstances, but they can affect irrigation system performance, particularly trickle systems. Water contaminated with sewage should not be used to irrigate berry crops.

Scheduling Irrigation

Once an irrigation system is in place, the major decisions are when to irrigate, how much water to apply, and how to use and maintain the equipment.

Crop rooting depth, canopy development, fruiting habits, and nutrition and water requirements in a given climate largely determine the irrigation schedule. Soil infiltration and water-holding characteristics (see tables 6.5, 6.6, and 6.7) help determine the rate and duration of water application and affect the soil's ability to make water available to plants. Actual water use will vary daily throughout the season, so develop a method to make sure the crop has an appropriate amount of water available. Never apply water faster than the soil can absorb it.

Several methods are used to determine whether or not to irrigate, some being more reliable than others. By the time plants show visible signs of water deficit, such as wilting, plant growth has already been severely affected. Irrigation at this point may save the crop, but production will still suffer.

Feel Method

With this method, the soil's appearance after being squeezed by hand is used to estimate water content. With a lot of experience, this method can be quite reliable, and charts are available to describe how different soils should look and feel at different moisture contents. However, a common mistake is to feel the surface soil layers rather than soil around the root tips, where most moisture is taken up. Avoid this problem by using a probe to sample soil in the crop root zone.

Water Budget Method

The water-budget method is an accounting process of daily water use and rainfall inputs. Plant water use is estimated daily based on crop development and climate conditions, and is compared to the soil's water-holding capacity. Often, pan evaporation is used to keep track of water losses. An evaporation pan is simply a pan containing a gauge, which calculates how much water has evaporated, and then correlates that amount with plant evapotranspiration, usually by multiplying evaporation by a factor of 1.2.

Assume that the rooting depth of bramble crops is 18 inches on a sandy loam, high-organic-matter soil.

After a soaking rain or after irrigation, the soil should hold about 2.7 inches of water (18 inches × 0.15 from table 6.7). Irrigation should begin when available water is depleted by 50%, or about 1.4 inches in this example. If evapotranspiration removes about 0.22 inches of water per day from the soil, then after about six days 50% of the available water is depleted and irrigation (or rain) is again required. With the water-budget method, moisture loss is monitored and continuously calculated, and water is replaced based on the calculations. (Evapotranspiration rates for your location can be estimated from table 6.4 on pages 56–57).

With experience, this method can be quite reliable. Automated weather stations and computer software programs using this budget method are available and can be adapted to particular site conditions. An irrigation system linked to computer can also be used to automate irrigation.

Rule-of-Thumb Method

Another method for irrigating most crops in the north is to assume that 1 to 1½ inches of water are required weekly, either through rainfall or irrigation. The irrigation schedule can account for average weekly precipitation and plan irrigation to apply the difference required. However, rainfall is still unpredictable and water-holding capacity of soil types vary, so this method can lead to deficits or excesses which may hold back crop performance. For bramble crops, growers may wish to raise the estimated water demand to 2 inches per week during fruit development, especially on well-drained soils. It is important to note that applying 2 inches in a single application on sandy, well-drained soils may not be very efficient because much of the water is subject to leaching from the root zone. This leaching will also carry nutrients such as nitrate, which is dissolved in the soil water. High application rates should be avoided especially when adding nitrogen to the irrigation water. During high-water-demand periods, it is better to reduce the application amount and apply smaller amounts more frequently to meet the water demand. For example, one could apply 1 inch every three to four days.

For drip irrigation systems, a rule of thumb for young bramble plantings on sandy loam soil is to apply 18 gallons per day per 100 feet of row. For mature plantings, the rate is increased to 27 gallons.

Other Tools for Measuring Soil Water

Many instruments have been developed to help growers schedule irrigation. Evaporation pans, atmometers, infrared thermometers, pressure bombs, and porometers monitor evaporative demand, plant stress, or leaf moisture status. Tensiometers, gypsum or ceramic electrical resistance blocks, conductivity probes, matric potential (heat-dissipating) sensors, neutron probes, and time domain reflectometry (TDR) probes are used to monitor soil moisture. Some of these tools, such as evaporation pans, atmometers, tensiometers, and gypsum blocks, are relatively inexpensive and easy to use. Others are more expensive and are used mainly for research. All of them require constant monitoring, maintenance, and calibration to be reliable for scheduling irrigation.

A tensiometer is a simple, inexpensive tool for measuring soil moisture status (figure 6.3). The ceramic tip of the tensiometer should be placed in the rooting zone of the bramble plant, approximately six to ten inches deep. When the reading reaches a critical level, irrigation is required. This critical level depends on soil type. Soil moisture should not be depleted below 50% of the soil's capacity. Irrigation should be started when the tensiometer reading reaches this level, about 20 to 40 centibars (cbars) in sandy soils, 40 to 60 cbars in loamy soils, and 50 to 80 cbars in clay soils. Tensiometers work well in sandier soils but may require more service. When the soil dries out too much, there is so much vacuum in the tensiometer that the water column pulls apart, and air enters to relieve this vacuum. Servicing involves refilling the tensiometer with water and extracting all of the air so the water column is again intact with the water in the soil.

Gypsum blocks are also inexpensive, simple to use, and can reflect moisture more accurately in drier soils than tensiometers. Practically speaking, however, they do not offer much advantage, since as mentioned previously, plants should be watered before soil moisture falls below 50% of capacity. The gypsum block contains two electrodes cast in a small block of gypsum. The gypsum protects the

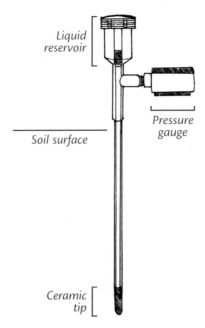

Fig. 6.3 **Tensiometer.**

electrodes from corrosion and confines the electrical path to within the block. A hand-held, battery-operated resistance meter is connected to the wires to indicate the electrical resistance. The more water there is in the soil (and in the gypsum block), the more the current will flow within the gypsum block between positive and negative charges. Gypsum blocks are sensitive to the total dissolved solids in the soil water so they can be affected by changes in fertility. They also decompose with time, especially in more acid soils, which may alter readings over time.

Some instruments have been developed for automated monitoring of water requirements and, when integrated with the appropriate irrigation system, can automate the entire irrigation process. More information regarding these tools or scheduling methods mentioned above is available in publications listed at the end of this chapter.

Trickle Irrigation System Components

The water-distribution hardware for trickle irrigation systems have several components, including a pumping unit, control head, mainline and submain pipes, laterals, and emitters (figure 6.4).

Pumping Unit

The pumping unit, which consists of a pump coupled to a power source, draws water from the supply source and pressurizes it for delivery through the irrigation system. A centrifugal pump or a submersible or deep-well turbine pump may be used.

Normally, a centrifugal pump cannot be placed more than 20 feet above the water line. Pumps are available in a wide range of flow capacities and delivery pressures. Selecting the correct style of pump and the proper size will depend on site characteristics and the final irrigation system layout.

Pump size depends on the discharge or amount of water to be delivered at a given time, and the head pressure required to lift the water and operate the trickle emitters. One reason trickle systems are more energy-efficient than sprinkler systems is that sprinklers usually

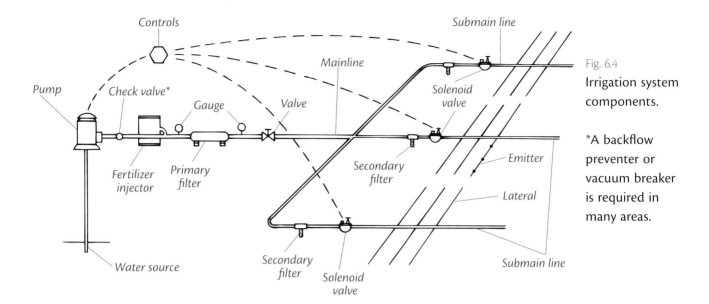

Controls

Submain line

Mainline

Pump

Check valve*

Gauge

Valve

Solenoid valve

Fig. 6.4

Irrigation system components.

*A backflow preventer or vacuum breaker is required in many areas.

Fertilizer injector

Primary filter

Secondary filter

Emitter

Lateral

Water source

Secondary filter

Solenoid valve

Submain line

require higher pressure to operate effectively and distribute the water uniformly. Consequently, pumps for sprinkler systems generally need to be larger than those for trickle systems.

Although the pumping units must meet certain hydraulic requirements, several options are usually available to meet site requirements and preferences. When growers can tie into municipal or household systems, where water is already pressurized, a pumping unit is unnecessary. The primary concern is that the supply (volume and flow rate) is large enough. Many municipalities limit the pipe size take-off to assure minimum disruption in pressure and flow to other users. They also generally require a flow meter and backflow prevention device.

Control Head

The control head is the combination of items that control, measure, or treat the water. Control heads can range from simple manually operated heads with a single valve to quite sophisticated heads with automatic controllers and sensors, water meters, pressure regulators, filters, and nutrient or chemical injection equipment. Control heads for trickle systems are often more complex than other systems because of the necessary water filtration equipment.

Automated pump controllers and accessory equipment can be adapted to some systems to measure soil moisture, start the irrigation system, and send water to the appropriate areas. The more complex and automated the control head and irrigation system, the greater the initial capital investment and maintenance costs.

Mainline and Submain Pipes

Mainline and submain pipes deliver water from the pump and control head to the laterals or other water distribution equipment. These pipes are usually classified as permanent, rigid and portable, or flexible and portable. Submain pipes are not always necessary.

Permanent piping is usually made of galvanized steel or plastic (either rigid PVC or polyethylene). This piping is installed below ground, with the exception of steel pipe, which can be installed above ground. For perennial crops such as raspberries and blackberries, permanent buried mainlines with hydrants spaced throughout the field offer several advantages, but they require high initial investment.

Rigid and portable (solid-set) piping is usually made of lightweight aluminum equipped with quick-coupler fittings. Although moving pipe is labor-intensive, portable piping systems offer flexibility and provide irrigation at a lower initial cost.

Flexible and portable pipe refers to conduits made with lightweight, durable rubber or synthetic compounds. These pipes are generally used with self-propelled sprinklers.

Although friction losses decrease per unit length from steel to aluminum to plastic pipe, proper pipe diameter is a more important factor to minimize flow velocity and subsequent friction loss. Pipe size is determined according to the discharge requirement, the allowable flow velocity within the pipe, and the trade-off between the tolerable friction loss and the total time of system operation in which that loss must be overcome. Since the total discharge requirements for trickle systems is lower than for sprinkler systems, pipe sizes are often smaller with trickle systems. A rule of thumb is that 2-inch diameter pipe is adequate for up to 60 gpm, 3-inch diameter for 60 to 125 gpm, 4-inch diameter for 125 to 250 gpm, 5-inch diameter for 250 to 425 gpm, and 6-inch diameter for 425 to 675 gpm.

Pipe type (its material and whether it is permanent or portable) is generally not a major factor in achieving desired flow characteristics. However, the pipe strength or burst pressure must be high enough to withstand the maximum pressure at which the irrigation system operates. The burst pressure of plastic pipe materials is sensitive to water temperature so the rating is the pressure at a given temperature (usually 75°F). A higher rating may be needed for plastic pipe exposed to direct sunlight. Common ratings include 60, 80, and 100 psi for layflat and polyethylene pipe; and 160, 220, and 360 psi for PVC.

Lateral Pipes

Lateral pipes deliver water from the mainline or submain lines to the trickle emitters. They are of the same three general types as the mainline pipes but are usually smaller. Lateral pipe sizes are designed to minimize pressure losses so that emitter discharge at the far end of the lateral stays within 10% of the emitter discharge near the mainline to provide uniform water application. Some trickle-system laterals combine the functions of a lateral and an emitter; these include porous pipe, row tapes, and multi-chamber (emitter) tubes. Lateral pipes are also rated for maximum or operating pressure, and row tapes come in different mil thicknesses. Laterals with built-in emitters are selected based on the emitter spacing and desired discharge to meet soil conditions and plant spacing requirements.

Emitters

Trickle-system emitters have very small openings, usually pinhole size. Different emitters have different internal flow characteristics that determine how sensitive they are to pressure changes and particles in the water. A 150- to 200-mesh screen is normally required for water filtration.

Some emitters have larger orifices, are self-cleaning, or can be taken apart and cleaned. Periodic chlorine injections can keep systems free of algae, bacterial slime, and iron precipitates. Chlorine treatment (resulting in 1 to 2 ppm residual chlorine at the emitter) should occur upstream from the filter in order to remove precipitated iron and microorganisms. This may require 5 to 10 ppm chlorine at the injector, especially if there are high levels of iron or microorganisms in the water. Swimming pool test kits can be used to calibrate the chlorine levels. If water pH is above 7.5, chlorine will not be effective. Separate acid injections, along with periodic flushing of the system, also help remove mineral buildup such as calcium carbonate precipitate.

Emitters normally operate at pressures of 5 to 40 pounds per square inch, with flow rates of 0.5 to 1.5 gallons per hour. Emitter spacing depends on the discharge rate and soil type because most of the water distribution is through the soil. The low pressure requirements of emitters result in more sensitivity to pressure losses along a lateral line or an elevation gradient. Pressure-compensating emitters may be necessary to achieve uniform water application on rolling terrain. Since the pressure and discharge requirements of emitters are usually smaller, the annual operating costs of trickle systems tend to be lower than those for sprinkler systems. Trickle irrigation systems should be sized for the mature planting.

Equipment Use and Maintenance

The appropriate use and maintenance of irrigation equipment, both in season and during storage, will increase its life and reduce operating and maintenance costs. An irrigation equipment dealer should provide an owner's manual and guidelines for operating and caring for the equipment.

The pumping unit and control head will require the most maintenance in terms of lubrication, cleaning, and protection from dirt, moisture, freezing, and animals. Leaking pump seals and pipe gaskets should be replaced as necessary. Emitters that are clogged should be replaced. Mains and laterals should be flushed periodically to remove buildup of precipitates and sediment. Equipment used in freezing weather must be properly lubricated and should be self-draining. The careful use and continued maintenance of irrigation equipment should ensure many years of trouble-free performance and the satisfaction of producing a bountiful berry harvest year after year.

Frost Protection

Though trickle irrigation is recommended for delivering water to bramble plants, sprinkler irrigation systems could be used to protect flowers and fruit on primocane-fruiting raspberries from early fall frosts. Enough water has to be applied to provide the needed heat exchange. It must be applied continuously over the entire protected area as long as freezing temperatures last. The amount of water required increases at lower temperatures, under windy conditions, and for taller-growing crops. Wet foliage and fruit can encourage disease and limit any benefits to this tactic.

Further Reading

Haman, D.Z., A.G. Smajstria, and F.S. Zazueta. 1990. *Chemical Injection Methods for Irrigation.* Circular 864. Gainesville, FL: University of Florida, Institute of Food and Agricultural Sciences. Also available online at HTTP://EDIS.IFAS.UFL.EDU/WI004.

Kramer, P.J. 1983. *Water Relations of Plants.* New York: Academic Press.

Ross, D.S. 1990. *Chemical Proportioners for Irrigation Systems.* Bulletin 179. College Park, MD: University of Maryland Cooperative Extension Service. Also available online at WWW.BRE.UMD.EDU/FACTS179.PDF.

Ross, D.S., and H.L. Brodie. 1985. *Soil Moisture Sensors for Irrigation Management.* Bulletin 312. College Park, MD: University of Maryland Cooperative Extension Service.

Ross, D.S., R.A. Parsons, and H.E. Carpenter. 1985. *Trickle Irrigation in the Eastern United States,* NRAES-4. Ithaca, NY: Natural Resource, Agriculture, and Engineering Service (NRAES). For more information, visit the NRAES web site WWW.NRAES.ORG, or contact NRAES at 607-255-7654 or NRAES@CORNELL.EDU.

CHAPTER SEVEN

Soil and Nutrient Management

Nutrition and fertilization are important components of the overall management of a berry planting. It is difficult to get accurate nutritional recommendations for a particular farm because many factors influence nutrient uptake and availability. For example, pH, moisture, organic matter content, clay content, and mineral composition of the soil all strongly influence nutrient availability. Management practices such as tillage, irrigation, herbicide use, and fertilization history also affect the plant's ability to take up nutrients. Finally, weather plays a role: conditions that reduce transpiration may cause temporary nutrient deficiencies. Since all of these factors interact to affect nutrient uptake, and since these factors differ from farm to farm, it is difficult to provide precise recommendations. An understanding of certain principles, however, will allow a grower to better manage nutrients according to the specific characteristics of his or her particular farm.

Soil Components

Soil is the substrate in which the roots grow and anchor the plant. Furthermore, it is the medium that provides nutrients and water to the plant. Soil is composed of solid particles (minerals and organic matter) and pore space (air and water) (figure 7.1). A balance among interrelated components is necessary for optimal plant growth. For example, too much water can reduce the oxygen content of the soil and cause roots to die. Insufficient water causes plants to wilt and inhibits nutrient uptake.

Soil particles are classified into sand, silt, and clay, in order of decreasing size. A sandy soil consists of large particles and, therefore, large pores. Drainage is good, but the ability to hold water and nutrients is poor. In contrast, a clayey soil consists of small particles and small pores. The capacity of clay to hold water can be low as well because the amount of pore space is small. Roots also have difficulty growing through clay because of the lack of space between particles. A loamy soil (a mixture of sand, silt, and clay) provides a mix of pore sizes, some of which retain water while others provide drainage and allow oxygen to penetrate; these soils are usually best for supporting plant growth.

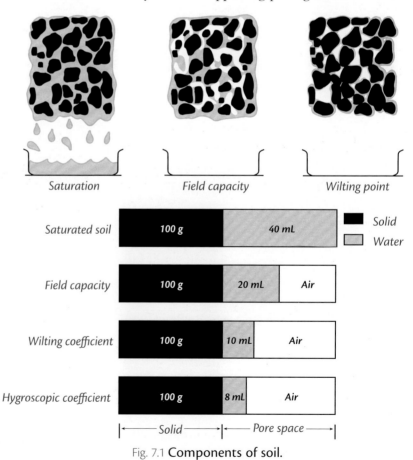

Fig. 7.1 **Components of soil.**

The composition and size of the mineral fraction of soil has a large influence on nutrient availability. Some minerals are very insoluble in water, so the associated nutrients may be relatively unavailable even if they are present in large quantities. Nutrient availability is increased if soil particles are small. The composition of the mineral fraction affects the release rate of nutrients; for example, certain clays have a lattice structure that traps ions between layers, rendering the ions unavailable. A soil high in phosphates or high in pH can also reduce the availability of certain nutrients, such as iron and zinc. Because the chemistry governing the availability of nutrients in the soil is complex, predictions about crop response to soil type or fertilizer addition are imprecise.

Organic matter consists of decomposing plant material, animal wastes, and microorganisms. Organic matter is a source of nitrogen, phosphorus, and sulfur and helps to increase the availability of positively charged ions, such as calcium, magnesium, and potassium. Soils that are high in organic matter content also have a large buffering capacity, are resistant to changes in pH, and tend to have a high water-holding capacity.

Some Basics

Often soil contains sufficient nutrients, but they are in a form that is unavailable to the plant. For example, a soil may contain 25,000 parts per million (ppm) of potassium, but the amount available to the plant may be just 500 ppm. Many of the factors discussed above influence the conversion of mineral elements from unavailable forms to available forms. Soil tests attempt to estimate the amount of plant-available nutrient, not the total amount in the soil.

Nutrients are available to the plant as individual ions that usually have either a positive or negative charge (table 7.1). The behavior of nutrients in the soil is influenced significantly by this charge. For example, ammonium (NH_4^+) tends to be retained by adsorption to negatively charged clays and organic matter, whereas nitrate (NO_3^-) is more readily leached. When ammonium is taken into a root, a proton (H^+) is excreted to maintain a neutral charge balance. The additional hydrogen ions that result from ammonium fertilization decrease the soil pH, which in turn, changes the availability and uptake of plant nutrients. Under warm, non-acid conditions, nitrogen tends to be converted to the nitrate form.

Some nutrients become more available at a low pH, others at a high pH, and others between pH extremes (figure 7.2). The recommended soil pH in a bramble planting in most locations is 6.0 to 6.5. Generally, in this range all essential nutrients are potentially available to the plant. In some sites certain micronutrients are present at unusually high or low levels and the optimal soil pH for availability and uptake of plant nutrients may fall outside 6.0 to 6.5. Lime can be used to raise and sulfur used to lower pH if it is outside the desired range.

It is also important to understand how plants respond to increasing levels of a nutrient. If a particular nutrient is very low, a plant will respond rapidly to increasing levels of that nutrient (figure 7.3). However, as levels continue to increase, the response becomes smaller and smaller until no further response can be measured. At very high levels, toxicity can occur, resulting in a yield decrease. Therefore, it is not the case that providing additional nutrients will always benefit the plant. In fact, high levels of some nutrients reduce the availability of others.

If the level of a particular nutrient is low, adding a small amount often results in a growth flush. This tends to dilute the concentration of the nutrients in plant tissues, although the total amount in the plant is greater. For this reason, it is not unusual to see foliar nutrient levels fall following fertilization.

Table 7.1 Ionic forms of plant-available nutrients supplied by the soil.

Element	Cations	Anions	Neutral
Nitrogen	NH_4^+	NO_3^-	
Calcium	Ca^{2+}		
Magnesium	Mg^{2+}		
Potassium	K^+		
Phosphorus		HPO_4^{2-} $H_2PO_4^-$	
Sulfur		SO_4^{2-}	
Copper	Cu^{2+}		
Iron	Fe^{2+}, Fe^{3+}		
Manganese	Mn^{2+}		
Zinc	Zn^{2+}		
Boron			H_3BO_3
Molybdenum		MoO_4^{2-}	
Chlorine		Cl^-	

Finally, realize that at least thirteen nutrients are essential to plant growth. Although nitrogen (N), potassium (K), phosphorus (P), calcium (Ca), magnesium (Mg), and sulfur (S) are the soil nutrients required in the greatest amounts, molybdenum (Mo), for example, is equally important, even though it is required at levels about 100,000 times less.

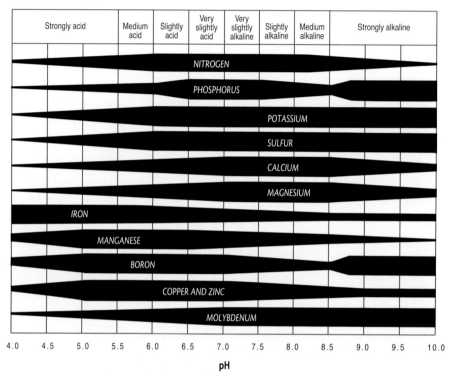

Fig. 7.2 **Nutrient availability as affected by soil pH.**

RESPONSE

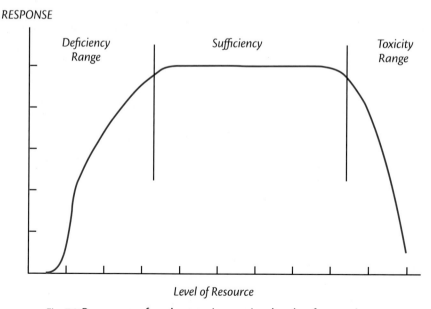

Fig. 7.3 **Response of a plant to increasing levels of a nutrient.**

Diagnosing Nutrient Problems

Visual Diagnosis

An obvious method for determining whether plants are receiving adequate nutrients is to look for symptoms such as pale foliage, poor growth, misshapen fruit, and discolored plant tissue. Often particular combinations of symptoms are associated with specific nutrients. The disadvantage of relying on visual diagnoses is that by the time symptoms appear, performance has already been compromised. Also, it is rare that only a single nutrient is deficient. For example, if the soil pH is too high, then iron (Fe), manganese (Mn), and zinc (Zn) become unavailable almost simultaneously. Multiple deficiencies make visual diagnoses difficult. Finally, symptoms of toxicity can sometimes resemble symptoms of deficiency. Basing fertilizer recommendations on visual symptoms alone is risky.

Soil Tests

Soil tests have been used for many years to estimate the amounts of nutrients available to plants. Once these numbers are known, a recommendation is made with the assumption that plant performance is related to nutrient availability. Using a soil test to assess nutritional status is much better than relying on a visual diagnosis of plant symptoms, but the test must be done correctly to ensure valid results.

Take soil samples for testing from the top 8 inches of soil. This is where most of the berry roots will grow. Collect samples from ten to twelve locations throughout the field (refer to figure 2.3 on page 12), and mix them together in a bucket. Remove about 1 pint of the bulked soil for analysis. More than one test is required when the soil changes within the field. No more than 10 acres should be included in any one sample.

Conduct soil tests the year prior to planting. With the exception of N, sufficient fertilizer and lime can be applied and incorporated prior to planting to meet nutritional needs over the life of the planting. In established plantings, complete soil tests every two to three years

Soil testing laboratories use different methods to extract plant-available nutrients and lack consistent standards for interpretation. For these reasons, results are not directly comparable from one laboratory to another. In addition, extractants used for estimating available P, K, Ca, and Mg are not appropriate for estimating levels of micronutrients. Therefore, soil test results for most micronutrients have little meaning.

Most growers assume a higher level of precision in soil tests than actually exists. Soil test recommendations for berries are estimates of fertilizer needs, as crop response data for each nutrient on different soil types has not been generated. Recommendations from soil test results give a good approximate estimate of the nutrient needs, but cannot be used to fine-tune a fertilizer program.

Foliar Analysis

Plant tissue analysis is used to measure directly the amount of nutrients in various plant parts. Recommendations are based on the levels of these nutrients at specific times of the year. In most cases, sufficiency ranges are known for brambles or are estimated from other crops (table 7.2). Unlike visual diagnoses, foliar nutrient analyses can alert the grower when nutrient levels are approaching deficiency so corrective action can be taken. Unlike soil tests, foliar analyses provide accurate results for all essential mineral nutrients.

Currently, recommendations are based on newly expanded leaves collected in mid-summer, usually the first week of August. Other sampling times or plant parts may prove to be more appropriate for certain nutrients; but until more detailed studies are done, foliar samples collected in midsummer are the standard.

Collect at least fifty leaves from randomly selected primocanes, remove their petioles, and wash them in distilled water. Dry them, place them in a paper bag, and send them to the laboratory for analysis. Samples should be representative of the entire field. If a particular area of the field looks poor or has been fertilized differently from the rest, sample it separately.

Terms Used in Interpreting Soil Tests

pH—The relative acidity or alkalinity of a soil. A pH of 7 is neutral, a pH less than 7 is acidic, and a pH greater than 7 is alkaline. (A pH between 6.0 and 6.5 is most ideal for raspberries and blackberries.)

Cation Exchange Capacity (CEC)—A measure of the ability of a soil to adsorb calcium (Ca), potassium (K), and magnesium (Mg) ions (among others) and of its resistance to change pH in response to liming or sulfur additions. Clays and soils high in organic matter tend to have a high CEC, whereas sands have a low CEC.

Cation—A positively charged ion. The most common in soils are calcium (Ca), potassium (K), magnesium (Mg), and aluminum (Al).

Base Saturation—The percentage of the exchange sites that contain a calcium (Ca), potassium (K), magnesium (Mg), or other cation. The higher the percent of base saturation, the higher the pH.

Table 7.2 **Sufficiency ranges for foliar nutrient levels in bramble leaves in midsummer (perennial systems).**

Nutrient	Deficient Below	Sufficient	Excess
N (%)	1.9	2.0–3.0	4.0
P (%)	0.20	0.25–0.40	0.50
K (%)	1.3	1.5–2.5	3.5
Ca (%)	0.5	0.6–2.0	2.5
Mg (%)	0.25	0.6–0.9	1.0
S (%)	0.35	0.4–0.6	0.8
B (ppm)	23	30–70	90
Fe (ppm)	40	60–250	350
Mn (ppm)	35	50–200	350
Cu (ppm)	3	6–20	30
Zn (ppm)	10	20–50	80

The Best Approach

A combination of soil testing, tissue analysis, and observation of crop response is the best approach to assessing nutrient status. Prior to planting, conduct a soil test and amend the soil according to recommendations. After planting, conduct a foliar tissue analysis at least every other year. The soil pH should be monitored regularly and a complete soil test performed every three years. Always be alert for any unusual-looking leaves and unexplained reductions in growth or yield.

Soil Amendments

Many materials are useful as soil amendments: fertilizers, lime, manure, composts, green manures, and others. Each has unique properties that are beneficial under certain circumstances.

Lime

Liming affects soil pH, which strongly influences nutrient uptake and plant growth. Proper liming can increase soil productivity and increase the efficiency of other fertilizers. Lime also provides Ca and possibly Mg, depending on the source. Lime is used to balance the acidification that occurs when certain fertilizers, manures, or composts are used (table 7.3), or when an area receives extensive acid rain. Other materials may contain Ca and Mg (for example, gypsum), but they do not influence soil pH significantly.

The proper amount of lime to apply depends on the soil test recommendation (see "Site Selection and Preparation," chapter two). Not all limestone is the same—some is less pure than others. The purity is indicated by the calcium carbonate equivalent (CCE). If a particular limestone has a CCE of 80%, then five tons per acre would be applied if the soil test recommended 4 tons (4 tons ÷ 0.80 = 5 tons). Limestone also differs with respect to the speed at which it reacts with the soil. The more finely ground the limestone, the faster it reacts, so particles should be smaller than a 20-mesh sieve—preferably a 100-mesh sieve. In addition, if the soil test recommends Mg, a high-Mg lime (dolomitic lime) should be used, even though it may be more expensive. Finally, lime is sold by weight; so if the limestone is not completely dry, adjust application rates accordingly (that is, increase rates by the percentage of moisture in the lime).

Manure

Manure is a source of both nutrients and organic matter and can significantly improve soil structure. If it is readily available, manure can replace some synthetic fertilizers and save the grower money.

The urea in manure is unstable and will volatilize quickly unless incorporated into the soil. The solid organic fraction decomposes more slowly and provides N over a long period of time—even into subsequent years. However, in most situations, insufficient N is released from manure to meet the total requirements of the berry

Table 7.3 Equivalent acidity and alkalinity of nitrogenous fertilizer materials.

Material	% Nitrogen	Pounds of Pure Lime for Neutralization	
		Per Pound of Nitrogen	Per 100 Pounds of Material
Inorganic sources of nitrogen			
Sulfate of ammonia	20.5	5.35	110
Ammo-phos A	11.0	5.00	55
Anhydrous ammonia	82.2	1.80	148
Calcium nitrate	15.0	1.35	20
Nitrate of soda	16.0	1.80	29
Potassium nitrate	13.0	2.00	26
Manufactured organic nitrogen			
Cyanamid	22.0	2.85	63
Urea	46.6	1.80	84
Natural sources of organic nitrogen			
Cocoa shell meal	2.7	0.60	2
Castor pomace	4.8	0.90	4
Cottonseed meal	6.7	1.40	9
Dried blood	13.0	1.75	23
Fish scrap	9.2	0.90	8
Guano, Peruvian	13.8	0.95	13
Guano, white	9.7	0.45	4
Milorganite sludge	7.0	1.70	12

plant during critical periods of crop growth (table 7.4); manure supplemented with N fertilizer has provided better results than manure used alone. Manure spread in fall should be applied over a cover crop, which helps retain much of the N from manure that otherwise might be lost to leaching and runoff.

Manure is also a source of organic P and K, but these nutrients are released slowly as the organic matter decomposes. However, in a field that has received manure applications over a long period of time, available P should be high. Growers who use manure for fertilizer should monitor Mg levels closely, because manure is not a good source of Mg.

Table 7.4 **Percentage of manure nitrogen available to crops in the current year.**

Time of Application	Poultry	Cow
Incorporation the same day	75	50
Within 1 day	50	40
Within 2–4 days	45	35
Within 5–6 days	30	30
After 7 days	15	20
Applied previous fall		
Without a cover crop	15	20
With a cover crop	50	40

Pathogen Contamination

Growers using manure should take practical steps to minimize the risk of pathogen spread onto the berries. To minimize the risk of pathogen contamination:

- Store slurry for 60 days in summer or 120 days in winter prior to field application.

- Compost fresh manure to kill most pathogens.

- In fall prior to the ground freezing, apply fresh manure onto a cover crop. Do not apply to bare ground.

- Incorporate manure prior to planting.

- Never side-dress with a slurry of fresh manure prior to harvest.

Compost

Compost is partially broken down organic matter that provides a source of nutrients and organic matter to plants. Because of the loss of water and carbon dioxide that occurs during the composting process, the quantity of the final product is much less than that of the raw materials, but compost materials will contain a higher concentration of N, P, and K. However, N is less available in compost compared to manure, because less is in the ammonium form and more is in the residual organic form. For example, whereas 35% of manure N might be available in the year the manure is spread, only 10% of the N in compost is available.

Compost has properties that make it potentially beneficial for berry growers beyond the nutrient contribution. Compost improves soil structure and water-holding capacity, and some composts suppress diseases because they have a high level of microbiological activity. Properly composted manure does not present a health hazard and is odor-free.

Green Manure

Green manure is a term used to describe a cover crop that is grown for the purpose of incorporation into the soil. An incorporated cover crop provides organic matter, which improves soil structure and water-holding capacity. Cover crops can also sequester residual N that is released from or applied to the soil. Green manures with a high N content (such as legumes) decompose quickly. Those with a low N content (such as cereal grains) decompose more slowly, tying up N for a period of time. Berries should not be planted immediately after incorporation of a green manure, or they could experience "nitrogen drag" (see "Site Selection and Site Preparation," chapter two).

Individual Nutrients

Nutrients are taken into the plant either actively by preferential uptake through membranes or passively through the mass movement of water (containing the dissolved nutrient) into the plant (called "mass flow"). Nutrients that are taken into the plant primarily through mass flow require adequate soil moisture to avert deficiencies.

Nitrogen (N)

Nitrogen makes up 2% to 3% of bramble plant dry matter. Brambles with less than 2% nitrogen in their leaves are

Table 7.5 Typical composition of some common chemical sources of fertilizer nitrogen and potassium.

Source	%N	%P$_2$O$_5$	%K$_2$O	%MgO	%S
Ammonium sulfate	21.0	—	—	—	24.0
Anhydrous ammonia	82.0	—	—	—	—
Ammonium chloride	25.0–26.0	—	—	—	—
Ammonium nitrate	33.0–34.0	—	—	—	—
Ammonium nitrate-sulfate	30.0	—	—	—	5.0–6.0
Ammoniated ordinary superphosphate	4.0	16.0	—	0.5	10.0
Monoammonium phosphate	11.0	48.0–55.0	—	0.5	1.0–3.0
Diammonium phosphate	18.0–21.0	46.0–54.0	—	—	—
Ammonium phosphate-sulfate	13.0–16.0	20.0–39.0	—	—	3.0–14.0
Calcium nitrate	15.0	—	—	—	—
Potassium nitrate	13.0	—	44.0	0.5	0.2
Sodium nitrate	16.0	—	—	—	—
Urea	45.0–46.0	—	—	—	—
Potassium chloride	—	—	60–62	—	—
Potassium sulfate	—	—	50–52	—	17
Potassium magnesium sulfate	—	—	22	11	22
Potassium nitrate	13	—	44	—	—
Potassium and sodium nitrate	15	—	14	—	—
Manure salts	—	—	22–27	—	—
Potassium hydroxide	—	—	83	—	—
Potassium carbonate	—	—	<68	—	—

usually not very productive. Leaves begin to yellow, canes do not grow vigorously, and the tips of older leaves may turn red. Plants with more than 3% nitrogen may be too vigorous and, as a result, will produce few flower buds and may not harden properly. Fruit firmness may also be reduced. Primocane-fruiting raspberries that will be mowed each spring, however, should have approximately 3% nitrogen in their leaves. For this crop, cold tolerance is not a factor, although excessively high nitrogen levels may delay fruiting and soften fruit.

Nitrogen sources include ammonium-based fertilizers, nitrate fertilizers, organic sources, and organic matter (table 7.5). The amount of N released from organic matter can be significant. Plants tend to grow better in soils high in organic matter (greater than 6%) than those low in organic matter (less than 2%), even with supplemental N fertilization. Most commercial growers apply synthetic fertilizers, even when organic matter is high. This ensures adequate amounts of N during critical growth periods. Nitrogen is released slowly from soil organic matter and

manures, so a sufficient amount may not be available at a critical time if one relies solely on organic sources. When added organic matter is high in carbon, N can become temporarily unavailable. This may occur when straw or other plant residues are incorporated into soil.

Fertilizer N is available in two forms: nitrate and ammonium. The brambles prefer nitrate N over the ammonium form. Nitrate N is very soluble in water and is readily available to the plant. However, nitrate fertilizers are subject to leaching and are generally more expensive than ammonium fertilizers. Therefore, many fertilizers contain the ammonium form of N because it is less expensive to manufacture and soil organisms eventually convert the ammonium form into the nitrate form. (Some ammonium-based fertilizers are coated with S or synthetic resin to further slow the release of N to the plants and extend its availability, but these fertilizers are expensive.) Because the ammonium ion has a positive charge, it tends to be adsorbed to soil colloids and is less easily leached. Even though they tend to acidify the soil,

Table 7.6 **Nitrogen guidelines for raspberries.**

Age of Planting (years)	Amount/Timing (actual N)	N Source	Comments
Summer-bearing			
0	25-35 lb/A 4 weeks after planting	calcium nitrate	Avoid touching plants after planting with fertilizers.
1	35-55 lb/A May or split between May and June	urea, ammonium nitrate	Use higher amount on sandier soils or if irrigation is used.
2+	40-80 lb/A May or split between May and June	urea, ammonium nitrate	Use higher amount on sandier soils or if irrigation is used.
Fall-bearing			
0	25 lb/A 4 weeks after planting and in August	calcium nitrate	Avoid touching plants after planting with fertilizers.
1	50-80 lb/A split between May and June	urea, ammonium nitrate	Use higher amount on sandier soils or if irrigation is used.
2+	70-100 lb/A split between May and June	urea, ammonium nitrate	Use higher amount on sandier soils or if irrigation is used. Adjust in response to leaf analysis.

some ammonium-based fertilizers are commonly used in berry production (table 7.3).

In newly planted fields, use calcium nitrate for fertilization, especially if the site was fumigated prior to planting. Calcium nitrate has a readily available form of N and is not subject to volatilization. On well-established plantings, other sources of N are suitable. Many growers prefer ammonium nitrate because it provides for both a rapid response (in the form of nitrate) and a slow release (in the form of ammonium). However, due to the potential explosiveness of ammonium nitrate, it is less available than in the past. Urea is usually the least expensive N source, but it is subject to volatilization under certain conditions. If volatilization occurs, N may be lost to the air. Volatilized ammonia can blacken berry leaves close to the soil. Incorporating urea will prevent this loss.

Foliar applications of urea are of limited value in brambles. Although a significant amount of N can be absorbed through the leaves, only a small amount can be applied at any one time, usually less than 2 pounds per acre actual N.

Soil tests are of limited value in estimating N availability, as large fluctuations occur from week to week. Some progress is being made to assess N status from plant sap using specific ion detectors, but the practical use of these tools is still years away. Growers must continue to rely on scheduled fertilizer applications and leaf analysis until more sophisticated methods are developed.

Nitrogen is more efficient when applications are split. Usually, the first application is made in May and the second in June. See table 7.6 for N fertilization recommendations for raspberries. Fertilizer should not be applied to brambles immediately after they are planted; root systems are very delicate at this time and fertilizers will likely burn them. Avoid touching plants with fertilizer. Recommendations are based on sandy loam soil with 3% organic matter content; plants growing on sandier soils might require more, and plants in heavier soils with high organic matter content will require less. Cultivar, plant age, length of season, cultural practices, and moisture status can also vary nitrogen requirement. Adjust application rates up or down depending on the results of a mid-summer leaf analysis. Nitrogen deficiency results in smaller plants with older leaves displaying a reddish color. Symptoms are most apparent in late summer.

Phosphorus (P)

The total amount of P in soil averages about 900 pounds per acre across all soil types, but only a fraction is available for plant growth. Much of the P is tied up in soil minerals, insoluble precipitates, and organic matter. Little P is dissolved in the soil solution, so most uptake occurs through diffusion. Good root growth is required for a plant to obtain an adequate surface area to facilitate P uptake. Berries tend to have a low demand for P relative to other crops. Only a small percentage of commercial fields are deficient in P; in most cases, excess P is more of a concern.

Table 7.7 Composition of phosphatic fertilizer materials.

Material	Total N (%)	Total K (%)	Total S (%)	Total Ca (%)	Total Mg (%)	Total P (%)	Available* (% of total)
Ordinary super-phosphate	—	—	11–12	18–21	—	7–9.5	97–100
Conc. (triple) super-phosphate	—	—	0–1	12–14	—	19–23	96–99
Enriched super-phosphate	—	—	7–9	16–18	—	11–13	96–99
Dicalcium phosphate	—	—	—	29	—	23	98
Superphosphoric acid	—	—	—	—	—	34	100
Phosphoric acid	—	—	0–2	—	—	23	100
Potassium phosphate	—	29–45	—	—	—	18–22	100
Ammonium phosphate nitrate	30	—	—	—	—	4	100
Ammonium poly-phosphate	15	—	—	—	—	25	—
Magnesium ammonium phosphate	8	—	—	—	14	17	—
Raw rock phosphate	—	—	—	33–36	—	18–32	2 – 3

* By neutral 1.0N ammonium citrate procedure.

Phosphorus tends to react with cations in the soil solution, forming insoluble precipitates with Fe, Al, Ca, and Zn. Excess P fertilization can result in micronutrient deficiencies.

Phosphorus availability is affected by soil pH, soil moisture, soil type, organic matter content, the amount of Ca and Al in the soil, and soil temperature. Extremes in pH, temperature, and moisture can limit availability, as can excessive Ca and Al. Soils with a large quantity of clay will fix more P than lighter soils. Certain microorganisms can increase P availability, including phosphobacteria and some mycorrhizal fungi. Humic acids from organic matter decomposition increase the solubility of P. Available P is increased after incorporating a green manure, even when no additional P has been added.

Because inorganic P has a low solubility in water, it is not subject to leaching. However, it must be incorporated to be effective. Phosphorus fertilizers (table 7.7) applied to the soil surface will not move into the root zone within a useful time period. Preplant incorporation is necessary. Large granules of fertilizers are slow to break down, so for maximum effectiveness, uniformly distribute small granules throughout the root zone. Keep soil pH near 6.5 to ensure that P is available.

Phosphorus can be applied though a drip irrigation system in the form of phosphoric acid. Materials containing P are incompatible with many other fertilizers. Use caution when applying through a drip irrigation system.

Plants deficient in P develop a purplish cast in older leaves. Younger leaves may turn dark green. Foliar P levels tend to decline after fruiting. If P levels are low, then apply 100 pounds per acre in a form that is readily available to the plant (table 7.7).

Potassium (K)

Brambles have a relatively high demand for K, as it is a component of fruit. Much more K is present in the soil than is available to the plant. For example, soils may average 25,000 ppm, but the concentration in the soil solution may be only 10 ppm. Soil tests estimate the amount of K on exchange sites, which is also available for plant uptake. This amount is variable but can be up to 600 ppm. Since little K is dissolved in solution, diffusion is the most important mechanism of uptake. Therefore, good root development is essential to increase the surface area through which the K can diffuse.

The availability of K is very dependent on soil chemistry. The amount of organic matter, the soil texture, the type of clay, and the mineral base also influence availability. In most cases, increasing the organic matter will increase exchange capacity, allowing more K to be adsorbed to the exchange sites. Negatively charged clays also provide exchange sites for K; however, certain clays can trap K ions between layers when they dehydrate. High levels of other nutrients, such as Ca and Mg, can replace K on the exchange sites. A balance among these three cations is necessary for proper nutrition.

Preplant incorporation of K (table 7.5) is most effective, while fertigation can be used to supply K in established plantings. Surface applications of K fertilizers are of limited value for short-term crops such as brambles. Foliar uptake is possible, although the total amount that can be supplied through this method in a single application is small. Sequential applications are effective but expensive.

Potassium is required for many physiological processes in the plant, including enzyme activation, transport of sugars, stomatal functioning, charge balance, protein synthesis, and photosynthesis. Deficiencies occur on older leaves first and result in marginal necrosis. Potassium levels in leaves tend to fluctuate during the season and decrease as crop load increases. If foliar levels are low, then supplemental K can be added with the amount dependent on soil type. The maximum amount of K that one should apply in any year is 250 pounds per acre; in a heavier soil, half that amount. Fall application is desirable. Excess K can induce a Mg deficiency, so if the K/Mg ratio exceeds 4, then additional Mg should be applied if K is also applied. Potassium sulfate or potassium magnesium sulfate are the best sources of potassium for brambles. Although muriate of potash (potassium chloride) is less expensive, brambles are sensitive to the chloride in this fertilizer if the application rate is high (>500 lb/A).

Sulfur (S)

Sulfur occurs in elemental form, as well as in sulfides, sulfates, and organic combinations with carbon and N. The majority of S comes from decomposing organic matter, although a significant amount is dissolved in rain, up to 100 pounds per acre annually. Most is absorbed by mass flow. Because S availability is associated with carbon and N cycling, large annual variations occur, giving soil tests limited value under most conditions.

Sulfur is an essential component of proteins; when S is deficient, overall plant vigor is decreased and leaves turn a reddish color. In the north, S has not been considered problematic, especially since the region gets more than its share of acid rain.

The major use of S for berry growers is for pH reduction. If soils are too alkaline, the addition of S will lower the pH. Sulfur is oxidized by bacteria into sulfuric acid, which helps to neutralize basic ions such as Ca and Mg. The size of S granules is the major factor influencing the rate of soil pH change. After ninety days, only about 1% of the S will react if the granules are unable to pass through a 10-meshes-per-inch screen (0.2 inch in diameter), whereas nearly half will react if the size is less than 100 meshes per inch.

Calcium (Ca)

Calcium is a major component of pectin, the strengthening agent of cell walls. Without sufficient Ca, fruit are soft, and leaf tips turn brown and do not completely expand. In severe cases, plants turn brown and new leaves develop interveinal necrosis.

Symptoms of Ca deficiency are common, but this is rarely due to insufficient Ca in the soil. Ca mobility is limited, both in the soil and in the plant, and the factors affecting mobility indirectly influence Ca uptake. Calcium can enter the plant only through unsuberized root tips—not along the entire length of root. Therefore, factors that limit mass flow, such as low soil moisture and cool, cloudy, humid weather, can reduce the amount of Ca entering the plant to below critical levels. Since Ca movement within the plant is also limited, deficiencies occur in new growth at points farthest from the root system.

Adequate Ca is usually present if the soil pH is within an acceptable range. With drip irrigation, Ca can be leached out of the wetted zone over time. In most cases, though, maintaining good soil moisture is the best way to prevent tip burn associated with Ca deficiency.

Apply adequate limestone prior to planting to adjust the soil pH to 6.0 to 6.5. In lighter soils, more Ca may be required than is needed for pH adjustment. If Ca is required but the pH is already high, gypsum can be used as a Ca source. Over a five-year period, as much as 2,000 pounds of Ca can be leached out of the root zone. Accommodation for this drop in Ca, and concomitant drop in pH, should be anticipated prior to planting.

Magnesium (Mg)

Magnesium is necessary in a plant for chlorophyll production and nitrogen metabolism. Its supply is quite variable from soil to soil. Deficiencies are common, especially on sandy, acidic soils. Cold, wet, cloudy weather induces Mg deficiency in marginal situations, since uptake is mainly by mass flow.

Magnesium availability increases with soil pH up to 8.5 (figure 7.2, page 66). Magnesium can be relatively unavailable at a low pH. Also, high levels of Al can reduce Mg availability, and excessive K can induce Mg deficiency. A K/Mg ratio of less than 5 is desirable. If this ratio is high, additional Mg could be beneficial even if Mg is within the desired range. Since Mg is fairly soluble, it can be effectively applied to leaves (depending on the formulation, at 5 pounds actual Mg per acre) or to the soil surface (at 40 pounds per acre). Apply in fall after plants are dormant. The least expensive source of Mg is dolomitic lime, but it must be incorporated prior to planting. A soluble form is magnesium sulfate (Epsom salts) at 20% Mg.

Iron (Fe)

Iron is the fourth most abundant element in the Earth's crust, but concentrations in soils vary widely. Much of the Fe in soil is in the insoluble ferric form (Fe^{3+}), which is unavailable to plants. Available Fe in the ferrous form (Fe^{2+}) is obtained from clays, minerals, and hydroxides. Root exudates, microbial byproducts, and organic matter are natural chelates that can increase Fe availability up to threefold.

Iron becomes more available with decreasing soil pH. Excessive liming can induce an Fe deficiency. Excess P can form insoluble precipitates with Fe. Nitrogen sources also affect Fe availability. Fertilization with ammonium sources of N tends to decrease soil pH around the root zone, thereby increasing Fe availability.

Rarely is an iron-containing, soil-applied fertilizer required to relieve a deficiency. Acidification of soil is the most cost-effective way to increase Fe availability. If plants are deficient, then foliar applications are useful during the time when soil pH is being lowered. Formulations vary, so follow the label directions.

Manganese (Mn)

Manganese is widely distributed in northeastern soils. With the exception of the mid-Atlantic coastal plain, few soils are inherently low in this nutrient. However, across the United States, Mn is the most commonly deficient micronutrient. Manganese availability is strongly

associated with soil pH, and deficiencies most often occur on alkaline soils or on soils that have been heavily limed. In some soils, toxicity can occur if the pH is too low. If Mn is deficient, soil pH should be lowered to below 6.5. Foliar sprays may temporarily relieve a deficiency, which is characterized by generally poor growth without distinguishing symptoms.

Boron (B)

Boron is the only nonmetal among the micronutrients and usually does not occur as a charged ion. This, coupled with its small size, makes it especially prone to leaching. In coarse-textured soils that are low in organic matter, up to 85% of the available B can be leached with only 5 inches of water. The level of B in soil varies widely, so B is one of the most commonly deficient micronutrients in berry plantings. Furthermore, soils naturally low in B occur throughout the United States and Canada.

Boron is essential for root growth. If root growth is poor, deficiencies of other nutrients can develop and plants become stunted. Foliar levels tend to decline during the season. If a foliar analysis indicates 30 ppm B or less early in the season, levels may be inadequate to sustain the plants through fruiting. To supplement soil B, apply no more than 1 pound of actual B per acre per year. Uptake occurs through leaves and roots, so the best time to apply B is prior to fruiting in primocane-fruiting brambles and mid-summer for other types. Blending granular B with other fertilizers makes application easier. A foliar application might consist of 2 pounds per acre soluble boron (20% B) in 100 gallons of water.

Mass flow is the most important mode of uptake for B, so conditions not favoring water uptake may induce a deficiency. Levels of other nutrients, especially Ca, K, N, and P, have been reported to affect B uptake.

A narrow range exists between deficient and toxic B levels. Toxic levels sometimes accumulate with irrigation in arid climates or where overapplication has occurred.

Zinc (Zn)

Zinc functions in enzyme activation and synthesis of growth regulators. Zinc deficiency is widespread in North America. Total soil Zn is not a good predictor of availability to plants, as Zn has a strong tendency to combine with anions in the soil to form insoluble precipitates. Zinc

Table 7.8 **Inorganic compounds commonly used as micronutrient sources.**

Micronutrient Source	Solubility in H_2O	Percent Element
Boron (B)		
$Na_2B_4O_7$ (anhydrous borax)	Soluble	20
$Na_2B_4O_7 \cdot 5H_2O$ (fertilizer borate)	Soluble	14
$Na_2B_4O_7 \cdot 10H_2O$ (borax)	Soluble	11
H_3BO_3	Soluble	17
Copper (Cu)		
$CuSO_4 \cdot H_2O$	Soluble	35
$CuSO_4 \cdot 5H_2O$	Soluble	25
$CuSO_4 \cdot 3Cu(OH)_2 \cdot H_2O$	Insoluble	37
CuO	Insoluble	75
Iron (Fe)		
$FeSO_4 \cdot H_2O$	Soluble	33
$FeSO_4 \cdot 7H_2O$	Soluble	20
$Fe_2(SO_4)_3 \cdot 9H_2O$	Soluble	20
$FeSO_4 \cdot (NH_4)_2 SO_4$	Soluble	22
Manganese (Mn)		
$MnSO_4 \cdot 4H_2O$	Soluble	26–28
$MnCl_2$	Soluble	17
$MnCO_3$	Insoluble	31
MnO_2	Insoluble	41–68
Molybdenum (Mo)		
Na_2MoO_4 (anhydrous)	Soluble	47
$Na_2MoO_4 \cdot 2H_2O$	Soluble	39
$(NH_4)_2MoO_4$	Soluble	49
MoO_3	Slightly soluble	66
$CaMoO_4$	Insoluble	48
Zinc (Zn)		
$ZnSO_4 \cdot H_2O$	Soluble	36
$ZnSO_4 \cdot 7H_2O$	Soluble	22
$ZnCl_2$	Soluble	47
$ZnSO_4 \cdot 4Zn(OH)_2$	Slightly soluble	55
$ZnCO_3$	Insoluble	52
ZnO	Insoluble	60–78

is also complexed by organic matter, which can reduce availability in certain circumstances. Zinc availability increases as soil pH decreases, so avoiding excessively high pH can help prevent deficiencies.

Zinc is relatively immobile in the soil, so preplant applications such as zinc sulfate, although effective, can be expensive. Soil surface applications are not effective. Fertigation also may be an effective way to increase plant Zn levels.

Copper (Cu)

Copper is one of the least mobile nutrients in soil or plants. For this reason, when Cu is deficient, corrections are difficult. Although a significant amount of soil Cu is insoluble, a significant pool may be complexed with natural organic chelates. This pool is available for plant uptake.

Only small areas of North America contain soils that are inherently low in Cu. However, high soil pH and excessive P, Zn, and Al restrict Cu absorption and translocation. Furthermore, Cu adsorption to Fe, Al, and Mn oxides can be significant. The dynamics of Cu in the soil are very complex.

Visual symptoms of Cu deficiency are not distinctive, although Cu is an essential component of many enzyme systems. Foliar levels above 7 ppm are considered adequate, but no response to applications have been reported when levels are above 3 ppm.

Copper is toxic to both roots and leaves, so remedial action can cause more harm than good. Foliar Cu applications can burn leaves, so only small amounts of chelated forms are recommended. However, because of low mobility, foliar levels may not increase in response to foliar applications.

Molybdenum (Mo)

Molybdenum is an important component of enzymes involved with N metabolism, but levels in the soil are very low. The plant needs only small amounts of Mo (less than 1 ppm), so deficiencies are common only in acidic, sandy, leached soils. Foliar applications are effective for providing the small amounts required.

Fertilizer Sources

Many types of fertilizer can be used in berry plantings provided that they meet the nutrient requirements of the plant. Organic sources of nutrients may be obtained easily (table 7.3) and often improve soil organic matter. However, the release rate of nutrients from organic fertilizers is often slow, and large amounts of fertilizer are required to meet requirements for optimum growth. Concentrated synthetic fertilizers usually are easier to apply, are more consistent in composition (tables 7.5, 7.7, and 7.8), and release nutrients quickly. The disadvantages of synthetic fertilizers are that they often have a high salt index (they can burn the plant), they are subject to leaching, and they may contain chlorides, which are toxic at high levels. Fertilizers should be used sparingly in young plantings because of sensitivity to salts. Calcium nitrate is recommended on first-year plantings as a N source, especially if the field was fumigated before planting. If more than 100 pounds per acre of K is required, potassium sulfate is recommended over potassium chloride to avoid chloride toxicity.

Many fertilizers tend to acidify the soil, so if large amounts are applied, additional lime may be necessary to buffer against pH changes (table 7.3). Fertilizers are available that contain micronutrients (table 7.9), but in many cases, micronutrients become fixed in soil and are unavailable to the plant shortly after application. For this reason, chelates and fertigation are the preferred application methods for micronutrients.

Chelated Nutrients

Chelate is derived from a Greek word meaning *claw* and is used to describe metallic cations complexed to large organic molecules. Complexed ions are protected from reaction with inorganic constituents that would make

them unavailable for uptake by plants. Plant roots exude chemicals that act as chelates. Chelates can result from the breakdown of organic matter, or they can be synthesized. Zinc, Cu, Mn, and Fe are among the essential plant micronutrients that form chelates with organic molecules.

Chelates vary in their stability and suitability as sources of micronutrients. Under most conditions, Fe chelates are more stable than those of Zn and Cu, which in turn are more stable than Mn chelates. This is because Fe has a higher affinity for chelates. If Cu chelate is added to a soil high in Fe, the Fe may displace the Cu, rendering the Cu subject to soil reactions. Therefore, the ability of chelates to increase nutrient availability depends on the level of other available cations. With foliar applications, the organic chelates are less reactive and cause less phytotoxicity. However, because of their large size, their movement into a leaf is more limited than with inorganic salts.

Fertigation

Fertigation is often the most effective way of providing nutrients to berries (table 7.9). Applications can be more uniform than with ground equipment and can be made during any weather. Less fertilizer is usually required as well. Disadvantages include the capital expense and time to set up and calibrate the system. The potential for leaching is greater with fertigation, and it is highly regulated by most states. Drip irrigation systems are susceptible to plugging if improper fertilizer materials are used. Although little is known about fertigation for perennial berry crops, an increasing number of growers are finding it worthwhile to install a fertigation system and experiment on their own.

The amount of fertilizer to apply is dependent on many factors, but a starting point is 8 pounds per acre actual N per week between early May and mid-September of the planting year, and 5 pounds per acre actual N per week between mid-July and mid-September of the fruiting year assuming granular fertilizer was applied in the spring. Other nutrients can be added if a leaf analysis indicates the need.

If fertigation is to be used, consider water quality and uniformity of water application by the system. Water low in salts, suspended particles, and bacteria is essential, as is a system designed to deliver equivalent amounts of

Nutrient Compatibility

Below are some rules regarding compatibility.

1. Do not mix Ca products with those containing phosphates or sulfates.

2. Do not mix Mg, Zn, Fe, or Cu products with products that contain phosphates. Water naturally high in Fe can be a problem, so the Fe must be removed prior to injection of P fertilizers.

3. Do not mix Fe chelates with other chelated products.

Table 7.9 **Materials for fertigation and their solubilities.**

	Solubility (pounds/gallon water)
A. NITROGEN	
Ammonium nitrate (33.5-0-0) [NH_4NO_3]	9.8 @ 32°F
Ammonium sulfate (20-0-0) [$(NH_4)_2SO_4$]	5.9 @ 32°F
Calcium nitrate (15-0-0 + 22%Ca) [$Ca(NO_3)_2$]	10.1 @ 64°F
Magnesium nitrate (11-0-0 + 9.5%Mg) [$Mg(NO_3)_2$]	3.5 @ 64°F
Potassium nitrate (13-0-45) [KNO_3]	1.1 @ 32°F
Sodium nitrate (16-0-0) [$NaNO_3$]	6.1 @ 32°F
Urea (44-0-0) [NH_2CONH_2]	6.5 @ 41°F; 10 @ 77°F
B. POTASSIUM	
Potassium chloride (muriate of potash) (0-0-60) [KCl]	2.9 @ 68°F
Potassium nitrate (13-0-45) [KNO_3]	1.1 @ 32°F
Potassium sulfate (0-0-48–54 + 16–18%S) [K_2SO_4]	0.6 @ 32°F; 1.0 @ 77°F
C. PHOSPHORUS	
Phosphoric acid (0-55–77-0) [H_3PO_4]	43.1 (liquid)
Mono-potassium phosphate (0-52-35) [KH_2PO_4]	2.75 @ 77°F
Diammonium phosphate (DAP) (21-54-0) [$(NH_4)_2HPO_4$]	3.5 @ 32°F
Mono-ammonium phosphate (MAP) (11-48-0) [$NH_4H_2PO_4$]	1.9 @ 32°F
Mono-calcium phosphate (0-53-0 + 16%Ca) [$Ca(H_2PO_4)_2$]	0.15 @ 86°F
D. CALCIUM	
Calcium nitrate [$Ca(NO_3)_2$]	10.1 @ 64°F
Hydrated lime [$Ca(OH)_2$]	0.02 @ 68°F
E. MAGNESIUM	
Epsom salts (10%Mg and 13%S) [$MgSO_4 \cdot 7H_2O$]	5.9 @ 32°F
Magnesium nitrate (9.5%Mg) [$Mg(NO_3)_2$]	3.5 @ 64°F
F. BORON	
Solubor (20.2%B)	1.0
Boric acid (17.5%B) [H_3BO_3]	0.5 @ 86°F; 2.3 @ 212°F
Borax (11.3%B) [$Na_2B_4O_7 \cdot 10H_2O$]	0.13oz @ 32°F; 14lbs @212°F
G. MANGANESE	
Manganese sulfate (24.6%Mn) [$MnSO_4 \cdot 4H_2O$]	8.7 @ 32°F
Manganese chelates (up to 12%Mn)	—
H. IRON	
Iron chelates (up to 10%Fe)	—
Ferrous sulfate (20%Fe + 11.5%S) [$FeSO_4 \cdot 7H_2O$]	1.3
I. ZINC	
Zinc sulfate (23%Zn + 11%S) [$ZnSO_4 \cdot 7H_2O$]	8.0
Zinc sulfate monohydrate (36%Zn + 18%S) [$ZnSO_4 \cdot H_2O$]	—
Chelated zinc products (up to 14%Zn)	—
J. COPPER	
Copper sulfate (25%Cu + 13%S)	2.6 @ 32°F
Chelated copper products (up to 13%Cu)	—
K. All water-soluble complete fertilizers (NPK) and commercial mixtures	

water throughout a field. Consult *Trickle Irrigation in the Eastern United States* for information on designing trickle irrigation systems for proper application of water and injection of chemicals.

Irrigation lines should be filled with water before injecting fertilizers, then flushed after injection is complete. Fertigation should occur near the end of the irrigation cycle to prevent leaching. Flush lines thoroughly between different fertilizers to avoid incompatibility problems (see sidebar on page 76). Chlorination may be required to control algae and bacterial slime that can plug emitters. Fertigation should not be used to correct major soil nutrient and pH problems; this should be done before planting.

Combinations of certain nutrients can form insoluble precipitates with each other, plugging the emitters and causing untold misery for the operator. To determine if chemicals are compatible, shake them together in a jar to determine if precipitation occurs before injecting them together in the irrigation system.

Further Reading

Magdoff, F.R., and H.M. van Es. 2000. *Building Soil for Better Crops.* 2nd ed. Washington, DC: Sustainable Agriculture Publications, United States Department of Agriculture (USDA). Also available online at www.sare.org/publications/soils.htm.

Ross, D.S., R.A. Parsons, and H.E. Carpenter. 1985. *Trickle Irrigation in the Eastern United States,* NRAES-4. Ithaca, NY: Natural Resource, Agriculture, and Engineering Service (NRAES). For more information, visit the NRAES web site www.nraes.org, or contact NRAES at 607-255-7654 or nraes@cornell.edu.

CHAPTER EIGHT

Insect and Mite Scouting and Management

Arthropods in the bramble planting can be beneficial (like pollinators or predators), benign (like transient fly species), or harmful (like tarnished plant bugs). Harmful insects and mites attack the fruit, buds, leaves, and roots of the bramble plant, and in some cases, transmit plant disease (e.g., aphids). They can also increase the susceptibility of damaged plants to other pests or environmental stresses. The grower's objective should be to minimize damage from harmful insects while preserving beneficial insects.

This chapter is designed to familiarize growers with the biology of bramble insects and mites, to help growers identify the damage pests cause, and to briefly outline ways growers can control pests. Emphasis is on cultural controls, since regulations and restrictions concerning pesticide use are continually changing and vary from state to state. Growers should consult their local extension personnel for recommendations concerning the most effective control procedures available in their area.

A pictorial diagnostic tool for berry crops is available online at WWW.HORT.CORNELL.EDU/DIAGNOSTIC.

Bees

Scientific names: *Apis mellifera* and others

Wind and bees are responsible for pollinating bramble flowers. Although a majority of flowers can be sufficiently pollinated without bees, bees are essential for the berries to reach their full size potential and achieve a good shape. Partially pollinated berries are small, crumbly, and tend to be misshaped as druplets fail to develop.

Many bee species are capable of pollinating bramble flowers, and most of these species occur in the wild. Bramble plants produce large amounts of nectar, making them attractive to wild bees and reducing their need for managed bees if wild populations are sufficiently large. If managed bees are needed, honey bees are the most commonly used for field grown bramble crops. One or two strong hives per acre are sufficient to provide for the pollination needs of brambles. A brood nest that spans five or six frames is optimal.

Place hives off of the ground, east-facing, in an area that receives maximum sunlight. Windbreaks near the hive are helpful. Do not allow grass to grow up around the hives. Avoid spraying nearby fields with pesticides while the bees are present, and avoid using highly toxic pesticides within a week of introducing the bees (table 8.1, page 80). Before introducing the bees, mow the field to eliminate competing flowers and thus further encourage the bees to visit the berry crop. Keep an ample supply of fresh water near the hive.

Some growers maintain areas near their fields exclusively for native and feral bees. The bees forage and nest in these sites and are available for the pollination needs of fruits and vegetables.

Fig. 8.1 **Bee pollination of raspberry flower.**

Table 8.1 Relative toxicity of pesticides to honey bees.

Chemical	Toxicity
Benlate (benomyl)	low
Brigade (bifenthrin)	high
Captan	low
Diazinon	high
Dibrom (naled)	high
Furadan (carbofuran)	high
Guthion (azinphosmethyl)	high
Kelthane (dicofol)	low
Lorsban (chlorpyrifos)	high
Malathion	high
Methoxychlor	low
Morestan (oxythioquinox)	low
Sevin (carbaryl)	high
Thiodan	medium
Thiram	low

Fruit and Leaf Damage

Eastern Raspberry Fruitworm

Scientific name: *Byturus rubi* Barber

The fruitworm adult is a small, somewhat hairy, light brown beetle, about ⅛ inch long (figure 8.2). Adults emerge in late April to early May from overwintered pupae in the soil, about the same time as raspberry leaves are unfolding. These adult beetles can be found along the midribs of leaves on which they feed. They also feed on flower buds and can reduce fruit set.

The adult females lay eggs on or near the blossom buds or, later, on the flowers and green berries (figure 8.3). After hatching, the larvae enter the blossoms or young fruit, where they feed on the fleshy receptacles (figure 8.4). The full-grown larva is yellowish-white, ¼ inch long, and has two transverse (crosswise) rows of stiff hairs. Larvae are full-grown by mid-July, when they fall to the ground and change to pupae, which overwinter in the soil. The adults emerge the following year (table 8.2).

 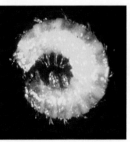 

Fig. 8.2 (*left to right*) Eastern raspberry fruitworm: adult, larva, pupa.

Fig. 8.3 ↗
Raspberry flower bud with eastern raspberry fruitworm adult, egg, and feeding damage (blackened hole).

◀ Fig. 8.4
Eastern raspberry fruitworm larva on raspberry.

Fig. 8.5 ➤
Raspberry leaf damage caused by adult eastern raspberry fruitworm.

Table 8.2 Life cycles of insects and mites attacking fruit and leaves of bramble plants.

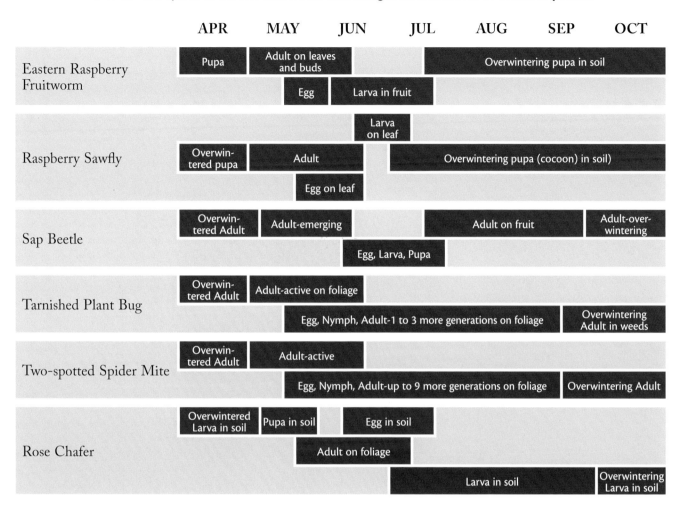

	APR	MAY	JUN	JUL	AUG	SEP	OCT
Eastern Raspberry Fruitworm	Pupa	Adult on leaves and buds			Overwintering pupa in soil		
		Egg	Larva in fruit				
Raspberry Sawfly			Larva on leaf				
	Overwintered pupa	Adult		Overwintering pupa (cocoon) in soil)			
		Egg on leaf					
Sap Beetle	Overwintered Adult	Adult-emerging			Adult on fruit		Adult-overwintering
			Egg, Larva, Pupa				
Tarnished Plant Bug	Overwintered Adult	Adult-active on foliage					Overwintering Adult in weeds
			Egg, Nymph, Adult-1 to 3 more generations on foliage				
Two-spotted Spider Mite	Overwintered Adult	Adult-active					Overwintering Adult
			Egg, Nymph, Adult-up to 9 more generations on foliage				
Rose Chafer	Overwintered Larva in soil	Pupa in soil	Egg in soil				
			Adult on foliage				
					Larva in soil		Overwintering Larva in soil

Injury is caused by fruitworm adults and larvae. In early May, the adults feed on the young leaves, skeletonizing the foliage (figure 8.5). As the leaf and fruit buds develop, the beetles feed on them, producing holes, which hinder fruit development. Later, the small larvae feed inside the flower buds and then bore into the young fruits, which may dry up or decay and fall off. The larvae can be found lying between the berry and its receptacle, and may remain with the berry after it is picked.

Because fruitworm larvae fall to the ground by the end of July, fall-fruiting brambles often escape injury. Cultivation of plant rows during late summer and early fall may kill the larvae and pupae in the soil; however, most commercial operations rely on chemical control. Insecticide sprays should be applied (1) early pre-bloom as blossom buds appear and (2) late pre-bloom just before blossoms open. Sprays applied for fruitworm control should also control the sawfly, described below.

Raspberry Sawflies

Scientific names: *Monophadnoides geniculatus* Hartig

The adults are small, black, thick-bodied insects about ¼ inch long and appear about the time the leaves begin to unfold in early May (table 8.2). The female has a yellowish-white band across her abdomen. She deposits eggs singly between the upper and lower epidermis of the leaves (figure 8.6, page 82). Eggs hatch into spiny, many-legged, pale green "worms." When fully grown, the sawfly larva is ½ inch long (figure 8.7, page 82). This species has one generation per season, overwintering as pupae in the ground.

In the last few years there have been reports of a second species of sawfly (*Priophorus morio*) present in the Northeast. Known as the small raspberry sawfly, it is similar in appearance to the raspberry sawfly. One difference is that it can have two or more generations per season. It has been reported to be a problem on greenhouse-grown raspberries.

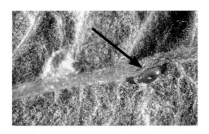

← Fig. 8.6 Raspberry sawfly egg.

▲ Fig. 8.7 Raspberry sawfly larva.

← Fig. 8.8 Raspberry leaf damage caused by raspberry sawfly larva.

in sheltered sites, generally after temperatures exceed 60–65°F for several days. They feed, mate, and lay eggs in the organic matter. After larval and pupal development is completed, new adult beetles appear from July to September when they feed on the ripe and overripe fruits (figure 8.10; table 8.2, page 81).

The sap beetle is also called the "picnic beetle" because it can become a nuisance at any outdoor function where food is present. It is attracted to fruit and any fermenting material. At any time from the start of fruit coloring through harvest, these small beetles may be found feeding on ripe or injured berries. They either feed near the surface or they bore into the fruit where they can be found next to the receptacle.

Because these beetles are attracted to injured and overripe fruit, control of other fruit-damaging pests and prompt harvesting of ripe berries can help in reducing damage caused by this pest. Raspberry cultivars that mature fruit later in the season tend to be more vulnerable to this insect. Remove harvested fruit from the field or cover it to prevent post-harvest contamination. Abundance of organic debris in neighboring fields may contribute to greater populations of sap beetles in the area. If necessary, sprays should be applied as fruit begins to color or as soon as beetles are seen.

Younger larvae usually feed on the outer edges of leaves but they chew irregular holes throughout the leaf as they become older (figure 8.8). In heavy infestations, the entire leaf surface is eaten, with the exception of the larger veins. Sawfly larvae may occasionally feed on the new bark, blossom buds, or young fruit.

Chemical control is generally recommended. Sprays should be applied early pre-bloom and late pre-bloom. Sprays for sawfly should also control fruitworm.

Sap Beetle

Scientific name: *Glischrochilus quadrisignatus* Say and *G. fasciatus* Olivier

Adults are about ¼ inch long and colored black, with four orange-red spots on their wing covers (figure 8.9). Overwintered beetles emerge in May from organic matter

Tarnished Plant Bug

Scientific name: *Lygus lineolaris* Palisot de Beauvois

Tarnished plant bug adults are about ¼ inch long, oval, somewhat flattened, and greenish-brown with reddish-brown markings on the wings (figure 8.11). A distinguishing characteristic is a small, yellow-tipped triangle on the back, behind the head. Nymphs are pale green when they first hatch and are very small, less than ¹⁄₁₆ inch long. Later, nymphal instars (a stage between molts) are successively larger, often brown in color, and have wing pads. Older nymphs have a characteristic pattern of five spots on their back (figure 8.12).

Tarnished plant bugs overwinter as adults and become active from late April to mid-May when they lay eggs in crop and weed hosts (figure 8.13). After hatching, nymphs feed on flowers and developing fruit. These nymphs molt to the adult stage by early summer, and the cycle is repeated; two to four generations occur annually (table 8.2, page 81).

Feeding by tarnished plant bugs on buds, blossoms,

Fig. 8.9 Sap beetle adult.

Fig. 8.10 Sap beetle adult on raspberry.

← Fig. 8.11
Tarnished plant bug adult on raspberry.

Fig. 8.14 →
Damaged fruit from tarnished plant bug.

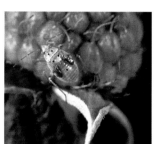

← Fig. 8.12
Tarnished plant bug nymph (late instar) on raspberry.

Fig. 8.15 →
Undamaged (*left*) and damaged (*right*) blackberries from tarnished plant bug.

← Fig. 8.13
Tarnished plant bug egg on raspberry leaf.

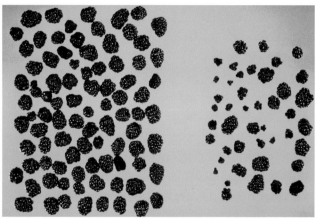

and developing berries results in deformed fruit, which lowers yields. Both nymphs and adults cause damage (figures 8.14 and 8.15).

Controlling weeds may help reduce populations of tarnished plant bugs. The area surrounding plants must be kept mowed to reduce populations. However, forage crops such as alfalfa near the planting should not be mowed when raspberry flowers or fruits are present. Mowing will encourage movement of insects to the raspberries. A reliable economic threshold has not been developed for tarnished plant bug in raspberries. If necessary, insecticides should be applied just before blossoms open and later as fruit begins to color.

Two-Spotted Spider Mite

Scientific name: *Tetranychus urticae* Koch

These mites vary in color from pale greenish-yellow to dark crimson red. As adults, they usually have two dark spots, one on each side of their bodies (figure 8.16). The mites are barely visible to the unaided eye. Adults or late instar nymphs overwinter at the base of brambles or weeds. After moving onto the foliage, the adults lay eggs on the undersides of the leaves, which are the prime feeding areas of young and adult mites. As many as ten generations per year can occur (table 8.2, page 81).

Mite feeding on leaf undersides first causes a fine gray or white stippling on the upper leaf surfaces (figure 8.17). Later, discolored blotches develop, webbing produced by the mites is apparent,

Fig. 8.16 **Adult** (*left*) and immature (*right*) two-spotted spider mites.

Fig. 8.17 Two-spotted spider mite damage to raspberry leaf.

and the leaves may turn yellowish-brown and then dry up and fall off. Older, less succulent leaves appear to be preferred by the mites, and injury is less serious on more vigorous plants. Damage is first seen and is more prevalent in drier areas of a field, and is more likely to occur during hot, dry seasons. Areas with mild growing seasons most frequently have mite problems.

Severe foliage injury to the fruiting spurs reduces the yield and quality of fruit during the current season. Feeding on primocane foliage stunts cane growth for the next year's fruit production, and because leaves are removed early, the canes are susceptible to winter injury. During certain seasons, the mites become so abundant that they swarm on the berries at harvest, resembling brown dust, and decrease the market value of the fruit.

Naturally occurring predatory mites can maintain spider mite populations at low levels, especially in fields not routinely sprayed with broad-spectrum insecticides (see table 8.3). In addition, researchers and practitioners are currently testing releases of predatory mites in an effort to control two-spotted mites in brambles. These can be ordered from commercial suppliers. Generally, predatory mites should be released prior to the onset of severe foliar symptoms. Miticide sprays are applied as the mite density on the leaf increases. Several sprays may be necessary, and thorough underleaf coverage is essential for good control.

Rose Chafer

Scientific name: *Macrodactylus subspinosus* Fabricius

The rose chafer beetles overwinter as larvae deep in the soil and migrate upward in the spring, pupating in early May. The adult is slender, long-legged, light grayish-brown, and about ¾ inch long (figure 8.18). Adults emerge from the soil in late May and early June. Feeding, mating, and egg-laying takes place into early July. The eggs are

Table 8.3 **Relative toxicity of pesticides to beneficial mites.**

Chemical	Toxicity
Benlate (benomyl)	medium
Brigade (bifenthrin)	high
Captan	low
Guthion (azinphosmethyl)	low
Kelthane (dicofol)	medium
Lorsban (chlorpyrifos)	medium
Morestan (oxythioquinox)	low
Ronilan (metalaxyl)	low
Sevin (carbaryl)	high
Vendex (hexakis)	low

deposited singly, a few inches below the soil surface. Hatching takes place two weeks after oviposition (egg laying), and the larvae (grubs) feed on grass and weed roots until cold weather, when they migrate deeper into the soil to overwinter (table 8.2, page 81).

Adults feed on leaves and blossoms in June and July. Light, sandy soil can promote high populations that can strip the plants. Larvae feed mainly on the roots of grasses and weeds, and do not damage brambles.

Chemical control is generally recommended. Sprays should be applied upon appearance of the beetles and/or damage.

Japanese Beetle

Scientific name: *Popillia japonica* Newman

Adults, about ½ inch long with a shiny metallic green head, (figure 8.19) emerge from pupal chambers in the soil from June to September and feed on ripe bramble fruit, in addition to hundreds of other kinds of plants.

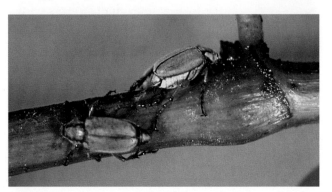

◄ Fig. 8.18 Rose chafer adults.

Fig. 8.19 ➤ Japanese beetle adult.

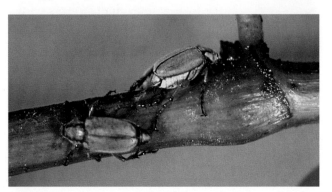

Eggs are laid on the ground, particularly in acidic soil. After hatching, the larvae feed on roots of grasses and other plants. The winter is spent as partially grown larvae. Growth and feeding continues in the spring. Pupation begins in June, with adult emergence following later in the month.

These beetles are serious pests of lawn, turf, vegetables, and nursery stock. Bramble plantings near turf may be especially susceptible to infestation. Beetles chew small holes in the fruit, which may then be more susceptible to diseases, particularly fruit rots. Sometimes the beetles may reach numbers high enough to cause leaf damage. Beetles are sometimes active before the fruit ripens, and as a result, the first damage noticed is skeletonization of the foliage.

A chemical spray may be needed at late pre-bloom, just before the blossoms open. Japanese beetles can continue to cause problems during and after bloom. However, it is much more difficult to avoid killing pollinators during this time.

Aphids

Scientific names: *Amphorophora agathonica* and *Aphis rubicola*

The two aphid pest species of brambles are (1) the large raspberry aphid, *Amphorophora agathonica* (figure 8.20), and (2) the small raspberry aphid, *Aphis rubicola*. They are both light green to yellow in color.

Aphids overwinter as eggs and hatch in May. Females,

Fig. 8.20 **Large raspberry aphids.**

which may be winged or wingless, give birth to live young throughout the summer. A number of generations may be produced. Males are produced in the fall and mate with females to produce the overwintering eggs.

Aphids are most important to bramble growers as transmitters of viral diseases, particularly in nurseries. Raspberry mosaic virus is transmitted by the large raspberry aphid, and raspberry leaf curl virus is transmitted by the small raspberry aphid.

All infected plantings must be removed and destroyed. New planting stock should be aphid-resistant cultivars that are certified virus-free. Also, a distance of at least 500–1,000 feet should be kept between new plantings and virus-infected plantings. Windbreaks between new plantings and wild brambles may hinder aphid movement. Special sprays can be applied to nursery stock to control aphids.

Blackberry Leafminer

Scientific name: *Metallus rubi* Forbes

The adult, a sawfly, emerges and lays eggs throughout June. After hatching, the larvae feed inside the leaf tissue (figure 8.21). When mature, they drop to the soil and pupate, usually in August. Second-generation adults are active from mid-August to mid-September, during which time they lay eggs. The hatched larvae feed in the leaves (figure 8.22), then drop to the ground where they overwinter. Pupation occurs in the spring, and adults emerge again in June. The larvae tunnel through leaf tissue and create "mines" that cause affected areas to turn brown.

This is a sporadic pest that can sometimes cause extensive leaf injury. Consult local extension personnel

Fig. 8.21 ▲
Blackberry leafminer larva on leaf.

Fig. 8.22 ➤
Damage from blackberry leafminer.

for recommendations and an assessment of damage severity.

Yellow Jackets

Scientific name: Family Vespidae

The adult female overwinters in isolation and starts a colony in the spring. Larvae in the colony feed on captured insects.

When local weather conditions are droughty, the adults are attracted to ripe or injured fruit as a source of moisture and sugar (figure 8.23). Yellow jackets will feed on the fruit and can be an extreme annoyance to pickers.

Prompt harvesting of ripe berries and "clean" picking practices (see "Harvesting," chapter twelve) will help decrease the fruit's attractiveness to the wasps.

Strawberry Bud Weevil (Clipper)

Scientific name: *Anthonomus signatus* Say

The adult is about ¹⁄₁₀ inch long and dark reddish-brown, with rows of pits or punctures along its back and two white spots with dark centers (figure 8.24). The mouthparts are black and extended into a snout.

Adults overwinter in fence rows, under mulch, or in wooded areas, and emerge when temperatures reach about 60°F in spring. The weevils move into bramble plantings

Fig. 8.23 **Yellow jackets on raspberry.**

and feed on immature pollen by puncturing the blossom bud with their snouts. This feeding produces many holes in the flower petals. After puncturing a nearly mature bud, the female deposits an egg in the wound. She then chews the bud stem until it nearly detaches. Larvae emerge from the flower buds in late June through July and pupate. Adults emerge in mid-summer, feed for a short time, and seek overwintering sites.

At one time this insect was considered a major pest in strawberries, but recent research indicates that many commercial cultivars can compensate for clipped buds. It is currently not known if raspberries compensate in a similar fashion. Holes in the flower petals indicate the presence of adults, but it is the severed buds which may cause economic damage.

If necessary, sprays are applied during the pre-bloom period after clipped buds are observed (figure 8.25). A reliable economic threshold has not been determined.

Potato Leafhopper

Scientific name: *Empoasca fabae* Harris

Damage from the potato leafhopper occurs throughout eastern North America and may reduce plant growth

Fig. 8.26 ➤ Leafhopper damage on Heritage red raspberry.

◤ Fig. 8.24 Adult strawberry bud weevil (clipper) on strawberry flower.

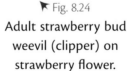

◀ Fig. 8.25 Clipped buds from strawberry bud weevil.

Fig. 8.27 ➤ Leafhopper adult with nymph.

in commercial plantings. Cultivars may differ in susceptibility (although more work in this area is needed). Adults and nymphs feed along the veins on the undersides of leaves by sucking up plant juices. In the feeding process, they apparently inject with their saliva a toxic substance that causes plugs to form in the vascular system of the plant. Margins of affected leaves develop a light yellow color, and new growth can be curled downward and stunted (figure 8.26). Potato leafhopper injury may be mistaken for herbicide damage, nutrient deficiency, or symptoms of viral infection.

The adult leafhopper is bright green and about ⅛ inch long (figure 8.27). It takes flight quickly when disturbed, so sweep-nets are used to catch and identify them. Young nymphs are smaller and light green and are easily identified by their habit of moving sideways when disturbed. Females deposit eggs within leaves and stems of plants, and nymphs develop on the undersides of leaves. Nymph activity is greatest from late spring to midsummer. Adult leafhoppers are highly mobile, migrating from the southern to northern states each year. The wide host range of this insect, nearly 140 plant species, facilitates the annual migration. Note that plantings near recently cut alfalfa may experience increased potato leafhopper numbers as they move out of the alfalfa and into other crops. The leafhopper is adequately controlled by several broad-spectrum pesticides.

Cane, Crown, and Root Damage

Raspberry Cane Borer

Scientific name: *Oberea bimaculata* Olivier

This beetle is slender, about ½ inch long, and black, except for a bright orange thorax that has two or three black spots. The long, black antennae are easily noticed (figure 8.28).

These insects require two years to complete their life cycle. The adults appear in raspberry plantings in early June and may be present until late August. They feed on the tender, green epidermis of cane tips and leave brownish patches or scars. Before laying an egg, the female punctures the stem with her mouthparts in a girdling fashion. She creates two puncture rings around the cane, about ½ inch apart and about 6 inches from the cane tip or lateral shoot (figure 8.29). After puncturing, the female deposits an egg into the cane pith in between the rings (figure 8.30).

Upon hatching, larvae burrow down through the cane (figure 8.31), reaching its base by the fall and down to the crown by the next summer. The larvae spend the

Fig. 8.28
Raspberry cane borer adult.

Fig. 8.29
Puncture rings and oviposition punctures from raspberry cane borer.

Fig. 8.30
Raspberry cane borer egg.

Fig. 8.31
Raspberry cane borer larva.

Fig. 8.32
Wilted stem caused by girdling practice of raspberry cane borer.

		APR	MAY	JUN	JUL	AUG	SEP	OCT
Raspberry Cane Borer	Year #1			Egg in stem				
			Adult-feeds on cane tips					
			Pupa		Larva in cane		Overwintering larva in canes	
	Year #2	Larva in roots and canes					Overwintering larva in roots and canes	
Flatheaded Cane Borer				Larva tunnels in cane-swelling apparent by July and August			Larva in canes (Overwintering)	
		Pupa in cane	Adult feeds on leaf, lays egg on bark					
			Egg					
Raspberry Crown Borer	Year #1	Larva in crown			Pupa	Adult		
						Egg		
	Year #2						Larva in base of cane or protected place	
		Larva in crown, roots, and canes						Larva in roots (Overwintering)
Tree Cricket		Egg (Overwintering)		Nymph and Adult (punctures stem)				
						Egg (Overwintering)		

next season underground, then pupation occurs the second spring, generally in an old stub from which adults emerge (see table 8.4).

The first observed damage usually is the wilting of cane tips and laterals in early June (figure 8.32, page 87). This is caused by the encircling rows of punctures made by the female before she deposits the egg. These rings restrict the sap flow, commonly resulting in blackening and abscission (cutting off) of the tip within a few days. Severe injury may cause the cane to die or fall over before fruit matures the next season. Larval burrowing can destroy the pith and fill the cane wall with holes.

During the growing season, remove and destroy the infested portion of the stem a few inches below the wilted tip. If this is done within a few days of initial injury, only a small amount of cane is lost. Also, damaged canes and roots should be removed and burned during the dormant season. Sprays are directed at adults and are applied at late pre-bloom, just before blossoms open.

Flat-headed Cane Borers

Scientific name: *Agrilus ruficollis* Fab. and *A. rubicola* Abeille

These two species of borers burrow through the canes of raspberries, blackberries, and dewberries. *Agrilus ruficollis*, the red-necked cane borer, has a reddish-colored thorax that contrasts sharply with its black head and wing covers (figure 8.33). *A. rubicola*, the bronze cane-borer, is similar except for its iridescent bronze or copper color. Adults of *A. ruficollis* are about ¼ inch long, while *A. rubicola* may be much smaller.

Fig. 8.33

Flat headed cane borer adults.

Fig. 8.34 ➤ Cane damage caused by flat-headed cane borer.

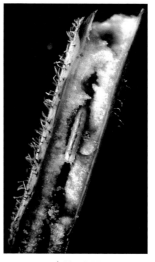

▲ Fig. 8.35
Raspberry cane maggot larva.

Fig. 8.36 ➤
Stem swelling from raspberry cane maggot.

The life cycles of the two species are nearly identical. Adults are present from late May to early August. They feed along leaf edges and can be most easily found on sunny days. Females deposit whitish, scale-like eggs along the bark of new growth in May and June. After hatching, the larvae construct long, winding tunnels which spiral around the cane several times in the sapwood, turn into the hardwood, and then end in the pith. A swelling usually develops where the tunneling occurs and is apparent by July or August (figure 8.34). Once the tunnel reaches the pith, it straightens into a path through the pith. The larva is full-grown by fall, remains in the tunnel during the winter, and pupates in the spring. Adults emerge in the summer (table 8.4).

The presence of these borers is indicated by a symmetrical swelling ¼ to 3 inches long on the cane. These swellings occur between 1 and 4 feet above the ground; those nearer the ground cause more damage. The affected cane is usually broken or severed near the swelling where the spiraling tunnels have weakened it. Many weak-caned cultivars of raspberries wither and die before the fruit matures.

Injured canes should be removed and burned during the dormant season. Insecticides are directed at adults only, and are applied at late pre-bloom just before blossoms open.

Raspberry Cane Maggot

Scientific name: *Pegomya rubivora* Coq.

The adult resembles a housefly, but is smaller. The maggot (larva) burrows into the pith (figure 8.35), then tunnels down the cane, later working toward the bark and gradually girdling the cane from the inside.

Injury caused by the maggot resembles that of the raspberry cane borer—new tips wilt, dry up, and die. However, unlike cane borer damage, no girdling marks appear. Tunneling produces a swelling of the stem which causes the plant to die above the injury (figure 8.36). A certain amount of injury may occur every season, but this insect seldom becomes an economic pest to growers.

The infested portion of the stem should be removed a few inches below the wilting tip and destroyed.

Raspberry Crown Borer

Scientific name: *Pennisetia marginata* Harris

The adult is an attractive, clear-winged moth resembling a yellow jacket, with a wingspan of 1–1¼ inches, and with bright yellow bands across the abdomen (figure 8.37). As with the raspberry cane borer, this insect requires two years to complete its life cycle.

Adults appear in early August and are present through most of September. Females can be seen during the day

Fig. 8.37
Raspberry crown borer adult

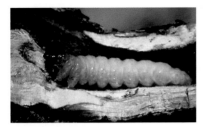

Fig. 8.38 →
Raspberry crown borer eggs.

↑ Fig. 8.39
Raspberry crown borer larva.

← Fig. 8.40 Cane swelling from raspberry crown borer.

Fig. 8.41 →
Raspberry crown with raspberry crown borer larva.

resting on the foliage where they lay their reddish-brown eggs individually on the undersides of leaves near the edges (figure 8.38). After hatching, the larva moves to the cane base where it either excavates a cavity in which to overwinter or finds a protected place in the bark. The next spring, the larva (figure 8.39) enters the crown and also the roots, but it usually tunnels into a new cane and girdles it before returning to the root tissue (figure 8.40). The second winter is spent in the roots. By the second summer, the crown can be extensively damaged. The larva transforms into a pupa by August of the second summer, and the adult emerges shortly thereafter (table 8.4, page 88).

Damage from this serious pest is often confused with disease symptoms. The first indication of injury is the withering, wilting, and dying of the cane foliage, often with half-grown fruit still attached. If damaged canes are pulled the second summer, they will break off at the damaged area, sometimes revealing the larva inside. Such injury to the canes may increase the incidence of diseases.

Workers in New England have seen swelling in the crown, and the entire plant with all its canes may be killed. Damage to the roots and crown is more difficult to find because the plants must be dug up to verify the cause (figure 8.41). Damage by this pest is indicated by girdled crowns and canes, and burrowed cavities inside the crowns. The crown must be opened to find the damaging larva.

During the growing season, dying canes and any others showing symptoms of infestation should be destroyed. All wild brambles in the area should be eliminated. Insecticides are applied as a heavy drench in the early spring to kill larvae, and as a spray between mid-October and mid-November to kill adults.

Tree Crickets
Scientific name: *Oecanthus* spp.

The tree cricket is a delicate-looking, greenish-white, slender-bodied insect (figure 8.42). It has dark antennae, which are usually longer than its body. During the summer, both nymphs and adults can be found on bramble canes (table 8.4). In late summer, females lay eggs in the canes, leaving several small punctures very close together and arranged in rows lengthwise on the cane (figure 8.43). There may be only a few punctures or up to 50 in a row. These rows are usually 2 to 3 inches long and may be anywhere on the cane, but are most common within 2 feet of the tip. Tree crickets have one generation per year, overwintering as eggs.

The punctures created by the female weaken the cane, causing it to split or break at the point of injury. Punctures on the lower part of the cane may weaken the entire cane,

Fig. 8.42
Tree cricket adult on leaf.

Fig. 8.43 Tree cricket damage to stem, showing oviposition punctures in whole stem (*top*) and eggs in sectioned stem (*bottom*).

preventing normal development of fruit the next season. Also, diseases may enter through the punctures.

Infested canes should be removed and burned. Old fruiting canes must be pruned out and wild brambles eliminated from nearby areas. Insecticides may be applied from late August to mid-September.

Root Weevils

Scientific name: *Otiorhynchus* spp.

The adult beetle is brown to black, with rows of punctures or pits along its back. Its mouthparts are extended into a snout (figure 8.44). Adults of the three species of root weevils range in length from 2/10 to 4/10 inch. They emerge from pupal chambers in the soil from late May through June, and feed on foliage at night. After 10–60 days, they begin to lay eggs in the soil. Upon hatching, the C-shaped larvae (grubs) (figure 8.45) feed on roots throughout the summer and overwinter in the soil. They start feeding again in the spring, pupate, and emerge as adults during the summer.

These insects are important pests in strawberries, but can also cause damage to bramble plantings. The presence of adults is shown by notches in the leaves, but this damage is seldom important. The real damage is caused by larvae which tunnel in the roots and crowns, thereby weakening, stunting, or killing the plant.

Few chemical spray options are effective. Maintaining weed-free plantings is an important practice for preventing egg-laying by adults. Soil fumigation, non-host rotation, and cultivation are effective as preplant control measures. Since the beetles cannot fly, place new plantings at least 1,000 feet from infested plantings, and avoid transporting weevils on equipment or plant material. Entomopathogenic nematodes have been shown to provide some control against root weevils in strawberries, but have not been extensively evaluated for raspberries.

Fig. 8.44 **Root weevil adult.**

Fig. 8.45 **Root weevil larva.**

Further Reading

Cornell University Department of Horticulture. "The Berry Diagnostic Tool." Ithaca, NY: Cornell University. WWW.HORT.CORNELL.EDU/DIAGNOSTIC. A pictorial diagnostic tool for berry crops.

Ellis, M.A., R.H. Converse, R.N. Williams, and B. Williamson (eds.). 1991. *Compendium of Raspberry and Blackberry Diseases and Insects*. St. Paul, MN: The American Phytopathological Society Press.

CHAPTER NINE

Disease Management and Physiological Disorders

This chapter focuses on the biology of bramble disease organisms, identification and diagnosis of symptoms, and management of pathogens. Cultural methods are emphasized, since regulations and restrictions concerning pesticide use are continually changing and vary from state to state. Growers may or may not encounter the particular diseases described herein, depending on geographic region, local growing conditions, production systems, and cultivar. Growers should consult their local extension personnel for recommendations concerning the most effective management procedures available in their area.

Overview

Plant diseases have many causes. They are most often grouped into two categories: biotic (those caused by living things) and abiotic (those caused by non-living things). Biotic plant diseases are most generally caused by microorganisms, the majority of which are fungi. Other biotic diseases are caused by bacteria, viruses, and nematodes. Abiotic diseases or disorders are most frequently the result of adverse environmental factors. Symptoms of both biotic and abiotic diseases may be similar and are in some cases difficult to distinguish.

Fungi are responsible for many different plant diseases, including blights, molds, mildews, rusts, cankers, and rots. They are ubiquitous in the berry plantings. Most fungi are beneficial because they help with decomposition of dead plant material and make nutrients available. Some compete with other harmful fungi and microorganisms and keep their populations low. However, a small number of disease-causing fungi may be extremely harmful to brambles and can increase plant susceptibility to other pests. Most fungal diseases typically develop rapidly in warm, wet weather, when water remains on the plant or in the soil after rainfall.

Bacteria also cause various forms of plant disease, including wilts, blights, spots, rots, galls, and cankers. Two types of bacterial disease occur in brambles. The most serious bacterial disease attacking bramble plants is crown gall, a bacterium that produces tumor-like growths on the plant. Another relatively uncommon bacterial disease of brambles is fire blight, which causes cane tips to die and bend over, giving a characteristic shepherd's-crook appearance. Generally speaking, bacterial diseases are some of the most difficult to manage.

Brambles are susceptible to many viruses, although most virus-related economic losses in the Northeast are attributed to three viral diseases: raspberry mosaic, raspberry leaf curl, and crumbly berry. In general, growers must remember that all viruses are systemic, infecting the plant throughout its vegetative parts, with the exception of the meristems. Therefore, the virus is transmitted to any new plant derived from vegetative structures such as root suckers, tip layers, etc. The most important procedure for management of any viral disease is to establish a planting from virus-tested stock. All other procedures are worthless if this single step is not accomplished. In the field, viruses may be transmitted mechanically (through pruning, rubbing, or root grafts), in pollen, and via insect vectors (such as aphids and leaf hoppers) and nematodes. The specific mode of transmission tends to be a defining characteristic of a particular virus.

Nematodes are microscopic soil organisms that are worm-like in appearance. Several hundred species of these organisms have been identified as feeding on plants; two in particular may be found in association with brambles: root-lesion and dagger nematodes. In addition to direct damage to plants caused by nematode feeding, dagger and needle nematodes have also been identified as vectors of several bramble-related viruses.

Not all diseases are caused by living organisms such as a fungi, bacteria, viruses, etc. Abiotic diseases (disorders) often occur and may have symptoms similar to those caused by microorganisms. Probable causes of abiotic disease may include:

Nutrient extremes
   deficiencies, toxicities
Temperature extremes
   winter/frost injury, ultraviolet radiation/heat
Moisture extremes
   drought, flooding, relative humidity
Phytotoxicity
   adverse reactions to chemicals
Environmental damage
   wind, hail, lightning strikes
   air pollution, acid rain, wildlife
   mechanical injuries and wounds

The importance of correctly identifying a disease or disorder can not be overemphasized. The choice of management strategies is often dependent on which disease or disorder one is confronted with. To this end, a pictorial diagnostic tool for berry crops is available online at WWW.HORT.CORNELL.EDU/DIAGNOSTIC.

Cane and Lateral Diseases

Anthracnose

Scientific name: *Elsinoe veneta* (Burkholder) Jenk

Anthracnose is a common and potentially destructive fungal disease of blackberries, black raspberries, and to a lesser degree, purple and red raspberries. Although anthracnose often occurs on red raspberries, the severity of the disease is highly related to the variety. For example, Boyne or Killarney are very susceptible.

The most obvious symptom of anthracnose occurs on the canes. Anthracnose first appears on young canes of black and purple raspberries as small, slightly sunken purple spots. As these spots enlarge, they become oval in shape, turn gray in the center, and develop dark, raised borders (figure 9.1). The sites continue to sink into the woody portion of the cane, sometimes causing it to crack. Many individual infection sites (about ⅛ inch in diameter) may grow together to form large, irregularly-shaped diseased regions. Small, white spots may also occur on the foliage of infected canes.

Seriously infected canes are weak and very prone to winter injury. Cracks that begin developing during the first summer continue to deepen the following spring,

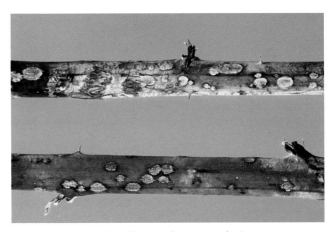

Fig. 9.1 **Sunken anthracnose lesions on canes of black raspberry.**

further weakening the surviving canes. Foliage produced from these canes is weak, and the fruit is often small and tends to shrivel and dry before harvest, especially during periods of water stress. The stems supporting individual fruits and fruit clusters may also become infected if the weather is wet while they are first developing. These infected stems may be girdled, resulting in significant yield losses. Individual drupelets of the berry may also become infected, turning brown and scabby.

Cane infections on blackberries are similar to those described on black raspberries. However, infection of individual drupelets can be a particularly serious problem on trailing blackberries under favorable weather conditions. The fruits of most erect blackberries are relatively resistant to infection. On red raspberry canes, individual infection sites may be smaller than on black and purple raspberries, and are sometimes only on the surface, not sunken. Many small surface infections may fuse together on primocanes during the late summer or early fall. This produces a graying of the bark, especially on the side most exposed to the sun. Such infections do not directly harm canes, but may provide spores for more serious infections of susceptible bramble types planted close by.

The anthracnose fungus overwinters within infection sites that developed during the preceding spring and summer. Spores produced from overwintered infections are spread by splashing rain. The spores germinate and infect young canes when they emerge in the spring. The severity of an infection period is proportional to both the temperature and the number of hours canes remain wet after rain starts.

New spores are produced from new infections. The disease will spread throughout a planting following rainy periods, as long as succulent, susceptible tissue is available. Disease risk is greatest between bud break and the preharvest period since infection appears to attack mainly young, actively growing parts of the plant.

Management

The following strategy is recommended for managing all cane diseases of brambles, including anthracnose:

1. When setting out new plants, cut off the handles of tip-layered cuttings at ground level and destroy them. These old stubs are potential entry sites for cane disease fungi and are not needed for the production of new shoots.
2. Remove and destroy all fruited canes and any heavily-infected primocanes after harvest. This is an important means of reducing the source of the next year's infective spores. This job must be completed before new canes begin to emerge in the spring.
3. Choose a planting site and use cultural practices that will allow good air circulation and rapid drying of canes after a rain. Cultural practices that promote rapid drying include good weed management, maintenance of narrow rows, removal of fruited canes after harvest, and certain trellising systems, such as the V-trellis. Suppression or thinning of primocanes will also contribute to better air circulation.
4. Apply an eradicant fungicide, such as liquid lime sulfur, just as buds are breaking in the spring; follow local recommendations and restrictions. The principle is to remove a significant amount of spores being produced on the overwintered canes before they can cause new infections. Thorough coverage and timing are critical. Cane disease fungi are generally resistant to fungicides while the canes are fully dormant. However, applications after leaves begin to unfold are likely to cause plant injury. Additional sprays of a locally recommended fungicide may be necessary during the growing season under extreme conditions. However, the single "delayed-dormant" eradicant spray usually gives adequate

commercial management of cane diseases in the Northeast if used in conjunction with recommended horticultural practices.

5. Grow brambles under cover in high tunnels or a greenhouse to reduce disease pressure.

Cane Blight

Scientific name: *Diapleella coniothyrium* (Fuckel) Barr

Cane blight is a potentially serious disease on all cultivated raspberries and blackberries in North America. This blight usually occurs as a result of specific cultural practices that create wound sites for the disease to enter. Cane blight occurs most commonly on black raspberries as a result of summer tipping. It also occurs on red raspberries, where it has been noted to be less common than spur blight but much more destructive. Up to a 30% loss of yield due to cane blight has been measured in heavily infested fields. Because spur blight and cane blight often occur together, some of the damage historically attributed to spur blight has probably been caused by cane blight.

Infections begin only on first-year canes at wound sites, such as pruning or tipping cuts, cane injuries created by rubbing against other canes or trellis wires, or insect-feeding punctures. A dark infected area develops beneath the surface of the cane and may extend up and down one side of the cane or may girdle it several inches

Fig. 9.2
Cane blight on thornless blackberry.

below the wound. Often, the infection extends along the cane for several nodes, in contrast to spur blight, which generally stays in the area around a single node. The wood of infected canes breaks easily and eventually becomes covered with tiny black fruiting structures of the cane blight fungus. Lateral shoots emerging from buds near or above infected regions are weak and may wilt and collapse. The entire cane can be killed if infection occurs near the ground (figure 9.2).

Spores from fruiting bodies in old, infected canes or dead canes are released during rainy periods, beginning in the spring. The spores are dispersed by wind currents or splashing rain, and they germinate and infect new canes if wound sites are available. New fruiting bodies are produced from these infection sites as the season progresses, providing many more spores for further disease spread.

Additional infections may occur any time during the growing season if wounds are present, and are particularly favored by extended periods of warm, wet weather. The fungus eventually overwinters within the infected canes, then produces new fruiting bodies the following spring, completing the disease cycle. The fruiting bodies produced from overwintering infections can continue to release infective spores for up to four years if the cane debris is not destroyed.

In addition to the strategies outlined for managing anthracnose, it is important to minimize cane wounding. In particular, any pruning, topping, or tipping during the growing season should be done during a period of dry weather, at least three days before any expected rain, to allow cuts a chance to heal before a potential infection period.

Spur Blight

Scientific name: *Didymella applanata* (Niessl) Sacc.

Spur blight is a very common disease of red raspberries throughout the eastern half of North America, but is rare on other brambles. Although spur blight has traditionally been considered a serious disease of red raspberries, its economic significance has probably been exaggerated.

Symptoms of spur blight first appear in early summer. Chocolate-brown or purple discolorations initially develop on new canes just below points of leaf attachment, usually on the lower portion of the cane. The discoloration then expands up and down the cane, but usually stops before

Fig. 9.3 **Spur blight on canes of red raspberry.**

it reaches the next bud in either direction (figure 9.3).

The leaves arising from within the infected region are often chlorotic (lacking green pigment). The leaves also may show dark, wedge-shaped, dead patches extending along the midrib or main veins out to the leaf margin. The blades of such leaves often fall off, leaving the petiole (leaf stem) attached to the cane.

Discolored areas of the cane remain brown or purple until early fall, when small, black, pimple-like fruiting bodies of the spur blight fungus form within the bark of infected regions. The bark turns gray and may develop shallow, lengthwise cracks. Canes that become severely defoliated or cracked are more susceptible to winter injury. Buds within the infected region may fail to break the following spring. If they do break, they produce weak, unproductive laterals. Healthy buds in the top of the cane, however, may compensate for this production loss when infections are only in lower cane regions, as is the case in most years.

Spores produced in fruiting bodies on overwintered canes start the disease cycle the following growing season. These spores escape into the air during rainy periods from mid-spring through early summer. They are carried by air currents to newly emerging canes where they germinate and cause infection if the canes remain wet long enough. A second type of spore is produced within new infection sites during the summer. This type is spread by splashing rain and can lead to an epidemic development of disease during excessively wet years.

Management strategies are the same as outlined for anthracnose above.

Cane Botrytis (Gray Mold Wilt)

Scientific name: *Botrytis cinerea* Pers. F.

Cane botrytis is caused by the same fungus that causes gray mold of bramble fruits. Red raspberries appear to be most susceptible to this disease, but it may occur on most *Rubus* species.

Cane botrytis is potentially more damaging than, and often confused with, spur blight. In fact both diseases may be present on the same cane; both occupy the same ecological niche and do similar things to plant growth. Like spur blight, buds at infected nodes are reduced in size and are less likely to produce healthy lateral shoots.

Cane botrytis infections first appear in mid- to late summer as pale brown leaf spots (lesions) on mature to senescent primocane leaves (figure 9.4). Younger, more vigorous leaves are not susceptible to infection by this pathogen. Infected leaves are usually shed prematurely. The fungus spreads over time from leaf lesions through the petiole and into the cane. Pale brown cane lesions develop and spread rapidly around the cane; on rare occasions these lesions may girdle and kill the primocane. Single leaf infections may lead to a lesion that covers three or four internodes. Where two cane botrytis lesions meet, a sharp boundary is always visible. This is also true where botrytis and spur blight lesions meet on canes infected with both diseases.

In spring, young lesions of both diseases are difficult to tell apart. As lesions mature, they become more distinguishable. Spur blight lesions are a much darker chocolate-brown color; cane botrytis lesions often display conspicuous banding patterns or a water-marked appearance due to fluctuating rates of pathogen growth. Healthy green vascular tissue is revealed under botrytis cane lesions when infected surface tissues are scraped away.

As botrytis-infected canes turn brown in the fall, lesions become indistinguishable from healthy tissue. They may take on a grayish-white appearance and become evident again after several weeks of low temperatures. Shiny, black, blister-like structures (sclerotia) form beneath the epidermis during winter. These erupt from underneath the bark in spring and produce gray masses of powdery spores (conidia) during periods of high humidity or rainfall. Conidia are dispersed by wind and water-splash (rainfall, overhead irrigation) to start new infections. Sclerotia are probably the principal source of inoculum in the spring,

Fig. 9.4

Cane Botrytis.

but most plant debris may be colonized by this fungus and produce conidia under wet conditions.

As only mature to senescent leaves are infected by this pathogen, disease is most severe inside dense, closed canopies, predominantly on the lower halves of primocanes. Pruning to open canopies, and keeping crop rows narrow and plantings weed free may help reduce or minimize development of this disease. Other production practices that promote rapid drying of foliage and canes will also be beneficial. Fungicides applied before harvest for control of botrytis fruit infections should give adequate control of this disease on canes if thorough coverage of all plant surfaces is achieved.

Fruit Diseases

Botrytis Fruit Rot and Blossom Blight (Gray Mold)

Scientific name: *Botrytis cinerea* Pers. F.

Gray mold is the most common cause of fruit rot of brambles. It is generally a more serious problem on blackberries and red raspberries than on black raspberries. This disease can cause very high losses if prolonged rainy periods occur during bloom or just before or during harvest.

Fruit may become infected at any time during development, but is most susceptible just before and after harvest. Infected berries first develop a watery soft rot,

▲ Fig. 9.5 **Gray mold on red raspberry fruit.**

◄ Fig. 9.6 **Blighting of red raspberry flowers by the gray mold fungus.**

but quickly become covered with a dusty mass of gray spores (figure 9.5). Infected fruits may occur singly, but often occur in clusters. If extended rains occur during bloom, blossoms may also be attacked and blighted. The infection will then move back into stems supporting individual blossoms or blossom clusters. If the weather turns dry after such attacks, the blossoms and stems will blacken and may not produce the gray spores usually found on the fruit. In such cases, this disease may resemble the fire blight disease of apples and pears.

The fungus overwinters in decaying leaves and fruit on the ground and in infected tissue on the cane. Masses of spores are produced during wet or humid periods the following spring and are spread throughout the planting by air currents. Flowers may become infected if they remain wet during bloom, either blighting completely during long rainy periods or having limited, "dormant" infections during more moderate wet periods (figure 9.6). These dormant infections may not resume activity until humid weather when they cause ripening fruit to rot. Ripening fruit may also become infected by (1) spores that blow onto them from overwintering infections, (2) spores produced upon recently infected fruit and flowers, or (3) direct contact with rotting berries in the same cluster.

Ultimately the disease severity will depend on a combination of factors, including (1) the number of spores present, (2) the number and duration of individual wetting periods, including mists and dews, and (3) the temperature—upper 60s and 70s are most damaging

if accompanied by wetness. The tremendous number of spores produced upon each infected fruit can cause an epidemic "explosion" of this disease if prolonged wet conditions occur during harvest.

Gray mold is managed through an integrated program, including (1) cultural practices that promote rapid drying of flowers and fruit, such as site selection, maintenance of narrow plant rows, trellising, and cane thinning; (2) timely and regular harvesting of fruit to prevent a buildup of gray mold spores on overripe fruit; and (3) fungicide sprays as necessary. Sprays are most important just before rainy periods that occur during bloom and before harvest. Growers should consult local extension personnel for recommendations for materials and restrictions. In addition to the above procedures, rapid removal of field heat by precoolers, followed by refrigerated storage is an important technique for reducing postharvest development of gray mold on berries intended for the wholesale market.

Crumbly Berry

Scientific name: *Tomato ringspot virus* (ToRSV)

"Crumbly berry" is a symptom with various causes, including poor pollination, genetic disorder, insect injury, nutrition deficiency, winter injury, water relations, or infection by *Tomato ringspot virus* (ToRSV). The focus here will be on tomato ringspot, which is widely distributed throughout North America. ToRSV can result in high economic losses in heavily infected plantings due to the production of small, poor-quality fruit and stunted plants. Only red raspberries are affected by ToRSV.

Although fruit symptoms are obvious, those on the foliage are not. During the first spring after plants become infected, yellow rings may form on the leaf blades, or a network of fine yellow lines may develop along veins, but in following years, leaf symptoms will be absent or appear on only one or two leaves. Plants are infected in circular or oblong patches, and after several years, plants within the center of the patch may be stunted and will take longer to break bud in the spring. The fruits on infected plants are small and crumble apart when they are picked. This "crumbly berry" symptom results from individual drupelets of the aggregate berry failing to form.

ToRSV is spread by the American dagger nematode, *Xiphinema americanum* Cobb (see figure 9.28 on page 108), a microscopic roundworm that feeds on plant roots. Initial infections result from either setting out infected planting stock or planting clean material in an already infested field. Dagger nematodes in the soil may have picked up the virus from infected weeds or crop plants. The virus has a wide host range including dandelion, chickweed, fruit trees, and grapes.

Once plants are infected, the disease spreads from plant to plant at a rate of about six feet per year, producing the circular or oblong patches associated with the disease. New pockets of infection may be formed if soil infested with virus-carrying nematodes is distributed to uninfested parts of the field during various management activities such as cultivation, harvesting, spraying, etc.

Nematodes thrive in the same light, well-drained soils that are best for bramble production. Soils should be tested for the presence of *Xiphinema* nematodes during the year before planting and treated with a preplant fumigant if test results are positive. Growers should check with their local Cooperative Extension offices for suggestions on sampling procedures and dates.

It may be practical to reduce spread by removing and destroying infected plants if there are only a few. In such cases, at least five plants beyond those showing symptoms should be removed in each row, including all weeds and suckers in the row. As many roots as possible should be removed, particularly the large ones which will be slow to decompose. The infected area should be kept absolutely free of vegetation for two years before replanting is attempted.

Raspberry Bushy Dwarf

Scientific name: *Raspberry bushy dwarf virus* (RBDV)

Raspberry bushy dwarf virus (RBDV) can cause serious losses in susceptible cultivars of red and black raspberries and blackberries, though it is less common in blackberries. RBDV occurs wherever raspberries are grown. The primary symptom of RBDV is crumbly fruit due to poor drupelet set (figure 9.7). Leaf chlorosis from very mild to bright yellow also develops on some cultivars of red raspberry and blackberry, but this

Fig. 9.7 **Crumbly berry of red raspberry caused by raspberry bushy dwarf virus.**

has not been observed on black or purple raspberries (figure 9.8). Plants infected with RBDV alone are rarely stunted. When RBDV occurs in mixed infections with other viruses, crumbly fruit symptoms generally are more severe and stunting may occur.

In many cultivars, infected plants are only recognized by the crumbly fruit symptom, though bright yellow chlorosis is very obvious in some cultivars. The name "Bushy Dwarf" is a misnomer since the virus rarely causes a bushy dwarf symptom in single infections. The disease name comes from plants that were doubly infected with RBDV and Black raspberry necrosis virus, but at the time only RBDV was isolated from the symptomatic plants.

RBDV is spread from plant to plant by pollen and, therefore, is difficult to control once the virus is present in

Fig. 9.8 **Raspberry bushy dwarf virus: infected Marion foliage and fruit.**

a field. The rate of spread is cultivar dependent. There are sources of resistance to RBDV, but in many cases resistant cultivars have inferior horticultural traits. Breeding for RBDV resistance is a high priority for most raspberry breeding programs around the world. The best strategy for growers is to use planting stock that has tested free of RBDV. Bees readily travel up to one-half mile, so isolation from infected plantings is also important. In larger plantings, blocks of susceptible cultivars should be isolated from one another with resistant cultivars planted between to serve as barriers for bee movement of pollen between susceptible cultivars. Wild brambles are often not a major concern for RBDV since pollination is inefficient across species, though planting black raspberries near wild black raspberries may be a problem since the native species, *Rubus occidentalis,* is also used commercially.

Blackberry Sterility

Cause unknown

Blackberry sterility is not fully understood, but is probably a symptom of a viral disease or a genetic disorder. Sterility occurs in all growing areas of the U.S. Although infected blackberries may grow more vigorously than healthy blackberries, they may either fail to set fruit at all, or if they do, the berries may be deformed.

To manage sterility, any blackberries that do not set fruit should be removed and burned. The roots should also be dug up to prevent new sterile shoots from growing. Only certified disease-free blackberries should be included in a new planting. The cultivar Darrow is known to be susceptible to this disorder.

Fig. 9.10 **White drupelet disorder of Heritage red raspberry.**

Fig. 9.9 **Sunscald on Royalty fruit.**

Sunscald (Sunburn)

Cause: Solar injury

While the exact nature of sunscald is not fully understood, it appears that berries exposed to direct, intense sunlight are especially prone to develop this condition. Affected drupelets have a bleached, whitened appearance at first, but eventually dry and collapse and are visually unattractive (figure 9.9). Sections of the fruit become brown and dry. Berries shaded by the canopy may also develop sunscald in the absence of direct sunlight when exposed to high temperatures.

This disorder is more common in blackberries than raspberries. There is some variation in susceptibility between types of blackberries; trailing types are less susceptible than erect or semi-erect blackberries. Variations in cultivar susceptibility also appear to exist within the same species.

White Drupelet Disorder

Cause: Solar injury

This disorder most commonly occurs on red raspberry and results from a combination of exposure to ultraviolet radiation and high temperature. Drupelets develop normally but remain white (figure 9.10). These white drupelets may occur singly or in groups. Since berries with white drupelet disorder vary from normal fruit only in the absence of pigment, they remain suitable for processing, but are usually unacceptable for fresh market sales. Research by Renquist and Hughes (1987, 1989) suggests that shading plants to reduce UV radiation may lessen the problem. Some differences in cultivar susceptibility to this disorder have also been noted.

Some have proposed other causes for white drupelet disorder in raspberries, such as tarnished plant bug feeding or powdery mildew infection. A certain mite feeding on blackberry drupelets causes them to discolor. The cause of white drupelets in blackberries is still unknown.

Fig. 9.11 **Early season symptoms of orange rust on blackberry.**

Fig. 9.12 **Masses of orange rust spores on the underside of a blackberry leaf.**

Leaf Diseases

Orange Rust

Scientific name: *Arthuriomyces peckianus* (E. Howe) Cummins and Y. Hiratsuka and *Gymnoconia nitens* (Schwein.) F. Kern & H.W. Thurston

Orange rust is a serious fungus disease attacking all cultivars of black and purple raspberries, erect blackberries, and most trailing blackberries. It does not attack red raspberries.

The disease is most easily identified in the spring. Young shoots that first develop are weak and spindly, with small, pale green or yellowish leaves (figure 9.11). Within two to three weeks, blisters form on the lower surface of the leaves and then rupture, producing masses of powdery, rust-colored fungus spores (figure 9.12). These leaves wither and drop off in late spring, and new leaves produced toward the tips of canes may appear normal, giving the impression that the plant has "grown out" of the disease. However, such canes will remain infected the following spring, producing a mass of spindly shoots with no blossoms.

The orange rust fungi overwinter within infected plants, which they colonize systemically (throughout the plant). Thus, new shoots arising from the roots or crowns of plants infected the previous year are already infected. The rust-colored spores produced upon the leaves of these shoots early in the growing season are spread by wind currents. The spores can infect the leaves of healthy plants under the proper environmental conditions. These conditions are not well defined, but are presumed to be relatively stringent.

On black raspberries, new leaf infections are confined to a small area, but they eventually produce a mass of brown or black spores in late summer or early fall. This second spore type then infects buds on cane tips that are just rooting, or new buds and shoots being formed

on the crowns of mature plants. The fungus grows down into the crown and root system. On blackberries, direct infection of healthy young shoots occurs by the rust-colored spores that are liberated in the spring, and then the fungus spreads into the below-ground portions of the new plant. In either case, infected shoots that arise during the following year produce a new crop of spores and the cycle continues. Disease spread may also occur through natural root grafting of adjacent infected and healthy plants.

Management of orange rust depends entirely on eliminating sources of new infections. New plantings should always be started from nursery stock known to be free of this disease. Any plants showing rust symptoms during the spring in which they are set out were already infected at the time of planting; they should be immediately destroyed before the fungal spores can be discharged.

Established plantings should be examined for orange rust every year during the first weeks of the growing season, when symptoms are easiest to observe. Any infected plants are economically worthless and should be dug up and destroyed promptly before they liberate a new crop of spores. The location of such plants should be clearly marked, and any new suckers that arise from root pieces left in the ground should be removed or sprayed with an approved systemic herbicide. Nearby wooded areas or fence rows should be searched for signs of wild brambles infected with orange rust, which should be destroyed.

Late Leaf Rust

Scientific name: *Pucciniastrum americanum* (Farl.) Arth. and *Pucciniastrum arcticum* Transzschel

Late leaf rust is a disease that affects only red and purple raspberries. It is a completely different disease than orange rust of black raspberries and blackberries, and the two should not be confused.

Because late leaf rust does not develop until late summer, it has traditionally been considered a disease of only minor importance on conventional floricane-fruiting cultivars. In some years, however, late leaf rust can cause significant economic damage on primocane-fruiting cultivars, which are in fruit during the period of disease development. Also, in New England, some floricane-fruiting cultivars contract late leaf rust as early as the green fruit stage, resulting in nearly 100% loss of marketable fruit. Festival, Nova, and Heritage cultivars appear to be extremely susceptible to late leaf rust.

Small, yellow spots develop on the upper surface of mature leaves in late summer or early fall (figure 9.13). Small blisters filled with powdery, rust-colored spores form on the undersides of these same leaves (figure 9.14). Heavily infected leaves may turn yellow and fall prematurely. Fruit infections may also occur during this period, developing as a mass of rust-colored spores on one to several of the individual drupelets of the aggregate berry (figure 9.15).

The disease cycle of late leaf rust is poorly understood. In most cases, the fungus appears to overwinter on the canes of infected raspberry plants, although it is not systemic like orange rust. Spores produced from the overwintering sites start a new round of leaf infections in the summer. The rust-colored spores produced from these infections then spread the disease to additional leaves and fruit.

Periods of free moisture are presumed necessary for infection to occur, but the specific effects of temperature and wetness duration have not been determined. In some locations, the fungus overwinters on white spruce trees, an alternate host, from which it infects raspberries the following year. However, the general presence of late leaf rust in areas free of white spruce suggests that the alternate host is not required for completion of the disease cycle.

Management measures are somewhat limited. Cultural practices that promote air circulation through the planting (such as thinning canes, narrowing rows, and weed management) help to quickly dry susceptible foliage and reduce the number of infections. Plantings should not be established in the vicinity of white spruce. If this is impractical, the removal of infected raspberry leaves and debris helps to prevent infections of the white spruce, disrupting the disease cycle and reducing (but not eliminating) disease pressure. The removal or eradication of white spruce in the vicinity of plantings is not recommended since the disease can occur in its absence. Fungicide options are limited. Although fungicides may be helpful for managing disease on primocane-fruiting cultivars, they are almost never needed on floricane-fruiting cultivars.

◄ Fig. 9.13
Late leaf yellow rust on the upper surface of a Heritage red raspberry leaf.

Fig. 9.14 ➤
Late leaf yellow rust spores on the lower surface of a Heritage red raspberry leaf.

◄ Fig. 9.15
Late leaf yellow rust infection of individual drupelets of Heritage red raspberry fruits.

Leaf Spot

Scientific name: *Sphaerulina rubi* Demaree & M.S. Wilcox

Leaf spot of raspberries affects susceptible cultivars of red, purple, and black raspberries. Blackberries appear immune to the raspberry leaf spot fungus, but are susceptible to a cane and leaf spot disease caused by a different fungus, *Septoria rubi* Westend., that does not infect raspberries.

Both diseases are most severe in seasons with frequent warm rains, such as those typically encountered in southern growing regions. However, highly susceptible cultivars such as Taylor may be heavily infected. The plants are prematurely defoliated and have increased susceptibility to winter injury. The following discussion will concentrate on the raspberry leaf spot disease.

Small, greenish-black spots first develop on the upper surface of young leaves, and then become whitish or gray with a distinct border as the leaf matures (figure 9.16). Individual leaflets may show anywhere from 1 to over 100 distinct spots, depending on the cultivar and severity of disease pressure. With time, infected tissue within these spots may fall out, producing a "shot hole" effect. Badly infected leaves may curl at the edges, dry up, and drop prematurely. Inconspicuous spots may also develop on the canes, particularly near their bases.

The fungus overwinters in inconspicuous cane lesions or infected fallen leaves. Spores produced from these sites are distributed the following spring by air currents and splashing rain, infecting young canes and leaves while they remain wet. Additional spores are produced from these new infection sites and are distributed by splashing rains throughout the summer, spreading the disease. Only young, growing tissues are susceptible to infection.

Management practices designed to promote good air circulation and rapid drying of foliage will limit disease severity. Where practical, fruiting canes should be removed immediately after harvest, and fallen leaves raked or cultivated before bud break to reduce fungal inoculum. Broad spectrum fungicides applied for managing other diseases also may provide control of leaf spot, but most materials specific for gray mold do not. Growers must check local extension recommendations and restrictions. Taylor is highly susceptible; Killarney, Canby, and Brandywine have also shown above-average levels of disease under New York conditions.

Powdery Mildew

Scientific name: *Sphaerotheca macularis* (Wallr.:Fr.)Lind.

Powdery mildew occurs on raspberries throughout North America especially when grown under tunnels or in greenhouses. However, only a few popular cultivars are highly susceptible to the disease, and the severity of disease can vary greatly from year to year.

Infected leaves may become covered with the white, powdery growth of the fungus, or may simply develop light green blotches on their surfaces (figure 9.17). Blotching that occurs early in the growing season is easily confused with the symptoms of mosaic virus. Infected shoot tips may become long and spindly with dwarfed leaves. Heavily infected plants may be stunted.

Fig. 9.16 **Leaf spot on red raspberry.**

The fungus overwinters within infected buds near the tips of heavily infected canes. Shoots that emerge from these buds the following spring are infected, and spores produced upon them are distributed by air currents to spread the disease. Repeated cycles of infection can continue throughout the summer. Unlike most fungal diseases, powdery mildew infections do not require periods of wetness in which to develop. However, they are more likely to become severe during humid weather conditions.

The easiest way to manage powdery mildew is to avoid planting susceptible cultivars. If susceptible cultivars are planted, cultural methods to promote good air circulation around canes will reduce disease severity. Removal of late-formed, mildewed suckers in the fall may also delay the start of the disease build-up in the spring. Some fungicides now registered for use on raspberries are effective against powdery mildew, but chemical control usually is not warranted.

Fig. 9.17 **Powdery mildew.**

Fig. 9.18 Leaf symptoms of raspberry mosaic disease on black raspberry.

Fig. 9.19 Stunting of black raspberry plant caused by raspberry mosaic disease.

Raspberry Mosaic Disease

Scientific name: *Rubus yellow net virus* (RYNV)*; black raspberry necrosis virus* (BRNV)*;* and an unnamed virus similar to raspberry leaf mottle virus.

Raspberry mosaic disease is caused by a complex of viruses. It is an extremely serious disease of black raspberries in the Northeast and is probably the most important factor limiting production where the disease occurs. Red raspberries are affected much less seriously, while purple raspberries are affected intermediately. Blackberries generally are not affected.

Symptoms are most prominent early in the season. On black raspberries, leaves show a mosaic pattern of light green blotches among the normal dark green background, and may develop large dark green blisters surrounded by yellowish tissue (figure 9.18). Such leaves are usually smaller than normal and may be deformed, although leaves produced during warmer summer weather are generally symptomless. Young shoot tips often turn black and die. Infected canes become progressively more stunted each year until they finally die (figure 9.19). The fruit on infected plants is small, seedy, and tasteless. Infected red raspberries may show varying reductions in vigor, and mild or inconspicuous leaf symptoms, depending on the cultivar.

Spread is almost entirely caused by a single insect, the large raspberry aphid, *Amphorophora agathonica*. The aphid picks up the virus as it feeds on infected raspberries, wild or cultivated, and then transmits it to healthy plants as it feeds on them. Spread can be very rapid, with

disease incidence increasing from a small percentage to a majority of the planting in a period of just two to three years. The activity of the aphid occurs primarily from mid-June through mid-August.

In regions where mosaic is common, management strategies are designed to delay rather than prevent the development of this disease, particularly on black raspberries. However, procedures that successfully delay the start of a mosaic epidemic by even one or two seasons can have a tremendous impact on the profitability of a planting.

First, a new planting of black raspberries should not be placed next to an old planting of black, purple, or red raspberries or blackberries. The old plants may be carriers of the disease, even if they appear symptomless. There is no absolute "safe" distance, but 150 to 200 yards between plantings should be a minimum, if at all practical. Similarly, a new planting of black raspberries must not be placed next to a wooded area containing wild brambles. All wild brambles in nearby fence rows or ditch banks should be destroyed.

Some newer purple and red raspberry cultivars such as Royalty and Titan are immune or highly resistant to colonization by the large raspberry aphid and are much slower to get the disease. Management of the aphid vector (carrier of disease) with insecticides may slow disease spread within a field, but is very unlikely to prevent its introduction.

Raspberry Leaf Curl

Cause: Uncharacterized virus

Raspberry leaf curl can cause serious yield losses where it occurs, but it is not as common as raspberry mosaic. Leaf curl is found throughout most of the Northeast, but reportedly is rare along the eastern seaboard south of New York. Both red and black raspberries are seriously affected, purple raspberries somewhat less so. Some blackberry cultivars show symptoms similar to those on red and black raspberries, but others remain symptomless.

Infected plants can be recognized in the field by their characteristic foliage—uniformly small leaves which curl downward and inward (figure 9.20). This symptom should not be confused with the leaf curling caused only by heavy aphid feeding. Growers should check the undersides of suspect leaves for the presence of large numbers of aphids. Leaves of infected red raspberry plants may be slightly yellow, whereas those of black raspberry often appear dark and waxy. Infected plants produce short, upright fruiting laterals, bearing small, crumbly fruit. New canes of infected plants become shorter each year until they may only reach a foot in height three to four years after the disease first appears. Chronically infected plants are always severely dwarfed, and produce few main canes.

Raspberry leaf curl is spread exclusively by the small raspberry aphid, *Aphis rubicola*. In New York, populations of this insect appear to reach a minor peak in late July and a major peak in early October. The small raspberry aphids are relatively inactive, and may spend their entire lives on a single leaf, although they are sometimes carried long distances on wind currents. Spread of leaf curl, therefore, is much slower than that of mosaic due to the different feeding habits of the respective aphid vectors. This fact, and the tendency of the small raspberry aphid to remain on affected foliage, makes a program of periodic inspection and removal of infected plants a practical means of limiting losses in fields where the disease does occur.

Cultural management strategies include the use of clean planting stock, not planting new fields near infected wild or cultivated raspberries, and quick removal and destruction of infected plants after they have been identified in a field. Insecticides may be used to limit populations of the aphid vector.

Root Diseases

Phytophthora Root Rot

Scientific name: *Phytophthora* spp., *P. fragariae* var. *rubi*, *P. megasperma*, *P. cactorum*, and others

Phytophthora root rot is caused by several related species of soil-borne fungi belonging to the genus *Phytophthora*. The disease can be very destructive on red and

Fig. 9.20 **Raspberry leaf curl on black raspberry.**

purple raspberries when conditions favor its development, but black raspberries and blackberries appear to be much less susceptible.

Although it appears commonly in the Midwest and Northeast, the disease has only lately been recognized as a serious problem. Phytophthora root rot has been identified as the cause of the decline of stands of red and purple raspberries previously thought to be suffering from winter injury or "wet feet."

The root rot is most commonly associated with heavy soils or portions of a planting where water accumulates, such as lower ends of rows, dips in the field, etc. Infections often occur in patches in the planting, which often expand over time.

Infected fruiting canes are often stunted with weak lateral shoots and leaves that yellow prematurely or scorch along the margins and between the veins (figure 9.21). Severely infected fruiting canes wilt and die as the weather turns warm before harvest (figure 9.22). Fewer new canes will emerge from within diseased patches, in contrast with normal numbers of canes that emerge when fruiting cane collapse is caused by winter injury, anthracnose, or cane blight. New canes may become infected, wilt, and die during their first year.

Because wilting and collapsing plants may be caused by other factors, the root systems of affected plants must be examined to diagnose Phytophthora root rot. Plants that are wilting but have not yet died should be dug up and the outer surface (epidermis) scraped from the main roots and crown. Tissue just beneath the epidermis should be white on healthy plants, but will be a characteristic red-brown on plants with Phytophthora root rot (figure 9.23). It will eventually turn dark brown as the tissue decays. A distinct line can often be seen where infected and healthy tissues meet, especially on the crown.

The fungi primarily persist in infected roots or as dormant resting spores in the soil. When the soil is moist, reproductive structures are formed on infected tissue or by germinating resting spores in the soil. Within each structure are many infective spores that are discharged into the soil when it becomes completely saturated with water. These spores then "swim" through the water-filled soil pores using specialized "tails" (flagella),

Fig. 9.21 **Leaf scorching and cane stunting on red raspberry caused by Phytophthora root rot.**

Fig. 9.22 **Wilting, collapsing red raspberry plants affected by Phytophthora root rot.**

Fig. 9.23 **Red-brown discoloration of infected root caused by Phytophthora root rot (*top*), healthy white root tissue (*bottom*); Root epidermis removed to reveal coloration.**

attach themselves to the plant's roots, and begin the infection process.

If water remains standing and oxygen is depleted from the root zone, the plant apparently becomes less capable of resisting the fungus's attempts at invasion. Infection becomes more likely and more severe. Thus, periods of excessive soil moisture effectively serve as infection periods for this disease. Each new infection site can serve as a source of additional infective spores, providing the potential for epidemic disease development in sites that are frequently wet or following a succession of several excessively wet seasons.

The keys to managing Phytophthora root rot are good soil drainage and proper cultivar selection. All brambles should be planted on well-drained soil, especially red raspberry cultivars that are highly susceptible to Phytophthora root rot, particularly Titan and Ruby. Canby, Taylor, Reveille, and Festival cultivars also appear to be very susceptible. Latham and Newburgh are the least susceptible red raspberry cultivars commonly grown in the Northeast and are the safest choices if red raspberries are to be planted on marginal ground. Royalty and Brandywine purple raspberries are also less susceptible than most reds. Black raspberries and blackberries appear to be relatively resistant to this disease, although they are not completely immune if grown in very wet soils. Growing plants on raised beds is one possible cultural method for minimizing root rot where drainage is occa-

sionally inadequate. However, supplemental irrigation must be available to get plants through drought periods. Amending soil with gypsum has also been shown to suppress Phytophthora.

The *Phytophthora* fungi are often introduced onto a farm by the movement of contaminated soil from runoff water, farm equipment, or symptomless nursery stock. Planting tissue-cultured propagules minimizes one potential source of contamination, although such plants may require extra care to get established. Tissue-cultured plants that were matured in a nursery field before digging are no less likely to be contaminated with *Phytophthora* than are conventionally propagated plants. Ideally, new bramble plantings should not be made on sites where brambles were previously grown. This minimizes the risk from *Phytophthora* and other soil-borne pathogens.

New fungicides have recently been developed that are very specific against *Phytophthora* and related fungi. These fungicides have effectively reduced the severity of Phytophthora root rot on red raspberries and may be useful as a component in an integrated management program on farms where the disease occurs. Consult local and state recommendations and restrictions.

Verticillium Wilt

Scientific name: *Verticillium albo-atrum* Reinke & Berthier

Verticillium wilt can be an extremely severe disease of black raspberries, but is generally much less serious on reds. Susceptibility among blackberry cultivars and types is variable.

During the first year of infection, leaves on the new canes of black and purple raspberry plants become pale green in mid-summer. These leaves may eventually turn yellow and drop prematurely, or the plant may appear to recover during cool fall weather. However, some buds will not break on infected fruiting canes the following spring. Leaves that do develop turn yellow, wilt, and die, starting at the bottom of the plant and moving progressively toward the top. Canes may eventually become completely defoliated, except for a few leaves at the top (figure 9.24).

Infected canes are usually stunted, and may develop streaks of blue in the bark before they finally wilt and die. Symptoms sometimes appear first on only one side of the plant, while the opposite side remains healthy for some time before also becoming infected. Symptoms on infected red raspberry canes are similar but less severe, and suckers arising away from the infected mother plant are often free of the disease, although their numbers may be reduced.

The fungus persists in the soil in an actively growing state or as dormant resting structures. Infection occurs when roots come in contact with the active fungus or a germinating resting structure. The disease is favored by cool, wet, spring weather. The fungus can infect through both healthy or wounded roots and root hairs. After initial penetration, the fungus grows into the water-conducting cells of the root (xylem). There, it produces spores that help spread the infection upward into the cane xylem with the normal flow of water. Infected xylem cells develop constrictions and become plugged by the growth of the fungus within them. Eventually,

the flow of water is so restricted that the canes wilt and die. Fungal structures are then returned to the soil as the dead roots decompose and spores become available to infect new plants.

Disease severity depends on the population of *Verticillium* in the soil at the time of planting, which is largely determined by the previous cropping history of the field. Fields with a recent history of highly susceptible crops are likely to contain dangerous levels of the fungus. Potatoes, tomatoes, eggplants, and peppers are particularly susceptible to Verticillium wilt. Squash, melons, strawberries, and stone fruit trees are less susceptible crops. Also, sites which have supported high levels of susceptible weed plants such as pigweed, nightshade, horse nettle, ground cherry, and lamb's quarters are also likely to contain high levels of the Verticillium wilt fungus. Such fields should be planted to a non-host crop for at least three to four years before raspberries, especially blacks and purple types, are planted. The fields can be fumigated with an approved material active against fungi. The risk of introducing the *Verticillium* fungus can be minimized by using planting stock from a reputable supplier.

Crown Gall

Scientific name: *Agrobacterium tumefaciens* (Smith & Townsend) Conn

Crown gall is a bacterial disease of plants that induces tumor-like growths. It occurs on a wide variety of plant species, including blackberries and red, black, and purple raspberries. (A similar disease, caused by the bacterium *Agrobacterium rubi* (Hildebrand) Starr & Weiss, also causes cane gall of black and purple raspberries; however, it is much less common in the north and will not be

◀ Fig. 9.24
Verticillium
wilt of black
raspberry.

Fig. 9.25 ➤
Crown gall on
roots of red
raspberry.

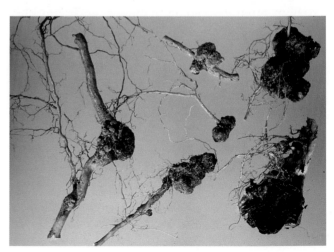

discussed here.) Crown gall may stunt and weaken seriously infected plants, but probably causes little economic damage in most fields where it occurs.

Galls produced on infected plants are rough, spongy-to-hard, tumorous growths up to an inch or more in diameter. On red raspberries, galls are found most often on the roots (figure 9.25). On black and purple raspberries, they are more common on the crown near the soil line. Galls are sometime produced on lower canes.

The crown gall bacteria persist in and on infected plant tissue in the soil. They are distributed throughout a field by any means that distributes soil. The bacterium enters a plant through wounds on the roots or crown caused by growth cracks, insect feeding, winter injury, or cultivation.

Once inside the plant, the bacteria cause nearby cells to begin multiplying and enlarging abnormally, creating the tumorous galls. As galls enlarge, they may disrupt the normal vascular system and interfere with the flow of water and nutrients. The amount of harm to the plant depends on the size, number, and placement of individual galls. The outer gall layers are filled with bacteria and provide inoculum for further disease spread as they are continuously shed into the surrounding soil.

Management procedures include: (1) planting only nursery stock that is free of any obvious galls on crowns or roots; (2) not planting into a field where crown gall has occurred previously, unless a non-host crop, such as strawberries or most vegetables, is grown for two or more years before replanting; and (3) minimizing injury to root and crown systems during farm operations such as cultivation.

Winter Injury
Cause: Cold temperatures

Winter injury is a common ailment of *Rubus* spp. in the north. Winter injury can manifest itself in a variety of ways. A late frost in the spring can result in the death of flower buds on floricane-fruiting varieties and lead to a total crop loss (figure 9.26). Similarly, early autumn frosts often terminate fruiting on primocane-fruiting cultivars. Very cold temperatures during winter can kill overwintering floricanes and may even damage the root system. The most common form of winter injury, however, results from fluctuating temperatures during the dormant season. This injury occurs after plants have achieved their chilling requirements, and plants are no longer fully dormant. Warm spells (i.e., fluctuating warm

Fig. 9.26 **Winter injury to floricanes.**

and cold periods) during the winter tend to damage the less cold-tolerant tissues. Often injury occurs in March when temperatures fluctuate more, rather than in midwinter, when plants are completely dormant.

Winter injury usually kills or damages the overwintering floricanes but not new primocanes. In contrast, plants affected by *Phytophthora* or *Verticillium* do not produce a healthy flush of primocanes. Occasionally, winter injury is not apparent until fruiting laterals begin to grow. This is because only part of the vascular tissue is damaged. With the onset of warm temperatures, the injured vascular connections cannot supply the laterals with water, so the laterals collapse. This can be mistaken for Verticillium wilt. However, winter injury rarely affects the roots whereas *Verticillium*-infected plants may produce distinct root symptoms.

The only reasonable means to preventing winter injury are avoiding frost pockets, establishing plantings in areas with good air drainage to minimize exposure to damaging spring frosts, and planting cultivars that are sufficiently winter hardy.

Nematodes

Plant parasitic nematodes can cause significant yield losses to many horticultural crops. The extent of loss depends on the crop, nematode species, and soil population level. Common nematodes in fruit crops are root lesion (*Pratylenchus*) and root knot (*Meloidogyne*). Pin (*Pratylenchus* sp.), dagger (*Xiphinema* sp.), bulb and stem (*Ditylenchus*), and cyst

Fig. 9.27 **Root lesion nematode damage on raspberry roots.**

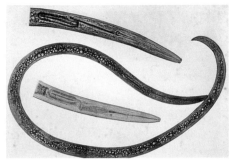

Fig. 9.28 **Microscopic dagger nematode.**

(*Heterodera* sp.) nematodes occasionally cause yield losses to some crops in isolated fields. The dagger nematode is mainly a virus vector on grape, raspberry and apple. Symptoms of nematode injury include:

a) uneven plant growth
b) poor plant establishment
c) weakening plants over time
d) poor root growth

Root-lesion nematode

The root-lesion nematode causes discoloration and tiny, brown, scratch-like lesions on younger white roots. These lesions merge to form large, brown areas. Initially, a proliferation of new young roots forms in response to root injury, giving the feeder roots a brushy, or witch's broom appearance (figure 9.27). Severely infested plants have thinner and fewer numbers of canes per crown. Up to 25% of the first-year canes may be killed by severe infestations of these nematodes.

Dagger nematode

Dagger nematodes (figure 9.28) spread Tomato ringspot virus, which causes crumbly berries, mottled leaves, and cane die-back (for more information on this nematode, see the section on Tomato ringspot virus, or "Crumbly Berry," on page 97).

Thresholds

Nematode populations above economic thresholds can significantly reduce yields (table 9.1).

Nematode problems are most often found in sandy loam and sandy soils. Always sample these soils for nematode populations before planting fruit crops. Clay or clay loam soils do not usually have root lesion nematode problems, but should be sampled for dagger nematodes before planting virus-susceptible raspberries, grapes, or tree fruit. Sampling soils for nematodes is especially important before planting in replant sites, or where susceptible crops have been recently grown.

Nematode Control

Use a combination of the following methods to manage nematodes:

a) Rotate susceptible crops with non-host crops for several years.
b) Plant nematode-suppressing cover crops.
c) Destroy residual crop roots.
d) Plant tolerant fruit cultivars.
e) Control weeds.
f) Use soil fumigation when necessary.

Suppressive cover crops—Examples of nematode-suppressing cover crops include the following: oilseed radish, certain oriental mustards (e.g., cultivars Forage and Cutlass), specific sorghum × sudan-grass hybrids, African marigolds (e.g., cultivars Crackerjack and Creole), and Canadian Forage Pearl Millet 101. These cover crops can reduce plant-parasitic nematode populations. Not all

Table 9.1 **Thresholds for nematodes on raspberry**

Type of nematode	Control when levels reach:
Root lesion nematode	1,000/kg soil
Root knot	1,000/kg soil
Pin	5,000/kg soil
Dagger	100/kg soil
Bulb and stem	100/kg soil

cultivars reduce nematode populations. One or more years of nematode-suppressing cover crops may be required to successfully reduce nematodes below economic thresholds.

Cover crops suppress nematodes in different ways. Canadian Forage Pearl Millet 101, for example, inhibits the ability of nematodes to reproduce in its root system. Certain cultivars of African marigolds produce a root exudate that kills nematodes in the soil.

Nematode-suppressing cultivars of oilseed radish and certain oriental mustards produce isothiocyanate in their leaves, stems, and petioles, which is toxic to the plant-parasitic nematode when released into the soil. To be effective, these crops must be cut green and immediately incorporated into the soil.

Exclude cover crops such as clovers and buckwheat from rotations since these are excellent hosts for root-lesion nematodes. If a cereal grain is to be used for one whole growing season, wheat or barley is the best choice. See table 2.1, "Characteristics of green manure crops and cover crops," on page 14 for more information.

Weed control—Nematode populations can build on many weed species. A good weed control program is essential the year before planting fruit crops. Weeds should also be controlled when nematode-suppressing cover crops are grown.

Fallowing—Keeping land fallow the year before planting also reduces nematode numbers. A disadvantage to fallow land is increased susceptibility to soil erosion. In raspberry plantings, choose ground covers between the rows that do not support nematodes, such as annual or perennial ryegrass.

Fumigation—Preplant soil fumigation is the most effective method of controlling nematode problems. Fumigants can be broadcast over the whole field or applied only in rows where raspberries will be planted. Check local state or provincial regulations regarding the choice and application of fumigants. Treat areas that harbor potential nematode problems before planting. CAUTION—Fumigants are toxic. Read the label and follow instructions regarding procedures for handling and application. Applicator permits are required in most regions. Always follow manufacturer's directions carefully concerning dosage and methods of use. A suitable respirator and protective clothing, etc., must be worn by the applicator.

In Summary:

Here is a checklist to assist in bramble disease management in both new and existing plantings:

Disease Control Strategies—Preplant

- ❏ Use preplant cover crops for suppression of weeds and soil-borne diseases.
- ❏ Select disease-resistant cultivars whenever possible.
- ❏ Plant only certified disease-indexed planting stock.
- ❏ Do not establish new plantings next to wild brambles.
- ❏ Select sites with good soil and air drainage.
- ❏ Orient crop rows with prevailing breezes.
- ❏ Space plants properly.

Disease Control Strategies—Established Plantings

- ❏ Maintain overall plant health.
- ❏ Thin to proper cane density.
- ❏ Maintain narrow rows.
- ❏ Avoid high rates of nitrogen fertilizer; succulent growth encourages disease development.
- ❏ Prune out old fruiting canes.
- ❏ Remove dead and dying canes after harvest.
- ❏ Promptly remove and destroy prunings, infected canes, fruit, and debris.
- ❏ Consider delayed-dormant applications of lime sulfur to reduce overwintering inoculum.
- ❏ Scout plants weekly for disease symptoms.
- ❏ Get a correct diagnosis.
- ❏ Take control measures promptly.
- ❏ Evaluate effectiveness of control measures; modify as needed.
- ❏ Keep records!

Further Reading

Converse, R.H. (ed.). 1987. *Virus Diseases of Small Fruits*. USDA-ARS Handbook 631. Washington, DC: Agricultural Research Service, United States Department of Agriculture (USDA).

Cornell University Department of Horticulture. "The Berry Diagnostic Tool." Ithaca, NY: Cornell University. WWW.HORT.CORNELL.EDU/DIAGNOSTIC. A pictorial diagnostic tool for berry crops.

Ellis, M.A., R.H. Converse, R.N. Williams, and B. Williamson (eds.). 1991. *Compendium of Raspberry and Blackberry Diseases and Insects*. St. Paul, MN: The American Phytopathological Society Press.

Funt, R.C., M.A. Ellis, and C. Welty. 2005. *Midwest Small Fruit Pest Management Handbook*. Columbus, OH: Ohio State University Press.

CHAPTER TEN

Weed Management

Managing weeds is a fundamental requirement for raspberry and blackberry production, and demands a significant amount of resource and attention from the grower. Without weed management, attempts at nutrient management and integrated pest management are obstructed, harvesting is difficult, and yields are depressed. Weed management is particularly important in the planting year, for if the berry plants establish well, then weeds are easier to exclude and manage in subsequent years.

Eliminate Weeds Prior to Planting

A combination of approaches is required to manage weeds effectively. Eliminating perennial weeds prior to planting is the most critical step. Planting cover crops, deep plowing, discing, spraying herbicides like glyphosate (e.g., Roundup), or covering the site with black plastic for several months can all help manage weeds prior to planting brambles. Once bramble plants are in the ground, though, these effective tactics cannot be used. There is no combination of herbicides that will remove all established perennial weeds in the row without significantly damaging the bramble plants.

A broad-spectrum, postemergent, systemic herbicide can reduce the number of perennial weeds in a field, especially if it is applied the year before planting. Growers generally find that two applications work best—one applied in late spring, then another applied in late summer of the year prior to planting. Applying the herbicide too early in spring could result in missing late-emerging perennial weeds, such as bindweed and nutsedge.

Preplant cover crops can be grown to compete with emerging weeds, provided they do not produce seeds themselves (see "Site Selection and Preparation," chapter two). Many cover crops are available that can be grown the year prior to berries to suppress weeds and to add organic matter to the soil. These can be effective at suppressing annual weeds after application of a broad-spectrum, postemergent herbicide like glyphosate (e.g., Roundup). Specific hybrids of sudan grass and marigolds have a suppressive effect on nematodes, and many cover crop rotations can reduce disease inoculum. Cover crops that are unrelated to berries (such as grasses and grains) usually make good rotational companions. Alternatively, food or fiber crops (other than brambles) can be grown to enable growers to use herbicides labeled for the primary weed species present in the field. This allows the grower to manage problem weeds on a site prior to planting brambles. In these situations, however, there is the possibility of herbicide carryover, depending on the herbicide used and the raspberry plant's sensitivity to it. Sweet corn, in particular, is a good rotational crop with berries, especially if the stover is worked into the soil to retain organic matter. For example, early sweet corn can be followed with oats to provide significant weed suppression in a single year. Fumigation also can reduce the weed seed bank prior to planting, but this option is expensive and is becoming limited due to growing environmental concerns and availability (see Site Selection and Site Preparation, chapter two).

Weed Management around the Planting

Growers may spend considerable time managing weeds in the berry field, but do little to manage weeds around the perimeter. These perimeter weeds can serve as a significant source of weed seeds. Mow the perimeters of the berry fields as one would a lawn to keep weeds from flowering and going to seed. Flowering weeds can also host tarnished plant bugs and other berry pests.

Weed Management in the Row

Herbicides labeled for bramble plantings are not effective against all weeds, and the application timing is restricted to narrow periods. Therefore, rotations, hand weeding, mulching in the planting year, hoeing, and

Fig. 10.1 **Mulching with straw or plastic during the first year.**

are sensitive to most postemergent herbicides for broadleaf weeds (particularly glyphosate), and are sensitive to preemergent herbicides early in the planting year (figures 10.2, 10.4, and 10.5).

When weeds do appear in the row during the growing season, growers must hand-weed to remove them. Cultivation is useful to a limited extent, but raspberries and blackberries have shallow roots. Damaging them can affect future cane production. Furthermore, cultivation that damages roots can increase the susceptibility of berry plants to disease.

cultivation are necessary supplements to chemical weed management. Herbicides alone will not rescue a weedy berry field.

Mulching raspberries the first year with straw or planting them through plastic are effective ways of suppressing weeds in the row (figure 10.1). However, mulches are only good for the first few months because canes have to eventually grow to replace those that will fruit and die. Do not mulch around bramble plants after the establishment year, especially if soils are heavy, as it may encourage root rot.

Herbicides are available that suppress weed seed germination. These are best applied in the late fall or early spring—not during the growing season. Attempting to kill weeds in the raspberry row with herbicides during the growing season is risky. Raspberries and blackberries

Weed Management between Rows

Growers either use clean cultivation between rows or plant grass and mow the alleyways to manage between-row weeds. Cultivation has limitations because it promotes further weed seed germination, degrades soil quality, and can disturb the shallow root system. Further, it is limited by weather and the location of the weeds in the beds. However, cultivation is a relatively simple procedure that can improve soil aeration. Cultivation can dilute any herbicide that was applied previously and can bring new weed seeds to the soil surface where they can germinate. Cultivation should be performed before applying an herbicide, unless the herbicide is meant to be preplant incorporated.

Shallow cultivation is preferred over deep cultivation in established plantings. When used every ten to fourteen

Fig. 10.2 **Sensitivity of tissue-cultured plants to simazine applied at planting (*left*) and to oryzalin applied at planting (*above*).**

days between rows in the establishment year, cultivation can eliminate most weeds. Cultivation before harvest can result in dirty fruit, so it is usually done prior to fruit set and at the end of the season in fruiting fields.

By seeding grass in the alleyways, growers can manage the vegetation with mowing (figure 10.3). Perennial ryegrass, a non-creeping fescue, or a combination of these, makes an attractive ground cover. Advantages of a grass alleyway include: increasing organic matter; helping to stabilize erodable soils; and using excess water, which reduces mud and soil compaction from machinery and allows field operations to continue shortly after a rain. A seeded cover crop also can displace weeds that would otherwise occupy the niche. Competitively displacing weeds with a more desirable species is better than allowing weeds to dominate, or destroying soil structure through repeated mechanized cultivation. The primary drawback

Fig. 10.3 **Grass middle in a young raspberry planting.**

of cover crops is that they can compete with bramble plants for nitrogen and moisture. Managing cover crops by mowing or chemical suppression can minimize this competition.

Companion grass mixes (a mixture of two or more compatible species) will harm brambles if allowed to crowd the rows. Experiments have shown that no amount of irrigation or nitrogen fertilizer will fully compensate for the impact of unmanaged weeds or sod grasses on perennial crops. Therefore, a weed-free strip approximately 3–5 feet wide should be maintained for the bramble row using shallow cultivation and/or preemergent herbicides.

Herbicide Specifics

Weeds are the major pest of berry growers, so most producers use all the tools at their disposal, including herbicides. Herbicides need to be applied correctly to maximize performance. Herbicide performance can be optimized by:

- using the right herbicide for the soil type, problem weed, and time of year
- using the appropriate rate
- timing the application properly
- properly placing the herbicide
- providing conditions most appropriate for activation

Preemergent herbicides interfere with weed-seedling establishment, so conditions must be favorable for weed growth (warm, moist soils) for these herbicides to work.

Herbicide glossary

Herbicide: any chemical substance designed to kill or inhibit the growth of certain plants that are considered undesirable, i.e., weeds.

Preemergent herbicides are designed to keep weed seeds from germinating.

Postemergent herbicides are designed to kill weeds that have grown to the seeding stage or beyond.

Selective herbicides are designed to kill only one type of plant, such as only broadleaf weeds or only grasses.

Nonselective herbicides are designed to kill a larger number of plant types or possibly any plant it contacts.

Contact herbicides kill only the plant parts on which the chemical is deposited. They are most effective against annual weeds.

Systemic herbicides are absorbed either by the roots or leaves of a weed and then travel within the plant system (**translocate**) to tissues that may be remote from the point of application. They are particularly useful against established perennial weeds.

➤ Fig. 10.4
Terbacil injury
in an established
planting of
Royalty.

Fig. 10.5 ➤
Simazine injury
in an established
planting of red
raspberry.

◄ Fig. 10.6
Glyphosate
injury in an
established
planting.

Herbicides must be moved into the top few inches of soil where the weed seeds exist, usually through rainfall or irrigation. Herbicides on the soil surface or in a zone below the weed seeds will not be effective. In most soils, about ½ to 1 inch of water is required to move the herbicide into the soil. In sandy soils, the water requirement is less. For some herbicides on sandy soils, 1 inch of water may be excessive because the herbicide is very soluble in water and does not bind readily to the sand particles. Herbicides that have a low solubility and bind to the soil particles are desirable, except where the potential for surface runoff exists.

Preemergent herbicides should be applied just prior to the seed germination period of most problem weeds. Unfortunately, weed seeds germinate over an extended period of time, but it is not practical to have high levels of herbicide residue present in the soil at all times. Some

weeds germinate during warm weather (such as foxtails), and others germinate in fall (such as chickweed); but the primary period of weed seed germination is in the spring. Most growers apply an herbicide in late fall or early spring to suppress spring weeds. Some herbicides applied in the fall will move into the seed germination zone during winter and be available to inhibit seedling establishment in the spring. Some very soluble herbicides applied in the fall may wash out of the seed germination zone during winter and consequently should be applied in the spring. Raspberries and blackberries can be sensitive to preemergent herbicides, so avoid contacting actively growing plants.

Postemergent herbicides should be applied on an as-needed basis. These selective herbicides are used to manage specific problem weeds, such as a grass or a broadleaf weed. They must be applied when weeds are actively growing. Apply grass herbicides when weeds are small in late spring. Application during a drought or when grasses are more than 8 inches tall results in limited control. Selective herbicides for grass control provide no residual activity and can be applied directly over established bramble plants.

Grass-selective herbicides can prevent alley sods or

grass weeds from invading the rows without much risk of accidental damage to canes. However, the fescues, especially fine-leaf fescues, are somewhat resistant to grass-selective herbicides. Herbicides that are effective against these grasses are also toxic to brambles and should not be used. Use non-creeping, fine-leaf fescues in alleys between the rows because these will not spread readily into crop rows and will minimize the need for herbicide sprays.

Some systemic herbicides are labeled for use for spot control of emerged weeds in established plantings. However, experience has shown that raspberries and blackberries are extremely sensitive to glyphosate-based materials (figure 10.6) and may show damage even when the herbicide is applied carefully. Nonselective contact herbicides that are not translocated also can be used for spot control, and are safer to use. Both types of herbicides can damage bramble plants, so avoid direct contact with the crop.

Summary

Use four strategies for managing weeds in bramble plantings. First, eliminate perennial weeds from the planting site one year prior to planting. Second, prevent weed seeds from migrating into the planting by keeping the area around the berry field mowed. Third, prevent weed seeds from becoming established by using cultivation, establishment-year mulching, and herbicides at the appropriate times. Fourth, eliminate weeds when they appear and before they produce seeds. A berry field with few weeds has fewer insect and disease problems and will be a pleasant place for customers to pick.

Further Reading

DiTommaso, A., and A.K. Watson. 2003. *Weed Identification, Biology, and Management.* Montreal, Canada: McGill University.

Uva, R.H., J.C. Neal, and J.M. DiTomaso. 1997. *Weeds of the Northeast.* Ithaca, NY: Cornell University Press.

CHAPTER ELEVEN

Spray Application Technology

Introduction

Applying crop protectants and foliar nutrients is an important part of bramble production. This chapter is designed to familiarize the grower with various aspects of spray technology as it relates to the application of spray products to bramble crops.

An increasing awareness of environmental pollution, along with concerns about operator contamination, has resulted in increased pesticide-use legislation. This in turn has exerted considerable pressure on the food and farming sectors to not only improve existing technologies, but to also develop many new and sometimes novel pesticide application techniques. Many of these new developments in spray technology have the potential to reduce both the direct and indirect costs involved in applying pesticides. The main expense associated with spray applications is product cost. Product cost in many cases continues to rise as the pool of available products shrinks due to resistance development and the fewer numbers of new products being developed. Other major costs to consider are those of labor, energy, equipment maintenance and/or replacement, and timeliness of application.

A full understanding of the principles of spray-application technology, coupled with informed decisions on product selection, equipment selection, calibration, operation, and maintenance will assist the grower to produce high-quality bramble fruit while minimizing crop protection costs, risks to operators, and impact on the environment.

Principles of Spray Application

Product Selection

As with many other undertakings, the best success occurs when the right tools are used for the job. Correct identification of the insect, disease, or weed problem to be managed is critical to minimizing its impact on bramble production. Have good diagnostic resources and/or references at your disposal on the farm or online to help in making your initial diagnosis. Consult the local cooperative extension office or regional specialist if the pest or problem cannot be identified with the resources at hand. Alternatively, send a sample to a diagnostic lab for further testing or confirmation.

Once a correct diagnosis of the problem has been made, the product or products to be used in its management may be selected. Consider the potential alternatives in regard to formulation, re-entry interval, drying time, product durability, tank mix compatibilities, available application equipment, and product cost per acre. Carefully follow all label instructions when applying products and determining appropriate rates. Use sufficient volume of liquid and tank pressure to get thorough coverage of soil or plant surfaces. Store any unused product according to manufacturer instructions.

A Word of Advice Regarding Resistance Management

As brambles constitute a relatively small market share of sales for chemical companies, fewer pesticide products are being made available for use on these crops as compared to other major fruit crops, such as apples or stone fruit.

To maximize the efficacy and minimize resistance development of the limited products available, it is wise to alternate product chemistries whenever possible. See product label instructions for more specific information on managing resistance development.

Application Timing

Most products must be applied to the target at a specific growth stage of the crop, weed, insect, or disease. Timeliness is crucial if sprays are to be effective. Applying the spray mix too early may result in its becoming ineffective before the target pest or disease is present. Applying sprays too late may lead to increased disease levels or insect activity.

Existing or projected weather conditions must also receive serious consideration in terms of application timing. Is there sufficient time to get the application on before a rain event? Will the product have time to dry on surfaces before precipitation starts? Does the label list any concerns in terms of applications during temperature extremes?

Coverage

Good coverage of the target is essential. Poor spray coverage is a major factor contributing to poor pest control. Uneven coverage increases the amount of product that must be applied in order to provide adequate control and may increase the number of sprays required to keep the pest from becoming established. Plant canopy (leaf surface) size and shape will affect the application volume necessary to provide good coverage. The old adage "you should spray until the leaves drip" is misguided; this usually requires far more material than necessary for effective control. Likewise, lowering spray rates below label recommendations can lead to inadequate coverage and, consequently, poor control. Always use the optimum volume to provide thorough coverage and control, based on plant size and density, and the spray equipment used.

Drift Management

Drift of pesticide spray is an important and costly problem facing pesticide applicators. Drifting pesticide can result in damage to susceptible off-target crops, environmental contamination, and a lower-than-intended rate to the target crop, thus reducing the effectiveness of the pesticide. Pesticide drift also affects neighboring properties, often leading to concern and debate.

There are two types of drift: airborne drift, which is often very noticeable, and vapor drift. The amount of vapor drift will depend upon atmospheric conditions such as humidity, temperature, and the product being applied.

Vapor drift can even occur days after an application is made. Drift is influenced by many inter-related factors including spray pressure, droplet size, nozzle type and size, sprayer design, weather conditions, and the operator. Drift may be reduced by: applying sprays only under calm conditions; using appropriate nozzle types, pressure, and orientation; adding adjuvants; and spraying at night.

Operator Safety

At all times, when handling concentrate or dilute pesticide, wear the protective clothing specified on the product label, which may include:

- Face shield
- Respirator or Particle mask (change as recommended by manufacturer)
- Coverall (1 or 2 piece)
- Trousers
- Hood
- Gloves
- Boots

Also have:

- Adequate washing facilities—soap and water, paper towels
- First aid kit
- Access to an emergency contact (phone, radio)

Put on and take off protective clothing in an orderly manner avoiding contact with contaminated surfaces (figure 11.1).

Whenever gloves have to be removed, thoroughly wash their exterior with soap and water and wipe off surplus moisture before removal.

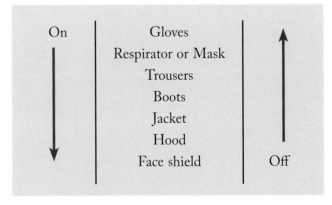

Fig. 11.1 **Follow a specific order for dressing and undressing prior to and after a spray application.**

Always remove gloves and thoroughly wash hands in soap and water, and dry well before smoking or attending to personal needs.

At the end of each work period (e.g., before meal breaks), thoroughly wash the outsides of gloves in soap and water and wipe off surplus moisture, thoroughly wash down overalls, then wash hands thoroughly as in specified above.

Always put on, remove, hang to dry, and store protective clothing away from restrooms and eating places, stored personal clothing, personnel areas of vehicles, and sources of contamination. Replace damaged items promptly, especially gloves.

Sprayer Basics

The basic purpose of the sprayer is to deliver nutrients and crop protectants from the sprayer to the desired target such as soil, crop, or non-crop plants. The basic components of a sprayer consist of a tank to carry the spray mix, and a pump to provide agitation and deliver the spray through a pressure regulator to the nozzles. The spray is carried from the nozzle to the target via hydraulic pressure or air assistance.

Bramble sprayers are usually air-assisted machines, either traditional airblast sprayers or modern directed-deposition sprayers, such as vertical booms. Growers of small areas may be able to use a back-pack sprayer or a hand-held system.

Sprayer Tanks

Sprayer tanks vary in size from a few gallons on a backpack sprayer to 500 gallons on a large, trailed machine. Modern tanks are made from corrosion-resistant materials such as plastic, fiberglass, or stainless steel. Stainless steel is the strongest but also the heaviest. A large hatch, fitted with a lid and a strainer, provides access for filling and cleaning. The use of tank rinsing aids (small spinning discs or nozzle heads) fitted in the top of the tank are recommended. They reduce the amount of washing water (rinsate) and time required to wash out sprayer tanks and reduce the potential for operator contamination.

Many modern sprayers are fitted with a self-fill hose for water and an induction bowl for filling to reduce the risk of operator contamination and environmental pollution caused by pesticide spills. An induction bowl consists of a bowl with a water flushing system, usually at knee-height, eliminating the need to climb onto the sprayer or lift pesticide containers over head. Induction bowls usually contain an integral rinsing system to clean empty containers. There is also a trend towards closed-transfer devices, a control that connects the pesticide container directly to a lid on the sprayer or induction bowl, again reducing the risk of contamination for the operator.

Sprayer Agitators

Tank agitation is extremely important to ensure that chemicals are well mixed and remain in solution (tank contents can settle out if agitation is insufficient or fails). The sprayer pump typically provides both flow for agitation and flow to the nozzles.

Sprayer Pumps

A sprayer pump should have a high capacity to ensure a good flow to the nozzles as well as providing good agitation for the tank contents.

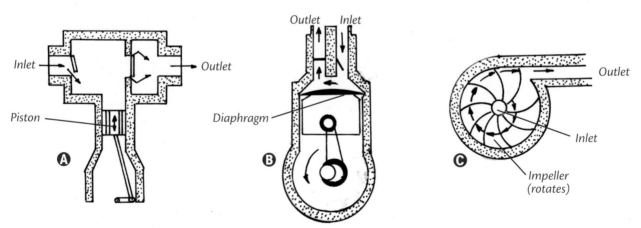

Fig. 11.2 ❹ Piston pump, ❺ Diaphragm pump, and ❻ Centrifugal pump.

Table 11.1 **Characteristics of different pump types.**

Pump Characteristics	Centrifugal pump	Piston pump	Diaphragm pump
Materials handled	Any liquid	Any liquid	Most liquids, although some product solvents may damage the rubber diaphragm
Durability	Long life	Long life	Long life
Pressure ranges (psi)	1-200	Up to 1000	Up to 600
Flow rates (gpm)	1-20	1-60	1-60
Operating speeds (rpm)	2,000-4000	600-1800	200-1200

Centrifugal, diaphragm, diaphragm/piston, or piston pumps are found on airblast or directed-deposition sprayers (figure 11.2, table 11.1). The use of a diaphragm or piston pump (a positive-displacement pump), while more expensive than a centrifugal pump, means fewer moving parts in contact with the solution. Growers tend to favor positive-displacement pumps because they are self-priming and can produce high pressures.

Centrifugal pumps are very simple in their construction, are generally inexpensive, and have low maintenance requirements. However, they are not capable of producing pressures in excess of 200 pounds per square inch (psi).

Strainers

Adequate filtration is very important to ensure that uniform sprayer output is maintained and remains accurate; inadequate filtration results in excessive nozzle wear and nozzle blockages. If a grower is intending to use wettable powders and fine sprays, then extra in-line filters should be fitted. Strainers should be fitted in three main places: the tank opening, before or after the pump, and at each nozzle (table 11.2). Filter accessibility is very important, and maintenance should be carried out at frequent intervals.

Table 11.2 **Recommended strainers for adequate filtration.**

Location	Mesh # openings per linear inch
Tank opening	12-25
Suction line: roller pump	15-40
Suction line: centrifugal pump	12-16
Pressure line	25-100
Nozzle tip	50 -100

Sprayer Nozzles

Nozzles are extremely important in creating the correct spray for a given target. Nozzles:

- Control the *amount* of spray—Gallons per acre (GPA).
- Determine the *uniformity* of the application.
- Affect the *coverage* of the target.
- Influence the *drift* potential.

Nozzles used on bramble sprayers are usually either hydraulic or air-shear type. Most airblast or boom sprayers use hydraulic nozzles although there are a number of airblast sprayers which use air-shear nozzles (figures 11.3 and 11.4).

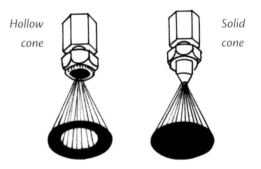

Fig. 11.3 Hydraulic sprayer nozzles.

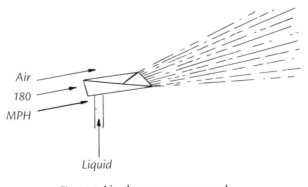

Fig. 11.4 Air shear sprayer nozzle.

It is the combination of optimum droplet volume and number that adhere to the leaves that will provide good insect and disease control. It must be stressed that too large a droplet will result in poor coverage, as much of the target will be missed; too fine a droplet will result in off-target drift and, equally important, lead to evaporation of droplets prior to reaching the target, especially in hot weather. A droplet with twice the diameter of another has four times the area and eight times the volume. Eight small droplets having the same total volume as one larger droplet will provide twice the coverage of the larger droplet. Conversely, for the same volume of liquid, when you halve the diameter of a droplet you increase the number of droplets eight-fold. For example, when a single 200 micron droplet is halved to 100 microns, you disperse its liquid into eight of these smaller droplets. Halve them again to 50 microns and you now get 64 droplets, etc. (see figure 11.5).

Hydraulic nozzles regulate the spray by the orifice size in the nozzle tip and the pressure of the system. Low pressure and a large hole create large droplets, small orifices and high pressures create small droplets. As the liquid passes through the orifice, the pressure forces the liquid to break up into droplets in the range of 10–350 microns (1 micron = 1/25,000 of an inch, 100 microns is the typical thickness of human hair). Application rate or flow rate is adjusted by changing nozzles.

Air-shear nozzles are found on some airblast sprayers and use the airstream to break up the spray liquid into fine droplets. The air passes a shear plate at 150–400 mph. Air-shear nozzles operate at low pressures, 15–35 psi and, as a result, have very low wear rates. The simple design is popular with some growers, and changing application rate or flow rate is only a matter of regulating liquid flow to the outlet via a valve or a disc with holes in it. However, the high-speed air can create many fine droplets which can lead to drift problems, especially if there is very little canopy present.

Nozzle Selection Technique

Correct nozzle selection is one of the most important, yet inexpensive, aspects of pesticide application. A nozzle's droplet size spectrum determines spray deposition and drift. Small droplets, less than 100 microns, drift in the air, whereas larger droplets, over 300 microns, tend to bounce off of leaves.

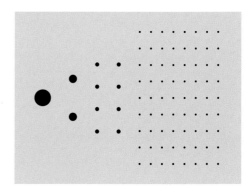

Fig. 11.5
Reducing droplet size increases coverage for the same volume of liquid.

A number of pesticide manufacturers have adopted the ASAE/BCPC nozzle selection system and now state on the pesticide label the spray classification needed for their product. Reference nozzles, tested in a laboratory using a laser analyzer, are classified according to the characteristics of the spray produced. Very fine, fine, medium, coarse, and very coarse are the categories of spray. Label recommendations now make nozzle selection far easier for the sprayer operator. A general guideline to follow for nozzle selection is:

- Fine spray quality for fungicides and insecticides
- Medium spray quality for herbicides
- Coarse spray quality for pre-emergent sprays

Weather conditions, particularly wind and its effect upon drift, must always be taken into consideration when selecting nozzles. If the label or supplier makes no recommendation concerning nozzles or spray quality, then a decision on desired spray quality must be made by the applicator, taking three matters into consideration:

- The target
- The product
- The risk of drift

Spray drift has long been a problem on many farms and neighboring properties. A number of nozzle manufacturers now offer low-drift nozzles to reduce drift.

Nozzle designs

Flat Fan Nozzles

Flat fan nozzles, when properly spaced along the boom and with the boom at the proper height above the spray surface, apply a uniform spray pattern. These nozzles are widely used in agricultural applications. Flat fan nozzles get their name from the shape of the spray pattern they produce, which resembles an inverted V or a hand-held folding fan (hence the name "flat fan").

Conventional flat fan nozzles—These nozzles produce droplets in the range of 10–450 microns. Nozzles with 80° angle produce coarser droplets than 110° at the same flow rate, but 80° nozzles require the boom to be set at 17–19 inches, whereas 110° nozzles can be set lower at 15–18 inches above the target. (The lower the boom is above the target, the less chance of drift.) Spray quality is fine to medium at 15–60 psi.

Pre-orifice flat fan nozzles—The internal design of this nozzle reduces the internal operating pressure compared to a conventional flat fan, resulting in coarser droplets (high pressure creates fine droplets, low pressure creates coarser droplets). The pre-orifice design contains a metering orifice (pre-orifice) that restricts the amount of liquid entering the nozzle. This is what drops the pressure within the nozzle. A number of manufacturers offer a pre-orifice flat fan, which produces a coarser spray at pressures between 30–60 psi. Low-drift nozzles such as the pre-orifice flan fan nozzle can reduce drift by 50%.

Air Inclusion Nozzles

Air inclusion, air induction, or venturi nozzles are flat fan nozzles with internal venturi to create negative pressure inside the nozzle body. Air is drawn into the nozzle through two holes in the nozzle side, mixing with the spray liquid. Air inclusion nozzles reduce drift by allowing air to be incorporated into the liquid flow. The -emitted spray contains large droplets filled with air bubbles and very few smaller, drift-prone droplets. The droplets shatter on impact with a leaf, the air bubble absorbing the energy, and produce similar coverage to finer, conventional nozzles.

Hollow Cone Nozzles

With hollow cone nozzles, the spray is confined at the outer edge of the conical pattern, the cone being formed by passages in a swirl plate or core to create a swirling motion. A disc with a hole in it forms the second part of the hollow cone nozzle. Varying flow rates are created by changing the disc (hole size), swirl plate, and system pressure. Most airblast sprayers are fitted with hydraulic hollow cone nozzles. The nozzles must be turned towards the target, and the airstream deflected towards the canopy, to maximize deposition and minimize drift.

Nozzle wear

As liquid passes through the nozzle tip orifice, the tip will wear. The rate of wear depends upon three major factors, nozzle material, pressure, and the products used. Nozzle material greatly affects wear rates. Brass and inexpensive plastics wear rapidly due to their soft material. Stainless steel and some high-quality plastics will last longer. Ceramic is the longest-lasting material. High operating pressure increases nozzle wear rates. Materials made of coarse powders cause nozzles to wear rapidly. If only liquids are used, nozzles will last longer.

Nozzle output should be checked frequently to ensure products are being applied properly. If nozzle output has increased by more than 10%, nozzles should be replaced. Nozzles are easily damaged if they are abused, and operators should *never* clear blocked nozzles with a nail or pin, but *always* with a bristle brush or airline. *Never blow through the nozzle with your lips!*

Sprayer Selection

The following factors should be considered by a grower before purchasing a sprayer:

1. Existing and Future Farm Plans and Equipment

Existing and future farm plans will dictate the area and crops to be sprayed. Different crops have different spraying requirements, such as application rates and the timing of applications. A field's layout dictates the available space for maneuvering equipment. A small area of brambles may only need a backpack sprayer, but as size increases, a small sprayer pulled by an ATV may be considered. Large-scale growers may consider a mounted or trailer-mounted airblast sprayer. Future plans may include expansion, and purchasing a sprayer today with excess capacity may be to your advantage in the future. Similar comments can be made concerning tractor size. For example, is your current tractor suitable to pull a new, larger sprayer over varying terrain?

2. Timeliness

Timeliness of spraying is very important. Pesticides must be applied at the correct time to ensure success in controlling disease and insects. A good rule of thumb is to be able to spray the whole area of brambles in a three-day period. The following will affect timeliness of application:

a) area to spray per season
b) capacity of sprayer
c) logistical support
d) frequency of spraying
e) land characteristics, e.g., topography
f) weather, seasonal variability
g) soil type, e.g., access to the field
h) workload of the farm, other demands, conflicting with staff time

3. Alternative Spraying Techniques

Growers need to consider novel sprayer designs which better direct spray deposition into the plant canopy. Each

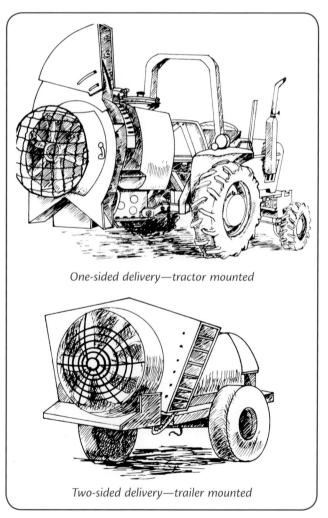

One-sided delivery—tractor mounted

Two-sided delivery—trailer mounted

Fig. 11.6 **Tractor-mounted and trailer-mounted air blast sprayers.**

new design needs to be carefully assessed: do the benefits outweigh the extra costs? With increasing legislation concerning the environmental aspects of pesticide application, techniques that improve spray coverage, reduce drift, and reduce tank rinsate must be considered.

Spray Equipment for Large Plantings

A variety of sprayer types are available for use in berry crops, including air blast sprayers, mist sprayers, and boom sprayers. The types of crop sprayer most commonly used are hydraulic boom sprayers for applying herbicides to control weeds, and vertical boom and airblast canopy sprayers to apply fungicides and insecticides to canes, foliage, and fruit.

Airblast and Directed-deposition Sprayers

Airblast and directed-deposition sprayers are either mounted on the 3-point linkage system of the tractor or are mounted on a trailer (figure 11.6). Mounted sprayers are lighter, causing less soil compaction, and are easy to maneuver. Care must be taken to prevent overturning when operating on hilly land. Weights are often added as ballast to lower the centre of gravity of the tractor and counter-balance the weight of the sprayer. Trailer-mounted sprayers allow a larger tank to be used, therefore increasing the available time to be actively applying pesticides. Most sprayers are powered by the tractor power take off (PTO), a shaft designed to power the pump and the fan.

The airflow generated by airblast sprayers can be most useful. It is used to:

Fig. 11.7 **Air blast sprayer— two-sided delivery.**

- produce droplets (pneumatic sprayers)
- transport droplets from the sprayer to the target
- protect droplets against wind effects
- shake the leaves of the canopy to aid penetration of droplets

However, too much air flow can:

- transport droplets past the target, resulting in drift
- excessively shake the canopy, leading to ground pollution
- remove droplets already present on the target

Directed-deposition sprayers (figure 11.8) comprise a system for delivering pesticide-laden air towards the target canopy. Two designs exist, one design uses flexible hoses or ducts to deliver air to the nozzle and then to the target, the other uses small fans mounted around the canopy. In both designs the outlets can be directed inwards towards the canopy, thus reducing drift and improving deposition.

Boom sprayers

Herbicide sprayers use horizontal booms fitted with nozzles to apply herbicides to weeds or the soil surface. The basic components—the tank, pump, controls, and filters—are similar to the airblast sprayer, but instead of using air to direct the spray to the target, they use pressure and gravity via a horizontal boom mounted approximately 18–20 inches above the target.

Fig. 11.8 **Directed-deposition sprayer.**

Fig. 11.9 **Mist sprayer.**

Fig. 11.10 **Vertical boom sprayers.**

Equipment Calibration

Calibrating a sprayer means making a test or trial run to determine the actual application rate. If the required application rate does not correspond to the actual rate measured, various adjustments (pressure, travel speed, flow rate, nozzle size, spacing, etc.) are made until they are comparable.

The application rate, in gallons per acre (GPA), is determined by:

> Forward speed
> Pressure
> Nozzle tip orifice size

To ensure accurate application, sprayers should be calibrated pre-season and during the season to be sure products are being applied at the desired application rate. Calibration should also be done before new nozzles are used for the first time or whenever pressure or speed is adjusted. Calibration requires only a few minutes and is time well spent (and potentially money saved by not applying too much or too little product to the target). *Important! Clean your sprayer thoroughly before beginning calibration and use only clean water during this process. Be sure to wear personal protective equipment (PPE)!*

Pre-Calibration Check

The sprayer must be operating properly before calibrating it. Check the following before you begin:

1. Check and clean all nozzles and screens. Replace any that are damaged.
2. Observe nozzle patterns using water; they should be continuously smooth with no skips or heavy streams. If more than one or two are suspect, they probably all need replacing.
3. Check the nozzles and their arrangement on the manifold. Follow manufacturers' recommendations. Generally nozzles in the bottom of the air stream have lower flow rates.
4. Check the pressure gauge. Pressure should be stable and at the desired level for spraying.

Airblast Sprayer Calibration Procedure

Step 1. Determine the forward speed of the sprayer (see sidebar) in miles per hour (MPH).

Step 2. Check nozzle output.
   a) Make sure your sprayer is clean, and use only clean water! Connect hoses to each of the nozzles and, using a stop watch, measure the flow from each individual nozzle for one minute into a calibrated jug or container.
   b) Compare your nozzle output at a given pressure with the manufacturer's output in a nozzle catalogue, or find the gallons per acre (GPA) listed on the label and use the following formula to determine the flow in gallons per minute (GPM):

$$\frac{\text{Speed (mph)} \times \text{width (ft)} \times \text{GPA}}{495} = \text{FLOW}$$

   c) Replace all nozzle tips which are less than 90% accurate.
   d) Remember to compare output from nozzles on each side of the sprayer.

Example

If a grower wishes to apply 50 gallons/acre at 3 mph on rows spaced at 10 feet apart, the total required through the nozzles will be:

$$\frac{3 \text{ mph} \times 10 \text{ ft} \times 50 \text{ GPA}}{495} = 3.03 \text{ gal/min}$$

Determining the forward speed of the sprayer
(Use for airblast or boom sprayer calibration.)

Mark out a 100-foot course with a stake at each end. Using a stop watch, record the time taken to drive the course at normal spraying speed. Record tractor engine revolutions and gear selected.

Determine your ground speed in miles per hour (MPH) with the following formula:

$$\frac{\text{Feet traveled}}{\text{Time traveled (seconds)}} \times \frac{60}{88} = \text{MPH}$$

Remember that there are 128 fl. oz. in one gallon. Therefore, if the output of one nozzle has been measured in ounces, then output is divided by 128 to determine GPM.

Step 3. Calculate the output of your sprayer using the following formula:

$$\frac{\text{Total GPM} \times 495}{\text{mph} \times \text{row spacing (ft)}} = \text{GPA}$$

Boom Sprayer Calibration Procedure
Step 1. Determine the forward speed of the sprayer (see sidebar) in miles per hour (MPH).

Step 2. Record the following inputs.

	Your figures	*Example*
Nozzle type on your sprayer (All nozzles must be identical)		110 04 flat fan
Recommended application volume (From manufacturer's label)		20 GPA
Measured sprayer speed		4 mph
Nozzle spacing		20 inches

Step 3. Calculate the required nozzle output.

$$\text{GPM} = \frac{\text{GPA} \times \text{mph} \times \text{nozzle spacing}}{5940 \text{ (constant)}}$$

Example:

$$\text{GPM} = \frac{20 \times 4 \times 20}{5940} = \frac{1600}{5940} = 0.27 \text{ GPM}$$

Step 4. Measure actual nozzle output.
Set the correct pressure at the gauge using the pressure regulating valve.
Collect and measure the output of each nozzle for one minute.

Step 5. Compare required output values to actual nozzle output values. The output of each nozzle should be approximately the same as calculated in Step 3 above. Remember that there are 128 fl. oz. in one gallon. If output has been calculated in GPM then output is multiplied by 128 to determine ounces used per minute. Replace all nozzle tips which are less than 90% accurate.

Alternative Calibration Procedures
Select a calibration plot that is between 0.1 to 1.0 acres in size (figure 11.11). There are 43,560 square feet in an acre. If row spacing is 10 feet, then 4,356 feet of row represents one acre (43,560 square ft ÷ 10 ft). Therefore 0.1 acre equals 436 feet of row. With a two-sided delivery sprayer, two "half" rows (one row equivalent) are sprayed on each pass, but with a one-sided delivery

Driving distance to cover desired area

Fig. 11.11 **Calibration course showing the driving area to be covered.**

unit, only half of a row is sprayed, so the sprayer must travel twice as far to spray an acre.

Tank Level Calibration Method

a) Fill the sprayer tank completely or with some known level of *clean water only*.

b) Spray the calibration plot selected and measured above.

c) Return to the filling site (exact location if possible) and accurately measure the amount of water required to refill the tank to the original level in a) above. An alternative is to weigh the sprayer before and after the calibration test to determine the amount of water sprayed. Water weighs 8.34 pounds/gallon.
CAUTION: Do not weigh the tractor since its weight will change with fuel consumption.

d) Determine the application rate by dividing the amount of water used by the area sprayed. For example, if 24.5 gallons were applied to 0.25 acres, the application rate is 24.5 gal/ 0.25 acres or 98 gallons/acre.

Time/Rate Calibration Method

This method is similar to the one above except the sprayer is operated in place, without moving between filling and refilling.

a) Determine the time needed to spray the calibration plot selected above by measuring the time required to drive over the plot at the selected speed.

b) Return to the filling site and fill the tank with *clean water only* to some known level.

c) Operate the sprayer, without moving, at the same pressure and pump speed for exactly the amount of time measured in a) above. It is not necessary to operate the fan.

d) Accurately measure the amount of water needed to refill the tank to the previous level.

e) Determine the application rate by dividing the amount of water used by the area sprayed. For example, if 30 gallons are required to refill the tank and 0.3 acres were sprayed (timed), the application rate is 30 gal/0.3 acres or 100 gallons per acre.

Preparing the Sprayer for Work

Early season, mid-season, or mid-winter, time spent maintaining a crop sprayer is never wasted. Surveys have shown that many farmers are using inaccurate sprayers. Faulty sprayers contribute to increased drift levels, and waste money through inefficiency and overuse of chemicals.

Sprayers must be regularly checked over to ensure that proper maintenance has been carried out and that no outstanding repairs need to be done. Before attempting any work on a machine make sure that it is fully supported on stands, it has been fully cleaned, and that all necessary protective clothing is on hand.

The cost of good maintenance is soon recovered. For example, replacing a faulty pressure gauge which has been indicating at 15% below the actual pressure will pay for itself in about two hours' operation. Maintenance measures such as fitting a new set of nozzles at the beginning of each season will also save money. Even when there is as little as 5% over-application, the cost of a new set of nozzles would be recovered in less than a day's work.

CAUTION

- Take great care when adjusting a sprayer while the tractor engine is running.
- Engage the handbrake whenever leaving the tractor seat.

Fitting the sprayer to the tractor

The selected tractor must always be powerful enough to operate the sprayer efficiently under the working conditions that will be encountered. All its external services—hydraulic, electrical, and pneumatic—must be clean and in good working order. Tractors fitted with cabs must have efficient air filtration systems. All protective guards must be in place. Trailer-mounted sprayers are often close-coupled to the tractor, so it is essential that the drawbar and the PTO shaft are correctly adjusted for turning. PTO shafts must be disengaged when making very tight turns.

Checking the operation of the sprayer

Partially fill the tank with clean water and move the sprayer to unplanted ground. Remove the nozzles. Although not using any chemical at this point, get into the habit of wearing a coverall, gloves, and a face visor when working with the sprayer. Engage the PTO and gently turn the shaft, increasing speed slowly to operating revolutions. Test the on/off and pressure-relief valves, and check the agitation system. Flush through the spray lines, then switch off the tractor. Refit the nozzles and check the liquid system again for leaks.

Pre-season maintenance

Before you begin spraying, the following components should be checked:

❏ Hoses
Should be checked for splits and cracks, particularly where booms fold, ensure connections are water-tight.

❏ Filters
Check for leaks, damage, and missing filter elements and seals.

❏ Tank
Inspect for fractures and any other damage, ensure that the tank sits firmly in its mount and that the securing straps are correctly adjusted. Agitation is very important; check that it is functioning properly and that the tank is clean.

❏ Controls
Check the control circuitry (electrical, hydraulic, or air) for correct operation and for both internal and external leaks.

❏ Pump
Ensure that the lubrication levels are correct and that the air pressure in the pulsation chamber (if fitted) is at the recommended level. Check that the pump rotates freely without friction or noise.

❏ Pressure Gauge
The pressure gauge is vital for indicating whether the nozzles are delivering the correct amount of chemical per unit time while spraying. Be sure it is operating accurately.

❏ Boom
The boom suspension must operate smoothly to ensure a stable "nozzle platform." Check the boom movement and stability, as well as the boom folding mechanism. Inspect the break backs for correct operation.

❏ Anti-drip valves
Avoid leaks by keeping small anti-drip valves, above or to one side of each nozzle, in good repair. Damaged diaphragms and seats will lead to faulty functioning. Examine all units under pressure to test for leaks and correct cut-off action.

❏ Nozzles
Ensure that all nozzles are the same model/size and are in good condition with no evidence of streaks or irregularities in the spray pattern. All nozzles must be clean and free from obstruction. (**Note**: Clean with a soft brush or airline—don't damage nozzles by using wires or pins.) Replace any nozzles that deliver ±10% of the manufacturer's chart value.

Routine maintenance

The following checks should be carried out routinely:
1. All hoses are tightly connected and free from sharp bends; cracked or damaged hoses must be replaced.
2. All controls move freely and are fully adjustable.
3. Pressure gauge reads zero.
4. The pump can be turned over by hand.
5. Air pressure in pump accumulator (if fitted) is correctly adjusted.
6. Drain plugs and clean filters are in position.
7. Tires on trailer-mounted machines are sound and correctly inflated; wheel nuts are tight.

Spray Equipment for Small Plantings

Although powered sprayers make bramble spraying easy and fast, they are relatively expensive and must be used on fairly large acreage to be economically justified. This acreage may include brambles or other crops, but the fixed (ownership) costs must be spread over many acres, even for the smaller air-blast units to be feasible. Growers with smaller plantings should explore alternative, less expensive spraying equipment.

Hand-Held Sprayers

Hydraulic hand-held sprayers or "handgun" sprayers may be equipped with single or multiple nozzles (figure 11.12). The multiple-nozzle guns are actually miniature hand-held booms. Handguns are connected by a relatively long hose to a powered pump. Most handguns require high pressure, so typically either piston or diaphragm pumps are used.

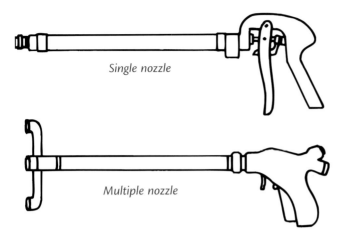

Single nozzle

Multiple nozzle

Fig. 11.12 **Hand-held sprayers.**

As with any hydraulic nozzle, the principle of handgun operation is that pressure is used to atomize the spray liquid into droplets. The energy of the droplet's velocity at the nozzle discharge projects the spray to the target. The farther the target is from the handgun, the higher the pressure needed to provide enough force to carry droplets to the target. However, as pressure is increased, smaller droplets are produced, which tend to slow more quickly.

Often, two people perform handgun spraying, one operating the handgun and one driving the tractor or other vehicle used to transport the sprayer through the field. This is convenient but increases labor needs. The quality of handgun spraying depends on the operator. Much practice is needed to become skillful enough to obtain a thorough coverage for adequate pest control without overspraying, and to obtain a uniform application rate. Factors such as temperature, fatigue, slope of the terrain, walking surface, and length and weight of the hose can increase the difficulty of handgun spraying.

Knapsack Sprayers

Another sprayer suitable for small plantings up to about ¼ acre is the knapsack sprayer (figure 11.13). They are also useful for making spot treatments where the pest problem is not spread across the entire field. This sprayer is operated manually and is carried on the operator's back with shoulder straps. Sprayer parts include the basic parts of most sprayers: a tank to hold the spray mix, a pump or pressurized gas canister to produce pressure and flow, controls to regulate flow, and an atomizer.

Tanks, which are typically plastic or steel, range from three to five gallons in size. Some have a mechanical agitator that moves when the pump is used to provide some mixing; others may have jet agitation. Before spraying, the entire sprayer can be shaken to ensure good mixing.

Hand-pump sprayers have a built-in piston or diaphragm pump. Some models can be adapted to either left- or right-handed pumping, with the free hand operating the flow control valve and the nozzle. The pumps are positive-displacement types and can produce relatively high pressures. There is only a very small chamber where the liquid is under pressure, which makes the sprayer a "pump-as-you-go" system.

The distribution system includes an on/off valve, usually with a pistol-grip handle, and one or more nozzles. The nozzle is often mounted at an angle on a 16- to 20-inch wand to aid spray placement on the plants. Some designs provide for interchangeable nozzle tips so that nozzles can be better matched to the job.

Using a knapsack sprayer to spray raspberries is a time- and labor-intensive method. From the standpoint of equipment investment, the cost is low, but the capacity is also very low. However, where labor is a minimal consideration, such as for many homeowners and hobbyists, the knapsack sprayer is effective, if properly used. Since the operator controls the travel speed, variations in application rate similar to those caused by handgun systems can be expected. In addition, extra care should

Fig. 11.13 **Knapsack sprayer.**

be given to coverage and uniformity because so little water is used to mix and carry the spray. It is not practical to apply a rate close to 100 gallons per acre with a hand sprayer.

Powered Knapsack Sprayer

Another version of the knapsack sprayer has a very small engine and fan to create a hand-carried air-assist sprayer. This sprayer is also known as a motorized knapsack mist blower (figure 11.14).

Powered knapsack sprayers are equipped with 3- to 5-horsepower engines. Two-stroke cycle engines are used to minimize the weight; however, they require a gasoline/oil mixture for fuel. Operators should follow the manufacturer's recommendation on the oil-to-fuel ratio, which may be given on the fuel tank or its cap. The engines operate at 5,800 to 8,000 rpm and are noisy—operators should wear ear protection. These sprayers are much heavier than manual models, weighing 17 to 25 pounds when empty.

The engine operates a centrifugal fan that delivers 200 to 450 cubic feet of air per minute. The discharge velocity is usually over 200 miles per hour. With this high velocity, air shear nozzles are practical and often used. However, hydraulic orifice and rotary nozzles are also used to form and inject the droplets into the air stream. The air from the fan is fed through a flexible

Fig. 11.14 **Powered knapsack sprayer.**

tube with an air nozzle on the end. The operator controls the direction of the air stream to place the spray on the target. Because of the high discharge velocity, the air nozzle should be at least 6 feet from plants. The air stream should be aimed downwind so that natural currents assist in dispersing droplets away from the operator. Spraying into even a slight wind may result in droplets being blown back onto the operator. Take care not to overspray the target, since it is often difficult to observe the spray coverage produced by these sprayers.

Motorized knapsack mist blowers can spray raspberries much faster than manual sprayers. The air stream will assist in delivery and coverage, even at lower application rates. However, the area that can be sprayed is still limited since the sprayer tanks are about the same size or even smaller than those on manual sprayers. Therefore, a full tank will cover only a relatively small area, and much time is required to refill the tank and measure chemicals.

Hand Sprayer Calibration

Hand sprayers need to be calibrated for the same reasons as power sprayers. The operator must first determine the percentage of an acre covered by one tank full of spray mix. By multiplying this percentage by the recommended application rate per acre, the operator can easily calculate the amount of chemical required per tank. Before calibrating a sprayer, operate it with only water to be sure all parts are properly working.

Handguns, manual knapsack sprayers, motorized knapsack sprayers, and other hand sprayers can be calibrated with the following method:

1. Select a calibration plot (row length) that represents $\frac{1}{100}$ to $\frac{1}{20}$ acre. A bigger plot will produce more accurate results. There are 43,560 square feet in an acre; therefore, row length per acre is 43,560 square feet divided by the row spacing (feet). For example, if the raspberries are planted in rows 10 feet apart, then there are 43,560 square feet ÷ 10 feet = 4,356 feet of row per acre. There are approximately 44 feet (4,356 ÷ 100) of row in $\frac{1}{100}$ of an acre, and 220 feet (4,3560 ÷ 20) in $\frac{1}{20}$ acre.
2. Fill the sprayer tank with only water and spray the calibration plot at a rate that achieves good

plant coverage. This requires good judgment; an inexperienced operator should get help or training from an experienced or trained pesticide applicator. The goal is to provide coverage to the entire plant without reaching the point of runoff (spray mix dripping from plants) to avoid waste and potential pollution.

3. Measure the amount of water required to refill the sprayer tank to the previous level. Calculate the application rate by dividing the amount of water used by the area covered. For example, if 1.5 quarts were applied to 1/100 of an acre, the actual application rate is 37.5 gallons per acre (1.5 quarts ÷ 4 quarts per gallon ÷ 1/100 acre).

A preferred alternate method for hydraulic handgun sprayers (not mist sprayers) (figure 11.13, page 128) is a modification of the above method.

1. Same as step 1 above.
2. Same as step 2 above, but also use a stopwatch to determine the time required to spray the calibration plot as measured.
3. With the sprayer in place, spray into a container for the time measured in step 2. Be sure to collect all the water for the exact time period. The water in the container will be the same amount applied to the calibration plot. Calculate the application rate as described in step 3 above.

Hand Sprayer Operation

Hand sprayers require much more labor to operate than the tractor-powered units, so hand sprayers are limited to small plantings. High application rates similar to those achieved with the powered sprayers are feasible with the powered handgun, because the spray mix is carried by the tractor or a trailer, and the pump is powered. However, with knapsack sprayers it is not practical to use such high rates.

A major problem with hand sprayers is the inability of an operator to walk along a row at a uniform rate. Variation in walking speed will vary the application rate. However, an experienced applicator may be able to compensate for variations of plant density in the plant row. For example, if a plant is missing in a row, the operator can skip that space and move immediately to the next plant. Inexperienced operators should practice with water until they can apply a spray uniformly at the recommended rate.

Hand sprayers necessarily place the operator near the nozzles and discharge point of the sprayer. This makes operator protection very important. Basic protection includes a hat, long-sleeved shirt, and trousers, or a spray suit. Depending on the toxicity of the chemicals, other protective gear, such as a respirator, goggles, waterproof gloves, or waterproof boots, may be needed. All operators should read the labels and follow directions for the specific material being applied. The spray should be discharged with the wind so that droplets are carried away from the operator. If spray is directed into the wind, some will be blown back onto the operator.

Drift can be a problem with hand sprayers and may be even more important where lower application rates are used. Since the spray mix is more concentrated, any loss means more active ingredient is lost. The best solution is to spray only when winds are slight or blowing at less than 5 miles per hour. Operators should use as low a pressure and as large an orifice as is practical to minimize the number of small droplets formed. Adding a drift-control additive to the spray mix may also be helpful.

Sprayer Maintenance

Like all other equipment, sprayers must be kept in good working order to last a long time. Cleaning is especially important because of the chemicals used. A very thorough cleaning should be performed whenever chemicals are changed and at the end of each spraying season. Sprayers must be protected from corrosion and freezing in storage during the off season.

Cleaning

All sprayers must be cleaned to prevent corrosion, cross contamination of pesticides, and crop injury. Trace amounts of one pesticide can react with another or carry over to the next spraying and cause damage. Long exposure to even small amounts of some pesticides can damage sprayer parts, even stainless steel tips and fiberglass tanks. If crops are sprayed that are sensitive to the herbicides used, maintain two sprayers—one for herbicides and one for all other spraying. No cleaning method is perfect, but careful cleaning will remove all but insignificant amounts of insecticides and fungicides.

Always try to end the day or a spraying job with an empty tank to avoid having leftover spray mix. Be careful when disposing of leftover mix or wash water; avoid contaminating water supplies and injuring plants or animals. Do not leave puddles that might be accessible to children, pets, farm animals, or wildlife. Two recommended methods of disposal are collecting the waste in a holding tank and recycling it during the next spraying, or spraying waste on another area with similar plants and problems while being careful to avoid overspraying.

When the sprayers are empty, triple-rinse the tanks with clean water, preferably after each day's operation. Also rinse the outside of the sprayer. Before changing pesticides or storing sprayers for the winter, clean sprayers thoroughly with a cleaning solution. Check the label for directions. A good detergent solution will remove most insecticides and fungicides. First, flush the tank with water; then add the cleaning solution to the tank and thoroughly agitate it before flushing again. Always flush with clean water to remove the cleaning solution.

Remove nozzle tips and screens; clean them in a strong detergent solution or kerosene, using a soft brush such as a toothbrush. Follow the same safety precautions during cleaning as for mixing and application. Use a respirator, waterproof gloves, or other protective gear as directed by pesticide label instructions.

Lubrication

Lubrication may be required, depending on the sprayer design. Some sprayers are built with sealed bearings that do not require additional lubrication. Wear points other than bearings may need to be greased or oiled. Some sprayer parts may need to be coated to prevent corrosion during nonuse periods. Follow the instructions in the owner's manual.

Winterizing

Sprayers must be protected from corrosion and freezing during winter storage. If a sprayer has no rubber parts, such as gaskets, diaphragms, or hoses, put new or used engine oil from a gasoline engine in the tank before the final flushing to prevent corrosion. As water is pumped from the sprayer, the oil will leave a protective coating inside the tank, pump, and plumbing. If the pump has rubber parts, disconnect the lines and put automotive antifreeze or radiator rust inhibitor in the inlet and outlet ports. Rotate or move the pump several times to completely coat interior surfaces.

Remove nozzle tips and screens and store them in a can of light oil such as diesel fuel or kerosene to prevent corrosion. Close nozzle openings with duct tape to prevent dirt, insects, or mice from entering. During the final cleaning, inspect the hoses, clamps, connections, nozzle tips, and screens for possible replacement. Store the sprayer in a clean, dry building.

CHAPTER TWELVE

Harvesting, Handling, and Transporting Fresh Fruit

High-quality raspberries and blackberries are those that are free from injury, decay, and sunscald, are uniformly colored, have a glossy appearance, and appear turgid. Unfortunately, raspberry and blackberry fruit quality can decline quickly in the field and even faster after harvest. Therefore, maintaining fruit quality after harvest requires special attention to preharvest and postharvest factors. The importance of various preharvest and postharvest factors will depend on your marketing plan; an operation that is marketing fruit through retail or wholesale outlets will need to pay closer attention to different factors than a pick-your-own operation.

Preharvest Considerations

Preharvest factors that influence berry quality include the choice of cultivar, growing site, plant health and nutrition, and fungicide and pesticide application.

Cultivars differ markedly both in storage life and shelf life. It is important to consider both characteristics in choosing cultivars for a specific market. Storage life is that time that a berry is stored at low temperatures, while shelf life refers to the period of time at ambient temperatures with or without storage (e.g., at a roadside stand or supermarket). A cultivar with an extended storage life would not be ideal for a roadside stand or supermarket if its berry shelf life was limited, as the fruit could deteriorate before it could be sold. This same cultivar might be good for a pick-your-own operation if customers promptly refrigerate fruit.

In a pick-your-own operation, the intensity of flavor that the fruit develops on the plant may be the principal consideration in choosing cultivars. Consumers harvest the fruit and eat them within a short time period. However, if fruit are to be marketed at the retail level, both fruit firmness and shipping ability becomes more important as the fruit have to withstand handling operations. Sometimes, flavor intensity is compromised for handling purposes.

Selecting a site that will provide good microclimactic conditions, such as good air drainage, and planting in a row orientation parallel to the prevailing summer winds will maximize plant health and improve the quality of harvested fruit. Proper plant densities will reduce disease pressure on fruit. Rain and dew increase the likeliness of infection by fungi, but this moisture will evaporate more quickly in a sparse canopy with good air circulation. Similarly, proper irrigation management (i.e., using drip irrigation) can minimize decay that might be induced from contact of fruit with water.

Nutrition is also an important component of good storage life. Fruit from plants that are nutritionally stressed, either because of under- or over-supply of fertilizer, will have a shorter storage potential than fruit from healthy plants. Adequate potassium and calcium should be available to the plant to assure good fruit health, and nitrogen should not be too high. While nitrogen encourages plant growth, high nitrogen availability can be associated with softer and faster-ripening fruit, and subsequently increased susceptibility to gray mold infection. Leaf analysis can be helpful in diagnosing deficiencies and, thereby, can help in fine-tuning the fertilizer program (see "Soil and Nutrient Management," chapter seven).

Fungicides applied during bloom and at petal fall can reduce the number of moldy berries. Gray mold (*Botrytis cinerea*) readily infects senescent petals and grows from the petals into developing fruit. Affected berries may have no visible signs of infection until harvest. Thus, timely petal fall sprays are essential, especially during damp, humid weather.

Some insects cause only minor physical damage when feeding on the fruit, but even small wounds are sites for fungal infection. Certain insects may spread bacteria and fungi from fruit to fruit. If insecticides are used to control pests, be sure to consider days-to-harvest restrictions.

Harvest Management

The stage of berry ripeness at harvest and how the fruit are handled are two critical factors in maintaining quality of the product. Fruit harvested before the fully ripe stage may have a longer storage and/or shelf life than those harvested at the fully ripe or overripe stage. However, there is usually a compromise between flavor and storage potential. Fruits harvested at a less ripe stage are unlikely to develop the same intense flavor as fruits harvested at the fully ripe stage. Appropriate cultivars should be selected to ensure that adequate flavor is realized for the type of operation. For example, some raspberry cultivars—e.g., Canby and Reveille—do not appear to be suited for commercial harvest because of poor flavor, soft berries, or dark color.

Quality of fresh market bramble berries usually declines as the season progresses. Be sure your marketing channels are open before the first and highest quality berries of the season are ripe.

Because raspberries ripen quickly and non-uniformly, frequent harvesting of the field (once every two days) is critical. Most raspberries grown in the East are harvested by hand for the fresh market as opposed to mechanically harvested for processing (figure 12.1). Pickers may need to be trained to identify the proper ripening stage and berry appearance for harvesting. The best stage of

Fig. 12.1 **Mechanical harvester for raspberries.**

maturity for the wholesale fresh raspberry market occurs when the berry first becomes completely red, but before any darker colors develop. Blackberries and raspberries should pull easily from the receptacle, yet be firm and not mushy.

Berries should not be touched before harvest. They are extremely fragile and easily damaged during harvest, e.g., by finger pressure, but the damage may not be visible until later. Studies in California have shown that the percentage of damaged fruit may vary significantly from one picker to another, and differences may be so great as to mask any other causes of deterioration. Training pickers is critical. Only undamaged berries with good appearance should be placed in the pack, and harvested fruit should not be exposed to direct sunlight. Growers might also find it economically worthwhile to turn the plug holes under when packing the top layer to offer a more attractive presentation.

Mixed ripening stages in the pack are less attractive in the marketplace. Under-ripe berries will be slow to develop acceptable color, whereas overripe berries lose their attractive "glossiness" and are susceptible to mold. Once the mold growing on overripe berries sporulates, large amounts of inoculum can infect other ripening fruit. Overripe berries also attract ants, wasps, and other pests. Pick overripe berries off plants and do not dispose of them near the field. It may be more economical in the long run to pay pickers to harvest rotten as well as marketable fruit, but at different times. Rotten berries must not be allowed to contaminate marketable berries with fungal spores.

Place only marketable berries into commercial containers. Marketable raspberries are at least 3 grams (0.1 ounce) in size and have no blemishes. Marketable blackberries are at least 5 grams (0.2 ounce) in size and have no blemishes. Small, overripe, or defective berries can be used for processing. This sorting process is best done in the field so berries are handled only once. Unlike many other fruits, grading standards do not exist for bramble berries, so it is less efficient to bring berries to a packing line for sorting and packaging.

The standard container for raspberries and blackberries at the supermarket is ½ pint, or 6 ounces. Pick-your-own operators usually offer pint containers to customers. Wide, shallow containers are better than deep containers. Never use a container which will hold more than four layers of berries, as berries on the bottom may be damaged from the weight of fruit on top. Pulp containers are inexpensive but stain easily, and may not be preferred by the market. Wooden containers also stain and are expensive. Solid, clear, vented, plastic containers (polystyrene clamshells) have become increasingly standard; they do not stain, they significantly reduce moisture loss when used with a cap, they enable customers to see all the berries they purchase, and they are inexpensive.

Postharvest Handling

Respiration of fruit is the process by which food reserves are converted into energy. The process uses carbohydrates and oxygen to produce carbon dioxide, heat and water, and therefore can result in shrinkage, reduced soluble solids (sugars), and deterioration. Good postharvest handling techniques will reduce the rate of respiration and, therefore, extend the life of the fruit.

The presence of ethylene, produced by a variety of sources including combustion engines, fruit such as apples, and any decayed and injured fruit, can stimulate respiration rates. Gray mold growth can also be stimulated by ethylene. Color of raspberries can be adversely affected by ethylene as it causes red fruit to darken to purple-red.

The rate of respiration, or the speed at which fruit deteriorate, can be measured by the amount of carbon dioxide produced per weight of fruit over time. Berry fruit, especially raspberries and blackberries, have much higher rates of respiration than fruit such as oranges and apples, which are stored for much longer time periods. Cooling berries after harvest is the most effective action a grower can take to maintain fruit quality. Each 10°F reduction in temperature reduces the respiration rate of

fruit by approximately 50% (Table 12.1). At 77°F and 30% relative humidity, fruit will lose water thirty-five times faster than it would at 32°F and 90% relative humidity. Clearly, prompt cooling and maintenance of proper temperatures and humidity are essential.

For blackberries, forced-air cooling to 41°F within four hours is recommended, and fruit should be transported at refrigeration temperatures of 41°F or less. Fruit can be held for two to fourteen days, depending on the cultivar, at 31 to 32°F with more than 90% relative humidity (RH).

Raspberries should be forced-air cooled to 34°F as soon as possible, no later than twelve hours after harvest. Fruit should be held for no more than two to five days, depending on the cultivar, at 31 to 32°F with more than 90% RH.

Berries will not freeze at 31°F because the sugars in the fruit lower the freezing point. Maintaining the storage at a slightly warmer temperature (32°F) will allow some room for error. However, major shippers report that storage at 40°F, as opposed to 30°F, reduces shelf life by 50%.

Cooling Methods

Only passive or room cooling, and force-air cooling are suitable for raspberries and blackberries because of their delicate nature and the need to avoid contact with water. The method of choice for cooling is forced-air cooling. The reason for this becomes quite obvious when comparing the "⅞ cooling time" (the number of hours it takes to remove seven-eighths of the field heat) of forced-air and passive cooling methods. In the case of passive cooling, the typical ⅞ cooling time for berries in twelve-quart flats on pallets is 9 hours, while the ⅞ cooling time for forced air cooling is 90 minutes—six times shorter.

Passive or room cooling, though relatively slow, can be used by any grower with cold storage facilities. The cooling process can be accelerated by spreading fruit out in the cooler, thereby exposing the tops of flats to cold air circulated by the cooling unit. Once cooled, the flats can be stacked and kept cool until the fruit is marketed. Growers can take advantage of night cooling by harvesting fruit as early in the morning as possible.

Forced-air cooling involves channeling refrigerated air through the containers holding the fruit (figure 12.2). For additional information see *Produce Handling for*

Table 12.1 Respiration rates (mg CO_2 kg^{-1} h^{-1}) of various fruits stored at different temperatures.

Commodity	Temperature (°F)				
	32	41	50	59	68
Raspberry	24	55	92	135	200
Blackberry	22	33	62	75	155
Strawberry	15	28	52	83	127
Blueberry	10	12	35	62	87
Orange	3	5	9	5	24
Apple	3	5	8	13	20

Direct Marketing listed in the Further Reading section at the end of this chapter. Large growers may have a separate forced-air cooling facility specifically designed for removing field heat, but inexpensive, effective improvisations can be adapted for any cold storage. If a grower only has a walk-in cooler, recently picked flats of berries can be set into a cardboard box that is opened at both ends, and a household fan can then be placed at one end of the box to draw air through the flats. Once the berries are cool, flats can be removed from the cardboard and wrapped in plastic.

Operation of a precooling system, whether on a small or large scale, requires that the cooling rate of the fruit be followed by checking flesh temperatures throughout the process. The fan should be cut off when the flesh temperature is within 5°F of the desired temperature to avoid dehydration of the berries.

The selection of a cooling unit is very important when a cooler is designed. If the temperature difference between the air and the cooling unit is too large, then the condensers will accumulate ice from moisture in the air. This drying of the air would not cause a problem for dry goods but would severely dehydrate fruit. The atmosphere around the fruit should be humid to prevent shrinkage, so a cooler should be able to maintain a relative humidity of 90–95% at 32°F. These types of coolers are more expensive and less common than those for dry goods. Consult a refrigeration specialist for help with selecting a cooling unit and building a storage facility.

Whatever method is used for cooling, condensation can be a problem. Cold fruit removed from storage on a warm day will become moist with condensation very quickly, resulting in loss of "gloss" and development of warm, moist conditions favorable to fungal decay. Condensation can be avoided, however. The best way is to maintain refrigeration during the entire marketing period; but this requires facilities for storage, transport, and display that many small producers do not have.

A simple method to avoid condensation is to cover flats

Fig. 12.2 **Forced air cooling unit.**

or pallets with plastic before they are brought out from cold storage. The plastic must be left on until the berries warm to a temperature above the dewpoint. Remember that the plastic must be removed if fruits are going to be refrigerated, as leaving the plastic in place will cause condensation to form inside the bag and create an environment for fungal decay.

High carbon dioxide concentrations, typically between 10 and 20% (in 5–10% oxygen), can reduce softening and fungal decay, and help maintain the quality of berries. However, the financial investment required for controlled atmosphere (CA) storage has limited the use of this storage method to extend raspberry and blackberry storage life. Also, most CA storages that are available have been built for large volume crops such as apples. Small portable units that can extend shelf life by several days are becoming available, but may still not be economically feasible. It is also important to recognize that different varieties respond very differently to high carbon dioxide atmospheres, and cultivar selection will be important if this technology is to be used.

Components of Forced-Air Cooling

1. **Vented containers** to allow air to flow past fruit
2. **Fan capacity** appropriate to the volume of fruit being cooled (2 cubic feet per minute per pound of fruit)
3. **Air ducts** to deliver cool air to the fruit and warm air back to the coils
4. **Control of escaping air** by plugging gaps and tarping the containers

Transporting Berries to Market

Many steps in the distribution chain can negatively affect fruit quality. It is estimated that deterioration from harvest to the consumer's table accounts for 40% of the berries lost. These losses occur from farmer to wholesaler, from wholesaler to retailer, and from retailer to consumer. Much of these losses are due to poor handling of berries after harvest.

A typical handling scheme after the berries are transported from the field and precooled might involve wrapping the flats after pre-cooling, loading them into a refrigerated truck, transporting them to a distribution center, unloading them into the warehouse, loading them into a truck, transporting them to a retail store, unloading them, handling them in the back room, and finally setting up the display. Mishandling, either by rough handling or by poor temperature management, at any point along this route can result in unacceptable loss of quality.

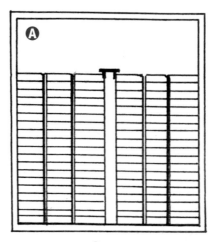 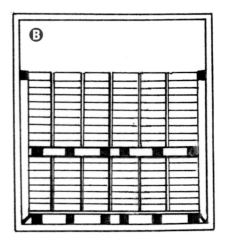

Fig. 12.3 **Ⓐ** Improper loading of flats within a truck—flats are in contact with the floor and walls; **Ⓑ** Proper loading—flats are not in contact with floor and walls and cold air is free to circulate.

Minimize the number of handling steps from field to display. Berries should remain cold and wrapped during each phase of transportation. Never allow the berries to sit on unrefrigerated loading docks. When loading a truck, stack flats on a palette and away from the truck walls (figure 12.3). Ensure that cold air is free to circulate around the sides of the pallet and across the top and bottom. When flats of fruit are allowed to touch the floor or side walls, temperatures in the flats can rise as much as 20°F. Do not stack flats directly over the rear wheels, and use strapping or stretch film around each pallet to stabilize the load. Transit vibrations can be reduced by using trucks equipped with air-suspension systems rather than spring systems.

Truck mechanical refrigeration equipment is designed to maintain temperature but currently lacks the air flow and refrigeration capacity for rapid cooling. Temperature regulating equipment in trucks does not have the accuracy to achieve temperatures below 40°F without danger of freezing. Furthermore, high-density loads are used to minimize transportation costs, even though they inhibit cooling during transit. Therefore, thorough product cooling before loading is very important. If possible, make sure berries are the last product in and first product out of the truck. Often, though, the transportation of berries is beyond the control of the grower. To develop new and distant markets, receivers must be educated in proper handling procedures. Personal contact with the receiver before the first delivery is often useful. In other cases, handling instructions may be attached to the flats.

Berries should be allowed to warm only when they are ready for display to consumers and before removing the plastic wrap over the flats. Any condensation will then form on the outside of the plastic wrap rather than on the berries inside. Fruit should be stored and displayed at the coldest refrigeration temperature possible, with no mist. As little as one day at room temperature can stimulate the growth of gray mold.

Further Reading

Bartsch, J., and G.D. Blanpied. 1990. *Refrigeration and Controlled Atmosphere Storage for Horticultural Crops.* NRAES-22. Ithaca, NY: Natural Resource, Agricultural & Engineering Service (NRAES). For more information, visit the NRAES web site WWW.NRAES.ORG, or contact NRAES at 607-255-7654 or NRAES@CORNELL.EDU.

Bartsch, J., and R. Kline. 1992. *Produce Handling for Direct Marketing.* NRAES-51. Ithaca, NY: Natural Resource, Agricultural & Engineering Service (NRAES). For more information, visit the NRAES web site WWW.NRAES.ORG, or contact NRAES at 607-255-7654 or NRAES@CORNELL.EDU.

Fraser, H.W. 1991. *Forced-Air Rapid Cooling of Fresh Ontario Fruits and Vegetables.* Bulletin 91-070. Ontario, Canada: Ontario Ministry of Agriculture, Food, and Rural Affairs. (To order, contact Ontario Ministry of Agriculture, Food, and Rural Affairs, Box 8000, Vineland Station, Ontario, Canada L0R 2E0.)

Gross, K.C., C.Y. Wang, and M.E. Saltveit. 2004. *The Commercial Storage of Fruits, Vegetables, and Florist and Nursery Crops.* USDA-ARS Handbook 66. Washington, DC: Agricultural Research Service, United States Department of Agriculture (USDA).

Perkins-Veazie, P. "Blackberry." In Gross et al. 2004. Also available online at WWW.BA.ARS.USDA.GOV/HB66/038BLACKBERRY.PDF.

Perkins-Veazie, P. "Raspberry." In Gross et al. 2004. Also available online at WWW.BA.ARS.USDA.GOV/HB66/121RASPBERRY.PDF.

CHAPTER THIRTEEN

Marketing Bramble Fruits

The key to marketing bramble fruits to the consumer is recognizing that growers are not just in the business of selling berries; rather, they are in the business of selling the sights, sounds, smells, and atmosphere that are associated with the total purchasing experience. This is the product that growers must promote and market to be competitive—not a low-priced produce item. Supermarkets are able to obtain large volumes of product and sell them for less than the local farmer can. However, supermarkets cannot offer a pleasant farm experience, even though many are now designing the produce section to resemble a farm market and are even featuring photos of local farmers in the stores.

Quality stands above all else in establishing and maintaining a profitable bramble fruit farm. But quality includes more than just the fruit; it includes the entire experience that is involved with obtaining the berries. For pick-your-own farms, this includes everything from the parking area to the greeter to clean restrooms to weed-free fields. For farm markets, it is the clean, wholesome atmosphere and friendly sales clerk, in addition to the product, that will bring return customers. High-quality fruit from a neat, efficient farm sold in a friendly atmosphere will reap much more profit than poorly handled, unsorted fruit in a cluttered farm stand.

Marketing Options

Which marketing channel you use to sell your product will determine the demand for your product, and how you price and promote your products. Invest time into marketing research to determine which marketing option is best for you. Consider the following question: Can you produce a better experience or provide a better service to customers in that market than those presently in the business?

Raspberries and blackberries are typically sold via one of three marketing channels: customer harvest (pick-your-own); fresh market (retail or wholesale); and processed (frozen, jams, jellies, wines, etc.). Each of these channels has advantages and disadvantages that should be carefully considered. Most growers use more than one marketing channel, which can be an advantage, as the demand in one market can make up for slack periods in another.

Due to the short season, no matter what marketing channel is chosen for your berry crop, customer contact should begin early, well before the harvest or picking season. Let buyers know what the product is, the quality of the crop, how much will be available, and when it will be available. Bramble growers who invest the time in advance marketing seldom fall into the frantic race to sell fruit before it rots, nor do they have to drop prices below the profit margin to get fruit harvested.

Marketing Fresh Fruit

Pick-Your-Own (PYO)
Experience has shown that raspberries and blackberries may not be as popular for PYO as other crops such as strawberries. This is probably due to the higher cost of raspberries and blackberries per pound, a greater difficulty in harvesting berries, and the later (hotter) season. In some locations, however, these obstacles may not deter customers, and PYO can be a successful part of an overall marketing strategy.

Success can be highly dependent on a farm's location. In order to attract enough customers to a PYO farm, the farm is best located within 20 miles of a densely populated area. Competition within that market area should be evaluated carefully. It could take 350 PYO customers to harvest 1 acre of raspberries. However, this number is influenced by the character of the community. Urban dwellers tend to pick less fruit than people living in the country, and certain local ethnic communities, such as Mennonites, may harvest large quantities of berries for freezing or making jellies.

It certainly helps if the fields are on or near a major roadway and easily accessible, though unlike a farm stand, PYO farm does not necessarily have to be on a well-traveled road. There are many examples of highly successful PYO farms that are in less-than-ideal locations. Developing a customer base on out-of-the-way farms requires patience, a great deal of promotional effort, including letting customers know when the crop is ready, and a reputation for providing a pleasant farm experience. For example, farm roads to the fields must be suitable for customer vehicles, or transportation should be supplied. Ample parking space should be available as well as toilet facilities, drinking water, shade, and some seating. An easy access area to accommodate the needs of older people or those with disabilities or strollers could attract additional customers. Some form of entertainment, especially for children, is becoming standard. Directions and rules should be clearly visible.

Although one of the major advantages of PYO marketing is reduced harvest labor, field supervisors must be employed to direct and help customers in parking, harvesting, and check-out procedures. Supervisors should be courteous and friendly and have a thorough knowledge of the farm. Check-out areas should be neat and efficient. Customers should not have to wait in long lines to pay.

It is generally better to charge by fruit weight than by volume (for example $2.50 per pound versus $1.90 per pint). This will curtail the inevitable arguments as to what constitutes a "full" pint and guarantees a fair price to all. On average a pint of raspberries or blackberries weighs 12 ounces. Electronic scales can make weighing proceed very quickly. If standard picking containers are supplied to customers, cashiers can easily subtract the weight of the containers and charge only for the fruit. Otherwise, containers must be weighed before customers go into the field. Supplying large picking containers

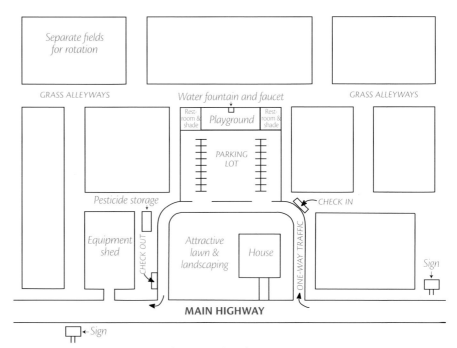

Fig. 13.1 **Map of a typical pick-your-own operation.**

(such as a 2-quart size) versus small containers (such as several 1-pint baskets) usually results in customers picking more fruit, because they tend to want to fill the container they have regardless of its size.

PYO farms are a common source of family recreation. Families tend to pick more fruit, so most operations allow children, but growers must ensure that children are supervised. Allowing children to pick fruit from the outside rows increases the likelihood that they will be advocates for return trips to the farm. It is also a good idea to have alternative amusement for children, such as a playground or petting zoo (figure 13.1).

Growers are strongly advised to consult their insurance agents regarding the potential liabilities involved in a PYO operation and to purchase appropriate coverage.

A bramble crop should be planned to fit into the overall farm operation. Add other crops suitable for farm retailing so that the customers will come back to the farm many times each year. For example, an early summer raspberry harvest could come after strawberries and be followed by blueberries or vegetables such as tomatoes, cucumbers, and sweet corn, and at the end of the season, pumpkins or even Christmas trees. PYO in conjunction with a farm market (even a small stand of pre-picked fruit) can be a powerful draw for customers who want convenience, local produce, and recreation all at one location. If the produce for the farm market

Fig. 13.2 **Rural farm market.**

Farm Markets and Farmers' Markets

Selling fresh fruit at retail is a potential option for growers whose operations are not suitable for PYO or who would prefer not to have PYO. As with PYO, marketing the experience of the farm stand is just as important as marketing the berries themselves. A clean, friendly atmosphere is essential, and consumers appreciate the convenience of being able to purchase food staples such as milk and bread along with their fruits and vegetables. An attractive exterior with a rural flavor is what consumers have come to expect (figure 13.2). Sometimes additional services such as café, ice cream, and/or a petting zoo could set the operation out to be a destination for customers. Adequate parking is essential for a successful farm market. As with any retail business, location is very important.

For growers who do not have a good retail location but would like to retail their berries, a farmers' market will be a good alternative. By selecting a well-managed farmers' market, growers can gain the access to consumers without bearing all the overhead and marketing costs of operating a farm market themselves.

Farmer's markets are becoming very popular throughout North America. Most markets charge fees to sell there and require that all produce be grown within a certain distance from the market. Prices received are often higher than at supermarkets because consumers are ensured that the product is local and fresh. Consumers also have an opportunity to talk directly with the producer. Selling at a farmer's market requires the farmer to arrive early to set up, and be available all day, usually on a Saturday, unless another person can be hired to do the selling. Some markets will sell on consignment, which eliminates the need to be present all day.

Fresh Market Wholesale

Wholesaling is another option for growers whose operation is not adapted to customer harvest or retail. Wholesaling usually involves harvesting large volumes of berries, cooling them to prolong shelf life (see "Harvesting, Handling, and Transporting Fresh Fruit," chapter twelve),

is to be grown on location, then a crew independent of the people who manage the PYO component must be hired for harvest.

Provide customers with recipes and instructions on how to handle fruit once it is home. Each year will bring new customers who may not have experience in the use and preparation of berries. Numerous recipes can be found by searching online or in the following publications:

- *The Best 50 Berries Recipes* by J. White, published in 2003 by Bristol Publishing Enterprises
- *Life's Little Berry Cookbook* by J. Bestwick, published 2000 by Avery Color Studios
- *Berries: A Cookbook* by R. Berkley, published in 1997 by Inc. Book Sales
- *Creative Recipes for Berries* by J. Donovan, published in 1991 by Salamander Books
- *Berries: Cultivation, Decoration, and Recipes* by M. Forsell, published in 1989 by Bantam

Providing information about making jams and jellies, or even wine, can increase sales and encourage repeat customers. Processing instructions follow in the processing section below or can be found by searching online and in the following publications:

- *Complete Guide to Home Canning and Preserving*, published in 1999 by USDA
- *Putting Food By* by J. Greene, R. Hertzberg and B. Vaughan, published in 1992 by Plume
- *Blue Book* by Ball.

and delivering them to a supermarket or warehouse. Buyers must be contacted well before the harvest season to set up delivery schedules, specify container preferences, and discuss payment policies. Some outlets may demand specialized handling or packaging. Wholesaling to other farm markets or restaurant chefs are other marketing opportunities growers might consider. Due to the specialty and perishable nature of brambles, growers could receive higher prices from these markets.

Combining wholesaling and direct marketing can be beneficial, as long as one of the markets is not getting the low-quality leftovers of the other. If one buyer is receiving lower-quality fruit, then that should be clearly understood by the buyer, and he or she should pay accordingly.

Postharvest handling of the fruit is a critical part of dealing with the fresh wholesale market. Growers must be able to deliver a high-quality crop with a maximum shelf life. This can mean a considerable investment in packing, storage, and transportation facilities ("Harvesting, Handling, and Transporting Fresh Fruit," chapter twelve).

Growers should follow up on their shipments to see that they are properly handled in stores. Improper handling there can ruin efforts to deliver a good product. A grower should discuss proper procedures with the produce manager, because the grower's reputation is at stake.

Reducing the Risk of Microbiological Contamination

Considering recent concerns over microbiological contamination of fruits and vegetables, take steps to reduce any risks of illness. Many steps can be taken to reduce risks of food-borne illness. Refer to www.gaps.cornell.edu for extensive information. Here are a few of the most important sources of risk and steps that can be taken to reduce them.

Most food-borne illnesses originate in fecal matter, either from humans or animals; therefore:

- Apply manure to fields only after composting and prior to planting. Never apply raw manure.
- Do not graze livestock next to irrigation ponds. Test irrigation water for pathogens.
- Do not allow animals or pets into the fields prior to or during harvest.
- Provide toilets and hand-washing areas for customers and workers to use before entering and after leaving the field (same applies to a petting zoo).

- Ensure that water is potable.
- Ensure that picking containers are clean or washed frequently.
- Keep garbage containers covered.
- Do not allow sick people into the field.
- Cool produce that is to be stored for any length of time.
- Ensure that transportation vehicles are clean and sanitized.
- Mark containers so they can be traced back if any problems occur.

Marketing Processed Fruit

Freezing

Selling frozen berries is a good way to sell excess fruit that might otherwise be wasted during the peak of the season. Few families have sufficiently large freezers to store all of the fruit they will consume during the off-season, so selling frozen berries can extend the season and add value to the product.

When berries freeze, ice crystals form inside the cells. The expanding ice crystals rupture the cell membranes, so when the berries thaw, they are softer and more flaccid. To reduce the amount of crystallization, mix berries with sugar prior to freezing. The sugar draws water out of the cells, so less is inside to crystallize. Berries frozen in a sugar solution will be more firm upon thawing than those frozen without sugar.

Most berries are packaged in a container with 6 ounces of berries to 4 ounces of concentrated sugar syrup (1 part water to 1 part sugar). High-fructose corn syrup is also used (4 parts fruit to 1 part syrup).

Freezing should occur rapidly after harvest to avoid losing flavor and to preserve color. Rapid freezing results in smaller ice crystals than slow freezing. IQF (individual quick frozen) berries are used in fruit salads because they maintain their integrity after thawing. Many processing plants have the ability to use IQF technologies.

Individual states and provinces have regulations regarding processing of fruit. In some states, freezing is not considered processing, so it does not come under guidelines from the health or agricultural and markets departments. Check with authorities about regulations before attempting to freeze berries for later sale.

Processing

Growing bramble fruit for processing entails many of the same efforts required for selling fresh fruit wholesale, such as contacting buyers, filling orders, and delivering. Growers who process the products themselves must follow appropriate state and federal sanitation, processing, and labeling regulations. This may include undergoing regular inspections, purchasing stainless steel equipment, and using water treatments. Contact your state or province department of agriculture and/or health department for details.

Value-added products, such as jams and jellies, may generate a higher profit margin than fresh fruit, but the inputs are much greater. Labor costs will be higher, and appropriate cooking tools will be needed as well as a steady supply of ingredients, jars, labels, shipping boxes, and so forth. Nevertheless, properly processed products provide the advantage of having year-round, quality, locally produced, specialty foods to sell directly to consumers or through wholesalers. Specialty foods are well suited for distribution in tourism areas such as wine trails, popular parks, and regional fairs.

Jams and Jellies

Jams (made with whole fruits or purees with and without seeds), preserves (made with pieces of large fruit), and jellies (made with filtered juice) comprise four ingredients: sugar, fruit, pectin, and acid. A balance among these is important. Fruit naturally contains all four of these, but the amount varies. Therefore, additional amounts must be added to bring the ingredients into balance.

Sugar sweetens the jam, suppresses microbial growth, sets the pectin, and makes the product glisten. The sugar content of a berry is generally between 5% and 15%, while the sugar content of a preserve must be between 65% and 69%. Obviously, additional sugar must be added to the fruit to make a preserve. Not all of the added sugar should be sucrose (table sugar) because of its tendency to crystallize. A portion of added sugar should be fructose (from corn syrup) or glucose. If the fruit contains enough acid, sufficient chemical inversion of sucrose will occur during boiling to make some glucose and fructose from the sucrose; this will prevent crystallization. The standard grade of jelly contains 45 parts fruit to 55 parts sugar. The fancy grade is 50/50, while imitation grade is 35/65.

Pectin is part of the cell walls of most fruit, but ripe berries have very little, and what exists is of poor quality for jam making. Green fruit contains more pectin, and up to 25% of a commercial jam can contain unripe fruit. Still, in most cases commercial pectin must be added for the jelly to set. One pound of 100-grade pectin will set a gel with 100 pounds of sugar at the proper pH. Fruit pectin can be purchased at most grocery stores in liquid or powder form. When using pectin, follow the manufacturers' instructions for proper set.

Acid balances the sweetness of the sugar and achieves the pH necessary to set the pectin. Fruits supply some acid, although with berries, additional citric acid is generally necessary to balance the jelly to a pH of 2.8 to 3.3. The most common cause of a jelly failing to set is insufficient acid.

The General Procedure for Making Jam*

From 2 quarts of berries (4½ cups). Makes 4 pints of jam.

1. Wash fruit.

2. Heat the fruit to near boiling.

3. Add 2 tablespoons of lemon juice (if pectin mix does not have added acid) and as much pectin as is specified in the manufacturer's directions (amount of pectin varies with the source). Let simmer for 2 minutes.

4. Add 7 cups sugar.

5. Bring mixture to a full boil for 15–17 minutes or until the temperature reaches 220°F or until the desired soluble solids level (67%–69%) is reached.

6. Turn off heat and remove the surface residue.

7. Fill containers with hot jam, close them, and turn them upside down for 5 minutes to sterilize the lid with the hot jam. Turn the containers back up for proper setting.

* See resources in the further reading section for specific details for making jams.

The entire mixture of fruit, acid, pectin, and sugar is boiled to catalyze the chemical reaction from liquid to solid. Boiling drives off some of the water in the mixture and destroys enzymes and microorganisms that would degrade the fruit.

Wine

Wineries may be interested in purchasing local raspberries, as fruit wines and fruit-flavored wines are increasing in popularity. The value of wine from a pound of raspberry can be ten times greater than the value of the fresh fruit. In addition, overripe fruit can be used to make raspberry wine, so long as the berries are not too moldy.

To make raspberry wine, you do not need fancy equipment—just a large pot, a fermenting bubbler, wine yeast, yeast nutrients, a hydrometer, a 5-gallon glass jug, and some cheesecloth. About 30 pounds of berries are required for every 5-gallon batch of wine. Berries are very fruity and acidic, so water and sugar are added to the berry pulp prior to fermentation to reduce the acidity to about 0.8% and increase the sweetness. The hydrometer is used to measure sugar content and to monitor the fermentation. If the desired alcohol content is 10%, then add more sugar to the mix to bring the mixture to 20° Brix, which is about 20% sugars (2% sugar for each 1% alcohol). In general, for every 2 pounds of berries, add 1 pound of sugar and 1 pound (pint) of water. Additional sugar may be required to obtain the desired sweetness. A simple rule of thumb is to add 0.1 pound of sugar per gallon of mixture to raise the sugar content by 1°Brix. At this stage sulfite might be added to prevent oxidation and to eliminate wild yeast. If used, add 50–100 ppm of sulfur dioxide (¼ teaspoon of potassium metabisulfite or 3 Campden tables per 5 gallon) and let stand overnight.

Next add the wine yeast and yeast nutrient. Wine yeasts, available from a wine supplier, can tolerate much higher alcohol content than wild yeasts. Dissolve the yeast in 100°F water (use 1 gram of yeast for every 1 gallon of liquid), and add it to the fruit-sugar-water mixture. The yeast nutrient is added directly to the mixture. Add the yeast to the mixture within thirty minutes of dissolving so a food source is available to the yeast. Also, be sure the temperature difference between the yeast solution and the fruit mixture is no greater than 5°F, or the yeasts may be killed. Fermentation should occur at 70°F for about

three to four days. This can occur in an open container, and the mixture should be stirred occasionally.

After three days, strain the mixture through cheesecloth and place it into a 5-gallon glass jug fitted with a fermentation bubbler. After another five to ten days, the wine will have reached an alcohol content of about 10%. When the wine reaches the desired alcohol and residual sugar content, stop the fermentation by placing the wine mixture in a cold room (30°F) or filtering it. Then decant the mixture and add sulfites (25–50 ppm) and sorbate to prevent oxidation and refermentation.

Berry wine can be allowed to ferment until the alcohol content reaches about 17% assuming that there was enough sugar to reach that level. However, wine with such high alcohol content is rather harsh and will require a significant amount of sugar to balance the alcohol. Stopping the fermentation process at 9% to 10% is recommended. Typically, wines will be fermented to dryness (no residual sugar) and sugar is then added before bottling to adjust the sweetness. Inexpensive kits are available to monitor sugar, acid, and alcohol content. Monitor sugar content daily, as alcohol increases rapidly when fermentation occurs at room temperature.

Berry wines sometimes develop an orange color or an off-flavor, but the cause of this is unknown. As with grapes, there may be cultivar differences among berries in their ability to make high-quality wines, but this has not been studied. A mixture of berry cultivars likely will produce better wine than a single cultivar.

Berry wine can have excellent color, balance, and flavor properties; however, it can be very unstable and should be consumed soon after bottling or kept refrigerated. Berry wine can be mixed with honey wine to produce another value-added product. Novice vintners may want to attend a seminar on wine making for more details on wine production.

To sell wine, you will need a license. The selling of wine is regulated by the state liquor control board and the Bureau of Alcohol, Tobacco, and Firearms.

Others Products

Products such as dried fruits, candies, syrups, flavored vinegars, dressings, beverages, sauces, and fruit beers provide other options for selling berries. Most states have marketing conferences for farm products, and the North American Farmers Direct Marketing Association

(317 West 38th Street, Vancouver, Washington 98660) has an annual meeting where many good ideas are brought forth.

Dried fruits are worth mentioning in more detail as consumers are looking for healthy snacks with great flavor. Berries can be dried whole or sliced depending on the final use. If the fruit has a waxy coat, it is necessary to "check" the skin by dipping in boiling water for 30 seconds. Berries are typically dried at 135°F in dehydrators that have good air circulation and a thermostat to control the temperature. Electric commercial dehydrators are common for low volume production but it is possible to build one to meet individual needs, as long as food grade materials are used. Forced convection ovens are suitable only if the temperature can be set accurately in the dehydration range (85° to 160°F is desirable). Drying time varies depending on fruit, air humidity, and type of dehydrator, and might take up to 20–30 hours. Berries are dried until leathery. Very acidic fruit will benefit from sugar infusion before dehydration. Mix the berries with a heavy syrup solution and let stand overnight. Drain and dehydrate. If better color is desired, fruit can be dipped for 5 minutes in an antioxidant solution made with lemon or lime juice (mix 1 cup juice with 1 quart water), ascorbic acid (known as Vitamin C, dissolve 1 tablespoon in 1 quart water), or commercial mixtures sold in supermarkets. Drain well before loading into the dehydrator. Dried berries should be stored in hermetic containers or bags to protect them from ambient moisture. For retail sale, choose an attractive plastic container or bag that allows the consumer to see the product.

Pricing and Labor

The price charged for the fruit must be fair to both the grower and the customer. For retailing a specialty product, price is not determined exclusively by supply and demand as it is for commodities. Raspberry and blackberry customers often do not shop around for the best price; rather, they develop a loyalty to a particular grower and trust him or her to set a fair price. Fair pricing requires a thorough knowledge of production costs (see "Budgeting," chapter fourteen). When calculating costs, growers must account for labor, including their own. Once production costs are determined, prices can be set that will meet costs and provide a reasonable profit based on consumer's willingness to pay for the

product. Of course, if a "fair" price for you is higher than prevailing market forces, it may not be profitable to grow berries.

Overcharging can result in disgruntled customers, especially if the perceived value of the farm experience is poor, but underpricing can cut deeply into profits. Reducing prices to undercut the competition may seem like a good idea, but in fact it is likely to cause more harm than good. First, a grower reduces profit by reducing price, because usually volume does not increase proportionally (table 13.1). Then, competitors may lower their prices in response, thus setting up a price war that can result in growers selling their crops at below break-even prices. Finally, customers may expect a drop in price later in the season and hold off buying until then, or expect to pay a lower price for your product which once again reduces profits.

In market surveys, individual customers as well as wholesale buyers rank quality and consistency above price in importance. Individual customers do little comparison shopping for produce. Lower-priced produce is often considered lower quality. The main reason customers visit a farm market or pick-your-own operations is to obtain fresh fruit and have a pleasant experience—not to get a break on price, especially for a specialty crop with a short season such as bramble fruits. So market forces have less of an impact on the price of direct-marketed raspberries and blackberries than they do on the price of many other commodities.

If considering outlets other than PYO, you must evaluate your harvest labor options. Depending on the

Table 13.1 Relationship among current profit margin, proposed price reduction, and increase in sales volume that would be required to retain the same profit margin.

% Profit Margin	% Price Reduction	% Required Increase in Sales Volume
10	5	100
15	5	50
15	10	200
20	5	33
20	10	100
25	5	25
25	10	67

location, there may be a shortage of willing and capable workers. Some operations have recruited children or senior citizens to harvest fruit; these workers can perform well if they are treated properly by the grower. Using imported labor may be an option for larger operations, but there are numerous state and federal regulations that affect this type of employment. Understanding these requirements demands a considerable amount of time and expense. Contact your state or province department of agriculture and labor for information about hiring temporary help and imported labor.

Most growers pay pickers piece-work by the pint, rather than by the hour. Bonuses offered for a certain number of pints will provide more incentive. Pickers should be trained to harvest only fruit of good quality at the proper stage of ripeness and to properly handle the fruit. Maintaining a good working environment is crucial to keeping good labor. Growers should generate enthusiasm for their farm and products and make workers feel like they are part of a team. Workers' attitudes will show in the quality of the harvested fruit.

It is best to start picking as early in the morning as possible, provided the fruit is dry, and quit before noon. This will ensure the fruit is picked at its best quality and that pickers are not forced to work during the hottest part of the day.

Advertising Basics

Advertising is the tool by which potential customers are contacted and attracted to your product. Without it, customers will never know that you exist.

First Impressions

Customers will first judge a farm and grower by the advertising they see. Advertisements should represent how you want the customers to view your operation, and they should focus on the entire farm and product experience—not just the price of berries. They should be tasteful and of high quality. The farm should have an attractive logo that is displayed prominently in ads, on signs, and on products; it should be simple enough to be easily recognized. Communicate with drawings rather than words as people may not read long ads. Contact your state or province department of agriculture to place your farm name and address on lists of farms selling berries.

Who Are Your Customers?

If you do not know who your customers are, you may be advertising to the wrong audience. A customer survey is a good way to determine who your customers are. Advertising can then be designed and targeted accordingly. For example, if most of your customers are home-makers with families, then ads should be placed where and when homemakers are likely to see or hear them. Surveys show that most customers come from within 20 miles of a farm. Advertising outside of this area may not pay off. Advertising also should be focused in the densest population areas.

Forms of Advertising

Word-of-Mouth: The Best Form of Advertising

The best form of advertising is the word-of-mouth recommendation that a satisfied customer passes on to others. This is true for both retail and wholesale customers. The potential benefit from this type of advertising is immense; it will generate lots of customers and many of a farm's best patrons. The quality of the fruit and the farm experience are both part of the perceived value that brings customers back. A bad reputation can develop quietly and ruin a business forever.

To satisfy a customer and make him or her happy enough to recommend a farm to other people, maintain a high-quality product and make buying the product a pleasure.

Roadside Signs

Roadside signs are often the first impression customers get of a farm. Signs should be neat, high-quality, attractive, and easy to read. They should represent the farm and farmers.

Select the color for signs with care. There should be enough contrast between the background and lettering to make the sign easy to read. For example, red or black letters are easy to read against a white background, while yellow letters are difficult to read. Signs and the letters on them should be large enough to be easily read by passing motorists. At 50 mph, a motorist has only three to five seconds to read a sign, so the sign must have only eight words or less to be readable. Symbols are often more effective than words. Use pictures or your logo on signs, if possible. Road signs are not the place to display prices. It is more important to catch the customers' attention—let them know what is available and how to get to it. Signs can be effective at directing people to the farm and attracting new customers. Some states have strict rules regarding roadside signs; contact your state department of transportation for details.

Signs and Advertising
- Dark letters on a light background are most legible.
- Letters should be 2 inches high for every 10 mph of posted speed. For example, if the speed is 40 mph, letters should be 8 inches high.
- Signs should be at least 100 yards away from the entrance to the market for every 10 mph of posted speed.

Direct Mailings
One of the most effective advertising tools is a customer mailing list. This provides a direct line of communication between customers and "their" berry farm. A direct mailing sent out at the appropriate time—such as a postcard indicating your opening date, the high quality of your fruit, and your desire to see the customer at your farm—gets better results than nearly any other media. Postcards are an excellent way to introduce new products, crops, or services; provide an update on events at the farm; and discuss the effects of the season's weather on the crop. A farm newsletter (electronic or hard copy) is also a good way to give product information, tell farm stories, and educate customers. It is important to make customers feel wanted and a part of the farm.

To establish a mailing list, collect the names, postal addresses, and email addresses of customers, either when they come to the farm or when they call regarding farm products. Surveys can be used to collect names for a mailing list, ask customers for feedback, and collect information about the consumers such as what newspaper they read or radio station they listen to. This information can then be used to help focus future advertising. Mailing lists of potential customers in a given area may be available for purchase from various companies. Such lists should be targeted for the region near the farm and to the type of customer most likely to be interested in your product.

> ### Advertisements for Berries
>
> Finger-Picking Good!
>
> Berried Treasures
>
> The Berry Best

The Media

What Should an Ad Say?
When designing an ad, promote benefits, not prices. Do not simply advertise "Jones' Farm"—that is not what a customer wants to buy. Emphasize the benefits of visiting the farm and the quality, freshness, flavor, and nutritional value of the farm's products. For pick-your-own operations and retail farm markets, emphasize the fun, recreation, and education that a trip to the farm provides. The ad should also give directions, list the days and hours of operation, include a phone number and Web site address, and state whether containers are provided (for PYO operations). Price is a relatively low priority among many of today's consumers. Finally, keep ads simple, attractive, and recognizable. Most customers will give an ad only a few seconds of attention.

Newspapers
Many people read the local newspaper daily, so newspapers are a good way to reach customers. Ads should be placed in the newspaper most likely to be read by potential customers for your product. Ads should be located in the section where your clientele is most likely to see them, such as the weekly food, marketplace, or recreation section. Ad space is usually sold by the column inch. A quarter-page ad could cost over $800; but depending on how many people see it, it could be an effective, worthwhile investment. Ads should be kept short and simple to prevent losing the customer's interest. Photos and logos can grab a reader's attention and increase the effectiveness of an ad. Offering coupons in an ad can provide further incentive to customers.

Radio
Radio is good for creating awareness but may not be effective at directing people to the farm if directions are complicated. Repetition is the key to radio advertising. It is better to buy twenty spots on one station than one spot on twenty stations. The cost of radio advertising varies according to the station, audience size, and broadcast time. Stations should be selected on the basis of what your target customers are most likely to listen to. Growers should

consider sponsoring morning weather reports, which could be followed by "picking reports" from their farms.

Television

Television advertising is typically quite expensive, including air time costs and production expenses. Consider a collaborative effort with area growers or your state or province organization for growers. The high prices may be cost-effective if a lot of potential customers are likely to be watching. Daytime ads can be effective at reaching the homemaker and are much less expensive than primetime ads.

Working with the Media

The local news media can provide some of the best advertising at no charge by running a feature story about a farm. Growers should get to know local reporters and give them advance notice about farm activities. Reporters may welcome a public relations story on a berry harvest or a local jam-making operation. They should be encouraged with an invitation to the farm or a press release promising good scenes for their cameras. Also consider offering an interview to build your operation's expert image and public relationships. A write up or report by the media is free and carries more weight than paid advertising. An advertisement associated with a report will also create more impact.

The most important rule when speaking to the media about your farm is—be positive! Has it been rainy this spring? Then the berries will be exceptionally juicy this year. Has it been dry? Then the berries will be smaller but sweeter. Everyone likes a winner; no one likes a whiner. Promote a quality farm experience in all interactions with the public—through advertising, interviews with the press, or one-on-one conversations with the customer.

Timing and Quantity of Advertising

Advertising should be timed around the crop. Light advertising should begin just before the harvest season. Advertising should be heaviest at the beginning of the season, and then taper off as the season progresses. Growers should not wait for slack sales to begin advertising. As a general rule, pick-your-own advertising should be budgeted at 5% of gross sales (up to 10% for a new operation). Keep records of money spent on advertising versus gross sales and number of new customers. Increase the advertising budget if competition in the area is great or if the farm location is far from the target audience. However, do not overdo it—too much advertising lowers returns and may bring in too many customers. Overcrowding and inadequate supplies are sure ways to lose patrons. Advertising is the tool that brings customers to the farm; the quality and perceived value of the farm experience are what bring them back.

Further Reading

Alltrista Consumer Products. 2004. *Ball Blue Book of Preserving.* Muncie: IN: Jarden Home Brands.

Konnerth, W.M., et. al. 1997. *Beginner's Book of Winemaking.* 4th ed. North East, PA: Presque Isle Wine Cellars.

United States Department of Agriculture. 1999. *Complete Guide to Home Canning and Preserving,* 2nd ed. Mineola, NY: Dover Publications.

University of Georgia Cooperative Extension Service. 2006. *So Easy to Preserve.* 5th ed. Book and Video Series. Athens, GA: University of Georgia in partnership with United States Department of Agriculture (USDA). Also available online at www.uga.edu/setp.

White, G.B., and W.L. Uva. 2000. *Developing a Strategic Marketing Plan for Horticultural Firms.* Ithaca, NY: Cornell University Department of Applied Economics and Management.

CHAPTER FOURTEEN

Budgeting

Developing a typical enterprise budget for a farm operation is relatively straightforward when most growers are producing the crop in a similar way, and the market price is nearly the same for all producers. However, there are no "typical" raspberry or blackberry operations. Each farm situation has unique characteristics, and the price a grower receives is determined by the mode of sale, perceived quality, population demographics, and the availability of fruit in the area. Further, raspberry or blackberry plantings usually fill niches in the overall farm operation; rarely is a farm completely dedicated to raspberry or blackberry production. Consequently, though one can develop a budget for an acre of raspberries, the *fixed costs* (those costs that do not vary with the level of production and management, including equipment, coolers, taxes, interest, insurance, and land costs) will vary tremendously from farm to farm. These costs should be allocated among the multiple crops on a farm to obtain an accurate enterprise budget.

The costs directly associated with the production of berries that vary in proportion to acreage or yield are called *variable costs*. These are often easier to determine for a given operation than fixed costs. Examples of variable costs include plants, fertilizer, hours of labor, fuel, and picking containers.

The simplest approach to estimating a budget is to calculate the costs of materials and paid labor (variable costs) that are involved in producing and selling the berries. Any income remaining after subtracting these costs from sales is considered profit. This method, which ignores fixed costs, can provide one estimate of profitability for growers who already own the land, tractor, sprayer, and cultivation equipment needed for bramble production.

One acre of raspberries yields approximately 2,500 pounds of fruit (this may be higher for summer-bearing raspberry plantings, lower for fall-bearing raspberry plantings). Berries sold pick-your-own may only require a small amount of off-farm purchases, such as fertilizer and pesticide sprays. If the raspberries are sold for $2.50/pound and the material costs are about $600 per year (table 14.1), one might conclude that raspberries are extremely profitable ($6,250 – $600 = $5,650 per acre). However, this calculation does not account for four key items: start-up costs, labor costs, marketing costs, and fixed costs. Failure to consider these costs greatly overestimates profit potential.

Start-up Costs

In the two or three years prior to harvesting the berries, a grower must invest in site preparation, plants, irrigation, and trellis. Site preparation costs for an acre field are approximately $600 including herbicide treatment for perennial weeds, soil testing, lime and nutrient amendments, plowing, tilling, and cover crop establishment (table 14.2). This number can vary within the same farm

Table 14.1 **Material expenses per acre during full production for a summer raspberry field that is part of a large fruit farm in the Northeast—not reflective of all costs.**

Operation	Month	Materials
Prune and trellis	March	$100
Fertilize	March	$40
Dormant spray	April	$75
Pre-bloom spray	May	$75
Post-bloom spray	June	$75
Cover spray	June	$75
Irrigate	June–September	$50
Leaf analysis	August	$30
Apply herbicide	November	$75
Total		**$595**

depending on the existing soil quality, site history, and the need for lime or drainage.

In the planting year, one must pay for the plants ($2,000 per acre), install irrigation within the planting ($500 per acre), mulch ($450 per acre), seed a permanent sod in the row middles ($125 per acre), and manage pests and weeds (table 14.3). An additional year after planting is devoted to plant establishment and includes the large material expense of a trellis system ($1,000 per acre or more depending on materials used) (table 14.4). Since there will be no fruit sold until the fourth year for floricane-fruiting raspberries, these pre-plant, planting, and establishment costs must be covered until the first fruit is sold. Unfortunately, it is unlikely that the sale of the first harvest will exceed the accumulated costs over the first four years; therefore, negative cash flow is likely for five or six years until accumulated profit exceeds accumulated expenses (figure 14.1).

Labor Considerations

To determine if raspberries are profitable, labor also should be included in the budget—even if the grower/owner does all the work. In the site preparation year, 8.5 hours per acre might be spent on the tractor spraying, plowing, discing, and seeding. If a grower assumes this labor is worth $15/hour, then an additional $130 in labor should be added to the preplant costs (table 14.2). During the planting and establishment years, three very labor-intensive jobs are planting, mulching, weeding, and establishing a trellis. Although a grower can do these tasks alone, it is much more efficient to have at least two helpers, and at least one helper is necessary if a tractor is involved. One can expect to spend about 40 hours or more of total labor during the two pre-harvest years on these specific tasks (tables 14.3 and 14.4).

In the fruiting years, a significant amount of labor also is required for harvesting. Even if one sells the berries PYO, one has to supervise and check customers in and out. For PYO, one supervisor can perhaps oversee 5 acres. In this case, when developing the budget, only ⅕ of the salary of the supervisor is allocated to an individual acre. An alternative to PYO is to pay individuals by the half-pint or pint to harvest the berries. Paying $0.50–0.75 per half-pint is typical, so an acre yielding 2,000 pounds (5,300 half-pints) would cost $2,670 to harvest. Because of the wide variation in potential

Table 14.2 **Expenses per acre, including fixed costs, fuel and labor, in the pre-plant year (Year 1) for a bramble field that is part of a large fruit farm in the Northeast.**

Operation	Month	Fixed Costs	Fuel	Labor	Materials	Total Cost
Sample soil	May			$5	$20	$25
Apply herbicide	June	$5	$3	$10	$75	$93
Plow field	June	$15	$3	$20		$38
Disc field	June	$25	$5	$15		$45
Apply nutrients	June	$5	$3	$10	$80	$98
Lime	June	$5	$3	$10	$100	$118
Disc field	July	$15	$5	$20		$40
Harrow field	July	$10	$5	$10		$25
Plant ground cover	July	$5	$3	$10	$50	$68
Incorporate cover	October	$15	$5	$20		$40
Overhead expense		Variable				Variable
Totals		**$100**	**$35**	**$130**	**$325**	**$590**

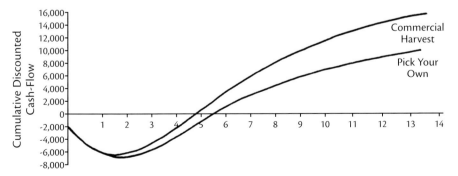

Cumulative Present Value per acre for Raspberries

Fig. 14.1 Minimum number of years required to recover the initial investment cost for pick-your-own and commercial harvest raspberry operations.

harvesting costs and yields, the full production budget in table 14.5 does not include an estimate for harvest costs. However, these labor costs should be included, plus the cost of containers and packaging if the grower is providing them.

In addition to routine fertilization, mowing, and pest management, pruning and tying canes to a trellis is a major job for summer raspberries and blackberries. One can expect to spend between 20 and 40 hours per acre on this task. So, even if one hires a laborer at $8/hour, once all the labor is included, the apparent high profit of a bramble operation is no longer as large as it may first have appeared. Detailed pruning and tying is not required for fall-bearing raspberries—they simply can be mowed in late fall or early spring—eliminating most of the 20–40 hour pruning requirement. However, yields are typically lower than summer-bearers, so net profit may be similar between the two types.

Let's assume that a farmer sells 2,000 pounds of raspberries through PYO at $2.50/pound, for a total income of $5,000. The grower spends $600 on materials (sprays, fertilizers) and up to 40 hours per year at $8/hour ($320) on routine maintenance (weeding, fertilizing, mowing, spraying). In addition, the grower pays someone $8/hour for 30 hours to prune and trellis the canes ($240). Of the remaining difference between costs and sales ($3,840), a portion will have to be used to cover the establishment costs described earlier (tables 14.2, 14.3, and 14.4), harvesting costs, marketing costs, as well as fixed costs.

Table 14.3 Expenses per acre in the planting year (Year 2) for a bramble field that is part of a large fruit farm in the Northeast.

Operation	Month	Fixed Costs	Fuel	Labor	Materials	Total Cost
Rototill strips	April	$25	$10	$20		$55
Lay out and stake field	May		$2	$20	$20	$42
Haul plants	May	$7	$3	$15		$25
Plant raspberries	May	$10	$10	$100	$1,880	$2,000
Planting year mulch	May	$40	$10	$100	$300	$450
Place field irrigation	May	$25	$15	$25	$450	$515
Irrigate	May–Sept.	$10	$20	$15	$150	$195
Fertilize	June	$3	$2	$10	$30	$45
Hand hoe/weed	June–July			$300		$300
Cultivate alley	June–Sept.	$20	$10	$25		$55
Seed permanent sod	September	$5	$5	$15	$100	$125
Apply herbicide	October	$5	$3	$10	$75	$93
Overhead Expense		Variable				Variable
Totals		**$150**	**$90**	**$655**	**$3,005**	**$3,900**

Table 14.4 Expenses per acre in the year after planting (Year 3) for a summer raspberry field that is part of a large fruit farm in the Northeast.

Operation	Month	Fixed Costs	Fuel	Labor	Materials	Total Cost
Install V-trellis	November	$10	$5	$350	$1,000	$1,365
Mow floricanes	Dec.–Feb.	$5	$2	$6		$13
Fertilize	March	$5	$2	$10	$40	$57
Replant (5%)	April	$5		$20	$90	$115
Hand hoe	June–July			$300		$300
Mow alley	June–Sept.	$15	$5	$20		$40
Cover spray	June	$5	$3	$12	$75	$95
Irrigate	June–Sept.	$10	$20	$30	$50	$110
Apply herbicide	November	$5	$3	$12	$75	$95
Overhead expense		Variable				Variable
Totals		**$60**	**$40**	**$760**	**$1,330**	**$2,190**

Fixed Costs

Fixed costs differ tremendously from farm to farm. The purchase of new or used equipment, such as a tractor or pick-up truck, can be a major contributor to fixed costs. Insurance is a fixed cost. Building a driveway or parking lot can be another major expense. Establishing a water source and irrigation deliver system is a fixed cost. Less obvious fixed costs are taxes, utilities, office computer, barn, tractor repairs, and record-keeping expenses. Economists also include the interest on capital equipment as an expense (since that money could have been invested in a bank and drawing interest) and the cost to rent the land (since the grower could have rented the land to someone else as an alternative to growing raspberries).

The more acreage one has, generally, the smaller is each acre's share of fixed costs. This is why large farms often have greater economies of scale than smaller farms. If the entire cost of an irrigation system, driveway, tractor, and barn is borne by just one or two acres of raspberries, then the operation will be less profitable than a farm with more acres, everything else being equal. Of course, one may not be able to expand the operation just to improve economies of scale. Limits may exist in available land, labor, capital, or market that preclude expansion. Raspberry budgets typically show a profit when only variable costs are considered, but they may be unprofitable when all of the fixed costs are included.

The tables estimate costs for a five-acre raspberry planting on a per-acre basis. An attempt is made to estimate fixed costs for various pieces of equipment, assuming they are used for other farm operations besides raspberries. Equipment used only on raspberries (e.g., an air-blast sprayer) will have a higher fixed cost than equipment that is used for many different crops (e.g., a tractor). The fixed cost of using a sprayer for a particular operation includes both the fixed cost of the tractor per hour, plus the fixed cost of the sprayer per hour, multiplied by the number of hours required to spray the acre of berries.

For budgeting purposes, the cost of capital equipment is not deducted from income in the year it is purchased, rather it is depreciated over the life of the equipment. For example, if a tractor is purchased for $30,000 and is expected to have a 30-year life, then only $1,000 is deducted from income in any one year for this purchase. If the tractor is used on 10 acres of crops, then only $100 of fixed costs are allocated to each acre in each year. (If the money was borrowed to purchase the tractor, then these interest payments also must be allocated proportionately.)

It is more accurate to calculate fixed costs on a per-hour basis, rather than a per-acre basis, because this allows the grower to allocate fixed costs depending on how much equipment use each acre requires. For example, if the tractor is used for 500 hours each year on various farm operations, the fixed cost for the tractor is then $2/hour. A sprayer costs $10,000 with an expected life of 20 years. It is used only 50 hours each year. The fixed cost of the sprayer is $10/hour. If it takes one

Table 14.5 Expenses per acre during full production (Year 4 and later) for a summer raspberry field that is part of a large fruit farm in the Northeast.

Operation	Month	Fixed Costs	Fuel	Labor	Materials	Total Cost
Prune & trellis	March	$15	$3	$350	$100	$468
Fertilize	March	$5	$2	$10	$40	$57
Dormant spray	April	$5	$3	$12	$75	$95
Pre-bloom spray	May	$5	$3	$12	$75	$95
Hand hoe	June–July			$300		$300
Mow alley	June–Sept.	$15	$5	$20		$40
Post-bloom spray	June	$5	$3	$12	$75	$95
Cover spray	June	$5	$3	$12	$75	$95
Irrigate	June–Sept.	$10	$20	$30	$50	$110
Harvest prep & cleanup	June			$15		$15
Harvest PYO	July	Variable			Variable	
Leaf analysis	August			$5	$30	$35
Apply herbicide	November	$5	$3	$12	$75	$95
Overhead expense		Variable				Variable
Total		**$70**	**$45**	**$790**	**$595**	**$1,500**

hour to spray an acre of raspberries, then the fixed cost is $12 ($10 + $2) for that particular operation.

Equipment is not the only source of fixed costs. Overhead costs (taxes, utilities, computer, barn, tractor repairs, and record-keeping expenses) need to be included in the budget as well to obtain a realistic accounting of expenses. On large farms, overhead costs can be in the range of $500 per acre. On smaller farms that only grow raspberries, the overhead per acre can be very high, perhaps in the thousands of dollars.

Marketing and Distribution Costs

Although word-of-mouth is the best form of advertising, it does not happen instantaneously and without some initial investment of time and money. For PYO, a grower often will have to advertise, at least during the first few years when the operation is becoming known in the community. In addition, the grower may want to have a picnic area, a few farm animals, or other attractions to aid in marketing the farm, and these all cost money to develop and maintain.

For sales to supermarkets or farm markets, a grower must transport the fruit and perhaps pay someone to attend to the farm market. Again, these costs should be included in the budget. Because of the extreme variability from farm to farm in these costs, they have not been included in the representative budget.

Considerations for Multiple-Year Budgeting

When developing budgets for a long period of time, such as ten years, some economists make an adjustment to future income (discounting future dollars) so the total profit in future years is expressed in today's dollars. A $2,000 profit today is worth more than a $2,000 profit ten years from now because of inflation. A common percentage for discounting future dollars is 6% annually. The sum of adjusted profit dollars over a period of years is called "net present value" and is a good measure of profitability.

The net present value must be positive for an operation to be considered profitable. Even if the net present value is positive, a raspberry planting still may not be feasible if a grower cannot obtain the money necessary to establish the planting. If the grower can obtain the money for establishing the planting, they may not be

in a positive cash flow situation for several years. For raspberries, most growers see a positive cash flow near year six (figure 14.1). The grower-investor must be able to function without any net return on investment for this period of time.

Putting It All Together

To construct a budget, list all of the operations for each year, from the preplant year through year ten. Then list the variable costs required to do those tasks (materials, labor, and fuel). Try to estimate the fixed costs associated with each step. This can be difficult when equipment is used for tasks other than raspberries. (Refer to tables 14.2 through 14.5 as an example of an enterprise budget for an acre of summer raspberries which is part of a larger farm in the Northeast.) Then include the costs associated with harvesting and marketing the berries. Lastly, include an estimate of overhead costs.

Once the total costs are known, estimated yields and prices can be used to determine profitability over time. A worthwhile exercise after calculating your operating budget is to determine the break-even price point. If the operation is profitable, the break-even price will be lower than the retail price for the berries. This difference indicates how much flexibility there can be in pricing, and guides in determining volume discounts.

Developing budgets also means making assumptions, including the assumption that the weather will cooperate, yields will be somewhat predictable, and no major pest outbreaks will occur. Some economists argue that although certain farming operations are profitable, the risk/profit ratio is too high in agriculture to attract investment. One might be better off investing money in a bank at a given interest rate, than to invest in farming at a similar interest rate but higher risk. If one must borrow money for agriculture, it will be important to convince the banker that you know these risks and can adjust to them.

Table 14.6 summarizes expenses in a production year by incorporating the cost scenario from the previous tables. It accounts for start-up costs (first three years without any income) by allocating them equally over the ten-year life of the planting. This simplification ignores interest on investment, but does provide an estimate of annual costs for the purpose of setting price and estimating profit. Assuming the planting yields 2,000 pounds

Table 14.6 Summary of total expenses and income per acre during full production for a summer raspberry field that is part of a large fruit farm in the Northeast.

Expense	Commercial	PYO
Variable costs	$1,430	$1,430
Fixed costs	$70	$70
Harvest cost	$2,670	$230
Harvest containers	$400	$0
Advertising	$200	$300
10% portion of start-up costs	$670	$670
Overhead	$500	$500
Total Expense	**$5,940**	**$3,200**
Income	$10,600	$5,400
Profit	**$4,660**	**$2,200**

per acre (5,300 half-pints) sold commercially for $2.00 per half-pint, one would realize a true profit of about $4,600 per acre. A PYO operation would have lower harvest costs, but the value of fruit would be less ($5,400 = 2,000 pounds × $2.70/pound or $1.00 per half-pint), realizing a smaller profit. With these assumptions, the "break-even" price for the commercially sold fruit would be $1.12 a half-pint, and $1.60/pound for PYO. Of course, a grower wants to make money rather than just break even. Assuming the start-up costs ($6,700) plus the fruiting year costs ($1,500) were invested in a bank drawing interest at 5%, one would receive a payment of $410 for doing nothing. So a grower would want to return at least this amount for all of the work, investment, and risk associated with the enterprise.

Detailed production costs have been developed for blackberries in the Southeast. The total cost of producing, harvesting, and marketing blackberries was estimated to be $15,514 per acre with a 10,000-pound-per-acre yield in the second year of production. Labor was the greatest expense category ($13,739), comprising 70% of total costs. Given certain assumptions about price and yield, a positive return on investment of about $3,900 per acre was realized once plants were in full production. Start-up costs were covered after five years, and revenues were positive after this time. Accumulated net cash flow after ten years was about $19,670. Break-even PYO prices ranged from $1.15 to $1.35/pound for yields of 12,000 to 8,500 pounds per acre, and $2.00 to $3.00/pound for wholesaling those same yields.

This analysis took into account many factors that growers often overlook. For example, the farmer was paid $16.39/hour, went to an annual meeting, subscribed to an Internet service, and budgeted for farm overhead and interest on investment.

To summarize, generally raspberries and blackberries have a high profit potential provided that fixed costs are not too high. Although yields are relatively low compared to some other crops, the price per pound is very high, particularly for ready-picked berries and those produced out-of-season. Gross sales of $8,000–$12,000 per acre are not unreasonable for raspberries, and up to $25,000 per acre for blackberries. Berries already harvested tend to provide a higher profit than PYO berries, provided that the grower can find harvest labor. Establishment costs can approach $7,000–$12,000, and a positive cash flow usually does not occur until the third or fourth fruiting year. If a grower has an aptitude for marketing and if labor is available, then raspberry and blackberry production can be a very successful agricultural endeavor.

Further Reading

Safley, C.D., O. Boldea, and G.E. Fernandez. January–March 2006. "Production & Marketing Reports: Estimated Costs of Producing, Harvesting, and Marketing Blackberries in the Southeastern United States." *HortTechnology* 16 (1): 109-117.

Glossary

adventitious bud—A vegetative bud that develops along the root of a bramble plant and that will grow into a primocane.

aggregate fruit—A type of fruit that develops from a single flower, but which consists of many smaller drupelets that fuse and ripen together.

air shear—Cutting with air; used to define a spray nozzle that uses air to break up the spray into the desired pattern and droplet size.

apical meristem—A group of cells at the growing point of roots and shoots from which all vegetative or reproductive growth originates.

aroma volatiles—Fragrant chemicals in fruit that quickly vaporize when exposed to air.

axillary bud—A bud which develops in the axil of a leaf, the point where the leaf attaches to the shoot.

backcross—A cross between a parent and one of its offspring.

biennial—A plant that requires two growing seasons to complete its life cycle; vegetative growth occurs the first year, reproductive growth the second year, and then the plant dies.

calyx lobe—The free, unfused, projecting parts of the base of a flower below the petals.

canopy—The leaf surface on a plant.

certified plant stock—Plants, from a nursery, which have been visually inspected by a state representative and found to be free of virus and other disease symptoms.

clean cultivation—Physically disturbing the soil between plant rows at regular intervals to eliminate weeds.

crown bud—A vegetative bud that originates from just below the base of a bramble plant and which will develop into a primocane.

cultivar—A "*culti*vated *vari*ety"; an entity of commercial importance, which is given a name to distinguish it from other, genetically different, plants.

cultural control—The use of production practices that are typically used to improve plant growth and yield, to control pests as well.

differentiation—The physiological and morphological changes that occur in cells, tissues, or organs during development and maturation.

double-cropping—Fruiting a primocane-fruiting raspberry in fall and again in summer, rather than allowing canes to fruit only once in the fall before removing canes.

drupelet—The small sections of a raspberry or blackberry fruit, each containing a seed.

entomology—The study of insects.

evapotranspiration—The total water lost through evaporation from the soil surface and from transpiration through the plant.

fall-fruiting—A raspberry which forms fruit on the tops of first-year vegetative primocanes near the end of the growing season; also known as *primocane-fruiting*.

fibrous root—A type of root system characterized by many branches of fine roots.

floricane—The second-year cane which overwintered and will fruit and die in the current year.

floricane-fruiting—A raspberry which forms fruit only on second-year canes in late spring or summer; also known as *summer-fruiting*.

germplasm—A collection of genetically diverse plants, including wild material, which can be used to improve cultivated plants through breeding.

green manure crop—A crop that will be incorporated into the soil for improving soil fertility and tilth.

hardiness—The ability of a plant to withstand cold temperatures.

leather bud—Buds at the base of a cane, often underground, which have the capacity to grow into a primocane.

node—The point of attachment of buds or laterals to the main cane.

oviposition—The laying of an egg by an insect.

pathology—The study of diseases and the organisms that cause them.

perennial—A plant or plant part that lives for more than two years.

pH—A measure of the acidity or alkalinity of the soil, ranging from 0 to 14; a low pH indicates acid soil, a pH of 7 is neutral, and a high pH indicates an alkaline soil.

photosynthesis—The process in a plant of making sugars for growth and respiration from the raw products of water, carbon dioxide, and sunlight.

phytotoxicity—The ability of a chemical substance to cause harm to a plant, often used to characterize the effect of a herbicide on crops.

pistil—The female reproductive organ of a flower from which the fruit will ultimately develop.

pollination—The act of placing pollen from the male reproductive organ onto the female reproductive organ of a flower, often carried out by bees or wind.

primocane—The first-year cane of a raspberry or blackberry.

primocane-fruiting—A type of raspberry that forms fruit on the tops of first-year canes near the end of the growing season; also known as *fall-fruiting*.

recommended daily allowance—Revised estimates of the amounts of vitamins and minerals that should be contained in the daily diet to ensure good health in human adults.

recommended dietary allowance—Original estimates of vitamin and mineral needs in human adults to ensure good health.

respiration—The process of converting sugars into carbon dioxide, water, and energy. Often, the energy is in the form of heat.

shoot bud—A bud on the aboveground portion of a plant.

stamen—The male part of a flower; it produces pollen.

stomata—Pores on the bottom of a leaf through which carbon dioxide enters the plant and water vapor exits.

sucker shoot—A young, vegetative cane originating from an adventitious bud on the root.

summer-fruiting—A raspberry or blackberry which forms fruit only on second-year canes in late spring or summer; also known as *floricane-fruiting*.

tip-layering—A method of propagation of black raspberries in which the ends of canes are buried in the soil so that new plants will arise from them.

tipping—The process of removing the tops of primocanes for the purpose of stimulating lateral branching; sometimes called *pinching*.

tissue culture—A method of propagation in which whole plants are obtained from meristematic tissue in indoor facilities.

topping—The removal of the top portion of cane after it has overwintered.

torus—The center of a fruit to which the drupelets attach; also called the *receptacle*.

transpiration—The process of water exiting the plant through the stomata.

Table of Conversions

	To Convert This:	To This:	Multiply by This:
Weight/Volume	quarts (fruit)	pounds	1.5
	pints (fruit)	quarts	0.5
	pints (fruit)	pounds	0.75
	pounds	kilograms	0.454
	ounces	grams	28.35
	quarts	liters	0.946
	gallons	liters	3.78
	gallons (water)	pounds	8.34
	pounds (water)	gallons	0.12
	tons (English)	pounds	2,000
	tons (English)	tons (metric)	0.907
Area	acres	hectares	0.405
	acres	square feet	43,560
	acres	square yards	4,840
	square miles	acres	640
Length	inches	centimeters	2.54
	feet	meters	0.305
	yards	meters	0.915
	miles	kilometers	1.6
Pressure	pounds per square inch (psi)	bar	0.069
	pounds per square inch (psi)	kilopascal (KPa)	6.895
Rate	pounds per acre	kilograms per hectare	1.12
	miles per hour (mph)	feet per second	1.47
	miles per hour (mph)	kilometers per hour	1.6

Temperature $°C = \frac{5}{9} (°F - 32)$

About Our Sponsors

The companies listed below provided funds to help pay for the production costs of this book.

Hartmann's Plant Company
PO Box 100 Lacota, MI 49063
Phone: 269-253-4281
Fax: 269-253-4457
Email: INFO@HARTMANNSPLANTCOMPANY.COM
Web site: HARTMANNSPLANTCOMPANY.COM
Products and Services: Wholesale raspberry and blackberry grower

Norcal Nursery, Inc.
P. O. Box 1012 Red Bluff, CA 96080
Phone: (530) 527-6200
Fax: (530) 527-2921
Email: NORCAL@SAKUMABROS.COM
Products and Services: Strawberry, Raspberry and Blackberry plants

Nourse Farms
41 River Road South Deerfield MA 01373
Phone: 413-665-2658
Fax: 413-665-7888
Email: INFO@NOURSEFARMS.COM
Web site: WWW.NOURSEFARMS.COM
Products and Services: We offer over 30 varieties of Brambles.
We also offer advice on variety selection and cultural practices.

Trellis Growing Systems LLC (TGS)
2427 South Hadley Road Fort Wayne, Indiana 46804
Phone: 260-241-3128
Fax: 260-436-3300
Email: RCBARNES@TRELLISGROWINGSYSTEMS.COM
Web site: WWW.TRELLISGROWINGSYSTEMS.COM
Products and Services: Trellis systems design and product including
posts, monofilament wire, anchors, and hardware. Also offer ground
cover, shade & wind cloth, and row cover for winter protection.